ASCETICISM IN EARLY TAOIST RELIGION

SUNY series in Chinese Philosophy and Culture
David L. Hall and Roger T. Ames, editors

ASCETICISM IN EARLY TAOIST RELIGION

Stephen Eskildsen

STATE UNIVERSITY OF NEW YORK PRESS

Published by
State University of New York Press, Albany

For information, address State University of New York Press,
State University Plaza, Albany, N.Y., 12246

Production by Cathleen Collins
Marketing by Nancy Farrell

Library of Congress Cataloging in Publication Data

Eskildsen, Stephen, 1963–
    Asceticism in early taoist religion / Stephen Eskildsen.
        p.   cm. — (SUNY series in Chinese philosophy and culture)
    Includes bibliographical references and index.
    ISBN 0-7914-3955-0 (alk. paper). — ISBN 0-7914-3956-9 (pbk. :
alk. paper)
        1. Asceticism—Taoism. 2. Taoism. I. Title. II. Series.
BL1923.E84 1998
299'.514447—dc21   97-50629
                                                           CIP

10 9 8 7 6 5 4 3 2 1

Contents

Acknowledgments

This book is a revised version of my doctoral dissertation that I completed in 1994 at the University of British Columbia (UBC). On this joyful occasion of its publication, I wish to thank everybody who has provided me with guidance, support, and encouragement. I am particularly grateful to the following people: Edward, Marion, Tom, Jane, and Lucile Eskildsen; Daniel Overmyer (my friend and mentor); Joseph McDermott (who first got me interested in Taoism); S. Y. Tse, Tsuneharu Gonnami and the rest of the excellent staff at the UBC Asian Library; Jerry Schmidt, Chen Jo-shui, Leon Hurvitz, E. G. Pulleyblank, Olivia Pi, Catherine Swatek, and Josephine Chiu-Duke (my teachers); Livia Kohn (for her helpful advice); Lingdanzi (the Master of the Miraculous Elixir); Franciscus Verellen, Harjot Oberoi, Paul Mosca, and Diana Lary (who graciously served on my thesis committee); the referees for my book manuscript (whoever you are); Nancy Ellegate, Cathleen Collins, M. Lansing, Betty Ross (and all of the other fine people at State University of New York Press); Margaret, Alan, and Boethe Lindgren (who provided me with lodging in my time of need); Maren Anderson, Mike Lebo, Katie Allston, Kate Wulff, and Ginger Flynn (my Baltimore comrades); Kenny McQueen and the Mudcats (Poco Over-30 Baseball League, 1994 Champions).

I also would like to take this opportunity to send out my prayers and best wishes for Project PLASE (Baltimore), the Lutheran Volunteer Corps, and all other organizations and individuals who strive to help the needy and underprivileged.

CHAPTER ONE

Introduction

The origins of the Taoist religion cannot be traced to a single founder or historical event. The religion emerged during the early centuries of the common era through the convergence of diverse elements of belief and practice. These elements were largely drawn from ancient immortality lore, macrobiotics, alchemy, Taoist philosophy, yin–yang/five agents[1] cosmology, state cult, popular religion, and Confucian ethics. Buddhist beliefs and practices also were eagerly incorporated into the mix, particularly from the fourth century onward.

Immortality has always been a cherished goal in the Taoist religion, and many Taoists have practiced asceticism in the hope of gaining everlasting life. One of the most salient features of early Taoist asceticism was the great emphasis on fasting and the amazing variety of techniques devised to suppress hunger. Celibacy, self-imposed poverty, wilderness seclusion, and sleep avoidance also were practiced. Of course, not all early Taoists were ascetics. As has been the case in most other major religions, severe forms of self-discipline and self-denial were carried out primarily by a spiritual elite who made religious self-cultivation their exclusive vocation. This spiritual elite probably represented a distinct minority within the ranks of the faithful.

My working definition of "asceticism" is that proposed by Walter O. Kaelber in *The Encyclopedia of Religion*. While admitting that the word has no universally accepted definition, Kaelber states that it may be defined as follows when used in a religious context:

> a voluntary, sustained, and at least partially systematic program of self-discipline and self-denial in which immediate, sensual or profane gratifications are renounced in order to attain a higher spiritual state or a more thorough absorption in the sacred.[2]

In most religions, the higher spiritual state and the absorption in the sacred are meant to help guarantee some form of salvation. For early religious Taoists, salvation meant not only a perfection or perpetuation of the spirit but also physical longevity and immortality. Their asceticism almost always purported to improve the

1

strength and health of the human body. Even though Taoist ascetics sometimes taxed their bodies severely, they believed that their strength and health would eventually be restored if they courageously persevered in their austerities. Ultimately, their austerities were supposed to perfect them both spiritually and physically, finally transforming them into superhuman, divine beings with limitless longevity and extraordinary powers.

Many of the ascetic practices of the Taoists, in their basic forms, predate the emergence of the Taoist religion itself. The practices originated among ancient immortality seekers who perhaps were active as early as the fourth century B.C.E., if not earlier. Unfortunately, the scarcity of sources makes it difficult to adequately discuss the practices as they existed during such an early period. Our study focuses on roughly the first six centuries of the common era, a period for which a detailed examination of asceticism is feasible, due to a relative abundance of sources. A full exploration of the earliest roots of Taoist asceticism must be left for a future study. Nonetheless some points should be touched upon at the outset concerning some of the early precursors of the Taoist religion and the origins of its ascetic current.

The precursors that first come to mind are the Taoist philosophers of the late fourth or early third century B.C.E. whose wisdom is preserved in the *Laozi* (also known as the *Daode jing*) and the *Zhuangzi*. We do not know whether these philosophers pursued lifestyles or training methods of an ascetic nature. In the first place, we know little about who they were, what they did, and who they associated with.[3] However, these texts do contain certain teachings that are compatible with an ascetic outlook and lifestyle. Prime examples from the *Laozi* would include the following:

> The five colors make man's eyes blind;
> The five notes make his ears deaf;
> The five tastes injure his palate;
> Riding and hunting
> make his mind go wild with excitement;
> Goods hard to come by
> Serve to hinder his progress (Ch. 12)[4]

> Exhibit the unadorned and embrace the uncarved block,
> Have little thought of self and as few desires as possible. (Ch. 19)[5]

> There is no crime greater than having too many desires;
> There is no disaster greater than not being content;
> There is no misfortune greater than being covetous.
> Hence in being content, one will always have enough. (Ch. 46)[6]

The *Laozi* conveys an apprehensive attitude toward stimuli that arouse the senses and enjoins its readers to decrease their self-centered desires and be content with what they have. Passages such as the aforementioned served as inspiration and justification for later Taoist ascetics. However, as we shall see, Taoist asceticism sometimes went well beyond what the *Laozi* recommends. Some religious Taoist texts teach one to eschew even the most basic necessities for a normal existence, such as food, rest, and companionship.

One of the most fundamental teachings of the *Zhuangzi* is that one should possess an outlook that "evens things out" (*qiwu*). While the profoundest subtleties of this outlook will not be explored here, it is relevant to point out that the *Zhuangzi* asserts that all things and circumstances that one may confront are of equal quality and desirability.[7] Based on this outlook, one is to abandon all value judgments, desires, and worries. By doing so, one simply experiences the universe as it is and willingly accords with its flux. Such a person is described as follows:

> The utmost man is daemonic. When the wide woodlands blaze they cannot sear him, when the Yellow River and the Han freeze they cannot chill him, when swift thunderbolts smash the mountains and whirlwinds shake the seas they cannot startle him. A man like that yokes the clouds to his chariot, rides the sun and moon and roams beyond the four seas; death and life alter nothing in himself, still less the principles of benefit and harm! (Ch. 2)[8]

A person who "evens things out" would presumably not get wound up in pursuits of pleasure, wealth, and fame. His inner freedom would enable him to be content in any situation, however bleak. However, this does not mean to say that one should purposefully eschew the simple pleasures and bare necessities of life. In saying that the "utmost man" is impervious to fires, freezing, thunderstorms, and death, the *Zhuangzi* describes his inner equanimity and freedom. Later Taoist immortality seekers hoped to gain invulnerability at both the spiritual and physical levels, and sought to do so through self-imposed austerities. In their view, the inner virtue acquired through the austerities would somehow be accompanied by the attainment of physical immortality and supernormal powers. The *Zhuangzi*, however, makes no such promise. It teaches its readers to see death as a circumstance no less desirable than life and to willingly accept it as one of the marvelous workings of nature. Later religious Taoist texts similarly assert that Taoist adepts must overcome their yearning for life and fear of death. However, paradoxically, gaining such a state of mind was somehow supposed to enable them to evade bodily death. But in the view of the *Zhuangzi*, the acceptance of death brings no such tangible reward; it simply liberates people from their anxieties.

Similarly, the *Laozi* contains no clear statements affirming the possibility of physical immortality. In certain places it does present its wisdom as a means for surviving worldly perils and reaching a ripe old age. Certain passages could be interpreted as endorsements of yogic practices of a macrobiotic nature. Still, there is no clear indication that the author(s) believed in physical immortality.

However, immortality beliefs certainly existed by the time the *Laozi* and *Zhuangzi* were written. By the fourth century B.C.E., people were beginning to entertain ideas about immortal, superhuman beings who lived in remote, inaccessible mountains or islands. One such being is mentioned in the *Zhuangzi*, within a conversation (probably fictional) recorded between two men named Jian Wu and Lian Shu. Jian Wu tells Lian Shu about the following "wild extravagances" that he had heard from an eccentric named Jie Yu:

> In the mountains of far-off Guyi there lives a daemonic man, whose skin and flesh are like ice and snow, who is gentle as a virgin. *He does not eat the five grains but sucks in the wind and drinks the dew* (emphasis added); he rides the vapour of the clouds, yokes flying dragons to his chariot, and roams beyond the four seas. When the daemonic in him concentrates it keeps creatures free from plagues and makes the grain ripen every year. (Ch. 1)[9]

Most important for our purposes is the italicized portion. As we shall see, phrases like this commonly refer to severe fasting methods where the adept shuns solid foods while attempting to nourish himself or herself on air and saliva. During this period, superhuman beings with unusual eating habits may have merely been objects of fantasy and admiration. There still may not have been adepts who aspired to become like them. But if there were such adepts, they may have been practicing some of the fasting techniques that were later pursued by Taoist ascetics.

The deficiency of sources hinders us from knowing much about the asceticism of the earliest immortality seekers. Most of the information on them is found in Sima Qian's (ca. 145–86 B.C.E.) *Shiji* (Chronicles of the Historian). There we are told about numerous court magicians (*fangshi*) from the kingdoms of Qi and Yan who offered their services to kings and emperors. Heeding their advice, several rulers during the fourth through the second centuries B.C.E. sent out expeditions to search for the legendary island dwellings of immortals.[10] The court magicians also endorsed various cultic observances and macrobiotic techniques as aids toward immortality. It should be noted that Li Shaojun, active during the reign of Han Emperor Wu (Wudi, 140–87 B.C.E.), included what was probably a fasting method (*gudao* or the "method of grains") among his practices.[11] However, even though fasting may have been included among the methods of the court magicians, the word "ascetic" would not seem to aptly characterize these men of worldly ambition. Still, it is not hard to imagine that there would have been some immortality seekers who observed their cults and honed their skills without seeking the patronage of the rich and powerful.

The *Xinyu*, written in 196 B.C.E. by the Confucian politician Lu Jia, contains an interesting criticism of immortality seekers.

> [If a man] strains and belabors his body, going deep into the mountains and seeking [to become a] Divine Immortal,[12] [if he] abandons his parents, does away with his blood relatives (lit., "bones and flesh"),

abstains from the five grains, and gives up the *Shi* [*jing*] and the *Shu* [*jing*] (i.e., classical learning), [thus] turning his back to what is treasured by Heaven and Earth in his seeking for the Tao of deathlessness; then he can no more communicate with [the people of] the world, or prevent what is not [right from happening].[13]

This passage strongly suggests that immortality seekers had already acquired a reputation for their austerities and unworldly tendencies.

At some point, immortality seeking and Taoist philosophy came to be intimately linked. When and how this occurred is unclear. However, magicians of the kind previously mentioned may have been responsible for this phenomenon, as perhaps were the scholars of the Huang-Lao school (the line of demarcation between these two groups is blurry; they probably overlapped). The Huang-Lao school originated in the Warring States kingdom of Qi—which covered most of present-day Shandong Province—and achieved its peak of influence during the early second century B.C.E. This school venerated two figures as its patrons; Laozi (the putative, most likely legendary author of the *Laozi* book) and the Yellow Emperor (a legendary emperor of remote antiquity). Its adherents interpreted and adapted the teachings of the *Laozi* to develop their own theories on statecraft and self-cultivation. They appear to have also promoted various macrobiotic measures such as alchemy, medicine, sexual yoga, light gymnastics, and dietetics.[14] The findings unearthed in 1973 at the tomb of the Lady of Dai (d. ca. 186 B.C.E.) in Changsha (Hunan Province) attest to the fact that Taoist philosophy and macrobiotics simultaneously held the interest of many members of the early Han aristocracy. Numerous books were found in the tomb, including two copies of the *Laozi* (the earliest manuscripts of the book available), a Huang-Lao text called the *Huangdi sijing* (Four Canons of the Yellow Emperor), diagrams of macrobiotic light gymnastic postures, and a fasting manual entitled *Quegu shiqi pian* (Chapter on Getting Rid of Grains and Eating Air). Most amazingly, the corpse of the Lady of Dai was found preserved with skin and internal organs intact.[15]

By the first century of the common era, immortality seekers had come to be known as "Taoists." This is apparent from evidence in the *Lunheng*, written by Latter Han skeptic Wang Chong (23–100 C.E.). In a chapter entitled "Taoist Untruths" (*daoxu*), Wang Chong endeavors to debunk the immortality beliefs and techniques of his time. In one passage, he writes,

There is a belief that by the doctrine of Laozi one can transcend the world. Through serenity and non-desire one nurtures the essence (*jing*) and cherishes the vital force (*qi*). The longevity of people is based on their spirits. If their spirits are unharmed, they will live long and will not die. After accomplishing his affairs (his duties as royal archivist?), Laozi practiced this. After a hundred years he transcended the world and became a Perfected Being. (The text follows with Wang Chong's rebuttal of these beliefs.)[16]

This passage not only attests to the linkage between Taoist philosophy and immortality seeking, but also reflects how the philosopher Laozi was revered as a great adept who attained immortality through serenity and non-desire.

The Latter Han Dynasty (25–220 C.E.) represents a critical juncture in the development of the Taoist religion. Immortality-seeking Taoists continued to develop their beliefs and techniques. While some of them only considered Laozi to be one of the many adepts who attained immortality, others went further in glorifying him. They deified him as being nothing less than a cosmic super deity, virtually equating him to the all-creating, all-embracing first principle (the Tao) described in the *Laozi*.[17] They interpreted the *Laozi* along the lines of their own beliefs and utilized it to lend authority to their cosmology, macrobiotics, and mysticism.

The earliest known organized Taoist religious movements, the Great Peace School (*taiping dao*) and the Five Pecks of Rice School (*wudoumi dao*),[18] emerged in the latter part of the second century C.E.[19] The Great Peace School had a large following in the east, in portions of present-day Henan, Hebei, Shandong, Jiangsu, and Anhui provinces. The Five Pecks of Rice School—which later came to be known as the Heavenly Masters School (*tianshi dao*)—thrived in the west, in a region covering portions of present-day Sichuan and Shaanxi provinces. The discovery of the *Laozi bianhua jing* (Scripture on the Transformations of Laozi) from the Dunhuang manuscripts has provided evidence that there were other similar movements during this period.[20] This text apparently belonged to a popular sect—distinct from the Five Pecks of Rice School—that existed in present-day Sichuan Province at the end of the second century.[21]

The Great Peace and Five Pecks of Rice schools found most of their adherents among the peasantry. These schools emphasized ritual healing and rudimentary ethics based on the fundamental assumption that moral transgressions cause diseases. The Five Pecks of Rice School utilized the *Laozi* as its fundamental scripture, interpreting it along ethical lines to formulate moral precepts. Both groups entertained hopes of realizing a utopian age under an enlightened Taoist regime. To help usher in such a utopia, the Great Peace School took to armed revolt (the Yellow Turban revolt) against the Han dynasty in 184, only to be crushed. The Five Pecks of Rice School, situated at a remote distance from the seat of imperial power, enjoyed autonomous political control of its local area for roughly thirty years, before surrendering to military strongman Cao Cao in 215. Its cooperative stance toward its conquerors allowed it to survive as a religious body. An important, unresolved question is whether or not, and to what extent, the two schools propagated immortality techniques. While they may have included adepts of immortality techniques within their fold, it seems likely that most adepts functioned independently of these schools.

In the ensuing centuries, newer religious Taoist movements integrated immortality beliefs and techniques with the ethics and rituals of the Heavenly Masters School. At the same time, they increasingly imitated Buddhist doctrines and practices. Most influential among these movements were the Shangqing movement of the fourth century and the Lingbao movement of the fifth century. Each of these movements promoted new scriptures that they claimed to be revelations of supreme divine truth. By the fifth century, the Taoist religion and Buddhism had become bitter rivals, competing for the support of emperors and the souls of the people. Naturally, as the Taoist religion underwent this formative process, its asceticism transformed significantly in its form, meaning, and purpose.

Ascetics in various religions have shared the inclination to view spirit (or soul) and matter as being mutually alien and antagonistic entities. Bodily mortification often has been carried out under the assumption that the flesh does little else but hinder one's progress toward salvation. For example, Christian ascetics have tended to view the flesh as the source of sinful impulses that hinder the salvation of the soul.[22] The goal of Jain asceticism is to purify and liberate the soul from *samsara* by "burning away" the karmic matter that adheres to it.[23] Manichaean ascetics considered the soul a particle of light issuing from the true God and aimed to liberate it from the evil prison of flesh.[24]

However, Taoists sought to immortalize both mind and body, and they did not draw a stark contrast between spirit (or soul) and matter. This crucial fact strongly affected the content and nature of their asceticism.

Henri Maspero, the great Western pioneer in Taoist studies, adeptly argued that Taoist theories on souls dictated that Taoists seek eternal life through bodily immortality. To the Chinese, spirit and matter were different modes of *qi* (energy, ether, material force);[25] spirit was a rarefied mode, matter a condensed mode. They thus saw the world as a continuum passing from void to material things. As a result, they had no concept of a soul that played the role of an invisible, spiritual counterpart to the material body. The Chinese view on souls was that every person possessed multiple souls. Although theories about the multiple souls varied in their specifics, a common view maintained that there were two groups of souls; the three *hun* souls and the seven *po* souls. The two groups of souls were believed to separate at death; the *hun* souls were thought to disperse into the skies, and the *po* souls were thought to seep out of the buried corpse into the soil. According to this theory, since the souls separated and dispersed at death, they did not perpetuate the deceased person's personality in an afterlife state that could be properly described as "salvation" or "immortality." Consequently, Maspero argued, the only means by which the Chinese could envision immortality was through the perpetuation of the flesh that kept the multiple souls together in their bodily habitat.[26]

Yet it is possible that some early Taoist immortality seekers did not actually believe in the immortality of the flesh. To believe in it certainly requires a great leap of faith, since virtually all empirical evidence confronted in real life seems to contradict it. Some, in keeping with the spirit of the *Zhuangzi*, may have understood "immortality" strictly as being a metaphor for an inner freedom and peace of mind. Some may have believed only in the immortality of an entity more subtle than the flesh. Many Taoist texts of the Song dynasty (960–1279 C.E.) onward set forth as their highest ideal the immortality and heavenly ascension of the "internal elixir" (*neidan*), a divine, internal entity concocted from the pure, subtle forces latent in the body. When it ascends, this entity, which is also known as the "*yang* spirit" (*yangshen*) or the "body outside of the body" (*shenwai zhi shen*), is said to leave the mortal body behind. Rudiments of such later doctrines may have already existed in the minds of some Taoists during the period covered in this study.[27]

However, while some Taoists probably understood "immortality" in such metaphorical or abstract ways, the immortality of the flesh is not explicitly rejected in any religious Taoist text of the first six centuries C.E. (as far as I am aware). Most early Taoist ascetics probably believed in the possibility of avoiding death and sought to achieve heavenly ascension in the immortal body.

Taoists also developed doctrines wherein hope was maintained for those who had died. First, there was the belief that some adepts had merely feigned their death by employing supernormal techniques of illusion. Even when death was not "feigned," it was believed that one could eventually gain the status of a lesser immortal after a lengthy sojourn in the subterranean realm of the dead, or become resurrected into the realm of humans. (It should be noted that in these scenarios the corpse does not decay and dissipate for eternity; it is somehow preserved, transformed, or regenerated).[28] However, serious adepts who pursued ascetic practices generally aspired to the highest grades of immortality, which were to be attained only by bypassing death.

Because they believed that the body had to be kept intact for their goal to be realized, Taoist adepts usually avoided practices that they considered harmful to their health. They did not wound the body through self-flagellation. They usually emphasized cleanliness and took care of bodily hygiene. They did not malnourish themselves to the point of disease or death—at least not intentionally. Deviations from these norms were rare and tended to be met with criticism from fellow Taoists.

However, because the goal was to make the body immortal and superhuman, Taoist adepts needed to see tangible proof in the here and now that they were training and transforming it properly. The mental fortitude and physical durability to persevere in increasingly greater austerities were in themselves deemed as such proof, as were the trance experiences induced through painstaking measures. Thus practices such as fasting and sleep avoidance were carried out at an intensity comparable to, if not surpassing, the asceticism of other religions. In this sense, the Taoist mind/body view encouraged and intensified asceticism.

Severe forms of asceticism can thus occur even when the practitioner is not indifferent to the well-being of the body. Actually, this phenomenon is not unique to Taoism. For example, within the Christian ascetic tradition, attitudes toward the body have been both negative and positive. An interesting comparison can be made between attitudes expressed in accounts concerning two famous Christian ascetics, Ethiopian Moses and Simeon the Stylite. Ethiopian Moses (ca. 320–407 A.D.) was a monk active in Egypt. He was a black man (hence the description "Ethiopian") of great physical size and strength who, prior to his conversion and monkhood, had been a slave and a robber and had committed every sort of imaginable sin. Throughout his monastic life, he was obsessed with overcoming his predisposition toward sinful acts and thoughts, which were blamed on his physical size and strength.

> Still, because he boiled with bodily vigor from his former way of life and was excited by pleasureful fantasies, he wasted his body with countless ascetic exercises. On the one hand, he abstained from meat and ate only a little bread, accomplishing a great deal of work and praying fifty times a day. On the other hand, for six years he prayed the whole night standing, never lying down or closing his eyes in sleep. At other times, he would go to the dwellings of the monks at night and secretly would fill the pitcher of each one with water. This was very hard work, for the place where some drew water was ten stades away, some twenty, some even thirty or more. For a long time he continued to have his former bodily strength, although he made every effort to conquer it with many ascetic exercises and oppressed his body with severe labors.[29]

Here is an example where austerities were practiced for the precise purpose of weakening the body. Moses' bodily strength and vigor are described as things that had to be conquered, since they were the cause of his "pleasureful fantasies." The body is seen as the soul's adversary in its quest for salvation.

However, in the *Homily on Simeon the Stylite*, by Jacob of Serug (449–521 A.D.), a very different attitude toward the body is conveyed. Simeon (386–459) was a Syrian monk renowned for lengthy fasts and other austerities. He spent his last forty years praying, exposed to the elements atop a small platform on a pillar approximately sixty feet high. Jacob's homily vividly describes an occasion during Simeon's stay on the pillar when a gangrenous and putrescent ulcer developed on his foot, causing incredible pain. Jacob's account attributes the appearance of the ulcer to the work of the Devil, who was attempting to undermine Simeon's efforts. In spite of the pain, Simeon continued to pray, standing the entire time on his one good foot. The text tells us that while doing so, Simeon sang out the following words:

> My foot stands straight and does not bend.[30] For its Lord will sustain it that it may stand and support the burden of the two. For lo, it bears the palace of the body like a pillar of the master-builder who fastens and supports it so that it will not be shaken. O Evil One, the hurt that you are causing does not hurt me since it is sweet for me; you will tire yourself out as I am not going to leave my labor.[31]

Eventually, when the condition of the bad foot had worsened to where it had rotted to tendons and bones, Simeon cut it off and said to it, "Go in peace until the resurrection. And do not grieve, for your hope will be kept in the kingdom."

Here the adversary is the Devil. The body is Simeon's ally. Even though Simeon's austerities tax the body severely, their purpose is not to weaken the body. Simeon trusts in God to strengthen and sustain the body so it can overcome the challenges of the Devil. He reassures his amputated foot that it will be reunited with him when his body is resurrected on the day of final judgment. Because of this belief in resurrection, the body is seen as bearing an equal stake with the soul in the battle with the Devil and the attainment of salvation.

Thus in the Christian tradition, asceticism has been accompanied by both negative and positive perceptions of the body. Simeon's concern for his body's sustenance and salvation bears a certain resemblance to the attitude of the Taoists. However, Taoism went a step further by asserting that austerities such as fasting and sleep avoidance, even when carried out to the point of bodily weakening and emaciation, would eventually strengthen the body and imbue it with powers previously unknown. Ultimately, in the best case scenario, the body was supposed to directly gain eternal life without undergoing death and resurrection.

For Taoist ascetics, becoming immortal meant redeeming the body from its mortal state. Also, most hoped to ascend to a heavenly realm beyond the ordinary world. Many believed the world itself was approaching inevitable destruction and was becoming increasingly evil in the process. These beliefs undoubtedly heightened their desire to transcend the world. In this sense, Taoist asceticism may have at times been motivated more by negative sentiments toward the mundane world than by positive aspirations toward higher goals. This pessimistic mood is particularly understandable in light of the widespread social strife that existed throughout the period of the late Han and Six dynasties. The end of the Han dynasty was marked by political intrigue and corruption that engendered widespread hardship and dissatisfaction among the populace. The culminative result was the aforementioned Yellow Turban Revolt of 184 C.E. Political and social stability rarely existed throughout the ensuing centuries. Wars persisted during the Three Kingdoms period (220–280) when the Wei, Shu and Wu kingdoms battled for supremacy. After a brief reunification under the Western Jin dynasty (265–316), the north was conquered by non-Chinese peoples who fought incessantly among themselves. During the fleeting intervals of peace, the political scene was rife with corruption, intrigue, and danger, rendering the benefits of social power and status dubious. For the peasantry and aristocracy alike, it must have often been difficult to be pleased with what the world had to offer.[32]

On the other hand, it can be argued that one's outlook toward the world and society is determined more on a personal, psychological level. Under virtually all circumstances, there are always people who by temperament can only perceive the human condition in a negative light. Nonetheless, one must not disregard the impact the historical context can have in dictating the extent and degree to which an antiworldly mentality can find its expression.

At both the physiological and cosmological levels, Taoist asceticism can be understood as a struggle between the forces of good (*yang*) and evil (*yin*). The good forces, at the physiological level, are the body's pure *qi* and the multitude of internal bodily deities that are activated through austerities. The austerities also serve to subdue the evil forces. The evil forces include the body's impure *qi*, along with its internal demons that try to undermine the adept's progress. At the cosmological level, the adept endeavors to communicate with divine beings (gods and immortals) and gain their support, while resisting the temptations of the mundane world and the demons that dwell in it. The enlightened mind and heightened spirituality of the ascetic are identified with *qi* in its refined, subtle forms that belong to the *yang* principle and possess a divine quality. The ordinary untrained flesh is seen to be full of gross, profane *qi* of the *yin* principle that hinders spiritual progress by obscuring the divine *qi* in the body. The uniqueness of this dualism lies in how the two sides of the duality are not completely alien to each other. Everything, regardless of which side it belongs to, is originally the same thing (*qi*) that has issued from the primordial state of non-being. The distinction between the things of the two sides lies not in their basic nature but in their degree of purity and refinement. This means that the untrained flesh, even though it is gross and impure, has the potential for transformation. Austerities act as the agent for this transformation.

Taoists fasted to purge the body of its impure *qi*. Because they considered all ordinary foods impure, they tried to eat as little as possible. To suppress their hunger they ingested special drug recipes and carried out techniques such as breath holding, air swallowing, saliva swallowing and talisman swallowing. The pure *qi* contained in the air and in their own saliva was thought to nourish the body in the best way possible, activating its latent divine forces in the process. Celibacy was practiced to retain seminal fluid. The vital forces that sustain life were thought to be concentrated in the semen, meaning that ejaculation could lead directly to the shortening of life.

Through their austerities, Taoists hoped to reach a higher spiritual state. By shedding all worldly desires and single-mindedly seeking immortality, they hoped to evoke the sympathy and assistance of gods and immortals. The elimination of sexual desire was considered particularly important in this regard. By employing meditation techniques that usually involved special visualizations, adepts entered trances, thereby hoping to encounter divine beings or gain a foretaste of heavenly realms. These trances also were partially induced and heightened by fasting and sleep avoidance.

Even though Taoist ascetics placed paramount importance upon health, it appears that overzealousness occasionally may have led to bodily harm and even death. The *Zhouyi cantongqi*, an alchemical text ascribed to Wei Boyang of the second century,[33] contains a passage that criticizes the excesses of ascetics.

[Adepts] eat air and make their intestines and stomach growl,
Exhaling the proper [*qi*] and inhaling the evil [*qi*] from the outside.
They never sleep during the daytime or night time,
And never rest from morning till evening.
Their bodies become more and more exhausted by the day.
With their consciousness obscure, they look like idiots.
[The blood in] their 100 blood vessels boils like water in a kettle,
Making them unable to reside in pure clarity.
They build walls and erect altars and shrines,
To engage in reverent worship from morning till evening.
Demonic entities manifest their forms to them in dreams,
And they become emotionally moved.
In their hearts and minds they rejoice,
And say to themselves, 'My life span will definitely be extended!'
Suddenly they die prematurely,
And their rotting corpses are exposed. (*Zhouyi cantongqi jie*
[HY1004/TT628], 1/21b–22a)

It is difficult to determine how often ascetic excesses lead to premature death. Usually, in most such cases, adepts probably fully intended to benefit—not harm—their health. The failure of such adepts could be rationalized by fellow adepts on the grounds that the failed adepts had pursued their methods incorrectly or had lacked inner devotion and moral virtue.

As we shall see, certain "immortality techniques" were tantamount to religious suicide. Theoretically, however, such methods were designed not to destroy the body but to create the illusion of death. The idea, particularly in instances where deadly quantities of poison were ingested, was that the corpse of the adept was merely an illusion fabricated for people to see. While creating this illusion of a corpse, the adept supposedly concealed himself from society to live on elsewhere as an immortal. However, it seems possible that in some cases ascetics may have abused and killed themselves as a result of more negative ideas and feelings. Some of them may have hated their bodies for the impurity of their untrained states. Some may have simply wanted to flee the agonies of worldly existence at all costs.

By the fourth century, and especially the fifth century, Taoists were eagerly incorporating Buddhist doctrines and practices into their religious system. Buddhist doctrines presented the Chinese with new and exciting possibilities for attaining spiritual perfection and transcendence. Taoists adopted the belief in *karma* and reincarnation and came to equate heavenly immortality with the liberation from *samsara*. The doctrine of *karma* accentuated the importance of suppressing and eliminating desires more than ever before. The doctrine of reincarnation caused Taoists to infer the existence of an individual spirit that survives successive bodily deaths. (This directly contradicted the Buddha's doctrine of no soul, or *anatman*.

Ironically, however, even Chinese Buddhists were initially unable to avoid drawing this inference from the doctrine of reincarnation.)[34]

As Buddhist influence became greater, there seems to have arisen an increased tendency among Taoists to emphasize spiritual enlightenment and transcendence more than physical longevity and immortality. Furthermore, the newly derived notion of an eternal, transmigrating spirit may have caused some to understand the ultimate salvation solely as the liberation of the spirit. This in turn may have caused some to abandon the ideal of physical immortality altogether. Among such Taoists, there may have arisen a tendency to devalue and abuse the body intentionally, in the hope of expediting the liberation of the spirit.

Apparently due to an awareness of such a problem, the *Yuqing jing* (HY1301/ TT1022–102431), an anonymous Taoist scripture of the sixth or seventh century, vehemently criticizes ascetic abuses. The *Yuqing jing* asserts that salvation must be realized within "this body," and insists that one must seek to perpetuate the life of the body, since the body is "the basis of the Tao." However, at the same time, the scripture does equate immortality with liberation from *samsara*. It also describes the ultimate salvation as an ascension and a union with a formless Non-Being. In other words, while vehemently asserting the need to keep the body intact, the *Yuqing jing* describes the greatest salvation as being a noncorporeal state. It thus presents us with an apparent contradiction and causes us to wonder what was supposed to happen to the flesh when the adept merged with the formless non-being. However, the idea seems to be that a good Taoist immortalizes the physical body by refining it into a formless state.

Over the centuries, historical writing—particularly that of traditional Confucian scholars, but also that of modern historians—has tended to cast a shadow of doubt upon the integrity of the Taoist religion. Prior to the latter half of this century, the Taoist religion had been a topic of little interest to historians, and mention was rarely made of Taoist religion aside from when it somehow affected political events. The Taoists mentioned in the standard histories have tended to be dubious characters; they include insurrectionists like Zhang Jue[35] and Sun En,[36] fawning political opportunists like Wang Qinruo[37] and Lin Lingsu,[38] and quack alchemists like Liu Mi.[39] The infamy of such characters has caused many to ignore or lose sight of the fact that most Taoists have practiced their religion in good faith. Historians of religion are now finally beginning to gain a more complete view through the texts of the Taoist Canon. We no longer rely solely on the accounts of those who were indifferent or hostile to the religion. This study focuses on a phenomenon that bears testimony to the earnestness with which Taoists practiced their religion. Taoist ascetics were willing to deny themselves the most basic worldly needs and comforts for the sake of their religious perfection.

CHAPTER TWO

The Lives of Taoist Ascetics (1)— Depictions in the *Liexian zhuan* and *Shenxian zhuan*

The *Liexian zhuan* (*Biographies of the Immortals*) and *Shenxian zhuan* (*Biographies of Divine Immortals*) are collections of fanciful stories about the lives and feats of famous immortals. Even though they bear virtually no credibility as historical sources, they nonetheless convey the cherished ideals of immortality seekers. While the general reader may have merely valued the stories for their entertaining quality, serious seekers of immortality saw the immortals depicted in the stories as inspirational figures and wanted to emulate them. It is therefore not unreasonable to speculate that many of the same austerities ascribed to the immortals were being attempted by real people, albeit without the same intensity or incredible results. Through the accounts of the *Liexian zhuan* and *Shenxian zhuan*, we can deduce much about the content and nature of Taoist asceticism up until the mid-fourth century.

The authorship of the *Liexuan zhuan* is ascribed to Liu Xiang (77 B.C.E.–6 C.E.). However, various scholars have found anachronisms in the text, and it appears that parts of it were written no earlier than the first or second century C.E. Although some of the stories could have been written by Liu Xiang or some other person of his time, additions have clearly been made at later periods. By the early fourth century, the text probably existed in a form resembling what we have now.[1]

The putative author of the *Shenxian zhuan* is Ge Hong (283–364 C.E.), the famous alchemist. It is beyond doubt that he wrote a book entitled *Shenxian zhuan*. However, much of Ge Hong's original work seems to be missing from today's editions of the *Shenxian zhuan*, which also appear to contain a certain amount of material written by someone else. The history of the text is truly complex. In fact, it had once been lost. It exists today as an independent book (in two slightly varying editions), only because somebody restored it by piecing together fragments preserved as quotes in other books. This apparently occurred some time in the seventeenth century or later. Various scholars have pointed out that some passages in today's text contain wording or convey attitudes that indicate interpolation by someone other than Ge Hong. Nonetheless, even though sizable portions of the text may not have been written by Ge Hong himself, nothing in its contents appears to be blatantly incongruent with the spiritual climate of the early fourth century.[2]

The *Liexian zhuan* and *Shenxian zhuan* provide us with a picture of the forms of training that existed in days when the quest for immortality was still loosely defined and structured. They depict men and women of diverse regions and periods who subscribed to various theories, methods, and ideals. The *Liexian zhuan* presents these personalities with no clear preference for any one approach toward immortality. The *Shenxian zhuan*, on the other hand, conveys a preference toward alchemy. Alchemy is described as the means that confers the highest grades of immortality, and other methods are described as "minor methods" that confer lower grades of immortality. The definitive distinction between higher and lower grades of immortality is that the higher immortals achieve heavenly ascension, while the lower immortals live eternally in an earthbound existence. Nonetheless, "minor methods" also are deemed necessary for the most ambitious adepts, since they enable them to acquire the mental and physical constitution worthy of concocting and ingesting alchemical potions.

It cannot be said that either text deems asceticism mandatory for attaining immortality. While many of the immortals depicted in them engage in austerities, quite a few exhibit traits that seem contradictory to the description of "ascetic." Perhaps most noticeably, the ideal of celibacy is contradicted in many places—especially in the *Liexian zhuan*—where sexual yoga (*fangzhongshu*) is mentioned favorably. In the *Liexian zhuan*, Laozi himself is described as being a master of sexual yoga.

> [Laozi] was fond of nurturing his *jing* (semen)[3] and *qi*. He valued the importance of copulating without ejaculating. (1/4b)[4]

The entry on Rongchenggong also conveys the following view of Laozi:

> [Rongchenggong] was able to adeptly practice the methods of supplementing and guiding, taking the *jing* (generative force) from the Dark Female. . . .
> His methods were the same as those of Laozi. It has also been said that he was Laozi's teacher. (1/3b–4a)

Even more striking is the story of a woman named Nü Ji.[5] Nü Ji, we are told, was a brewer and seller of exquisite liquor. One day, an immortal visited her saloon. After partaking in her liquor, the immortal left five silk scrolls as collateral for his unpaid bill. Nü Ji opened the scrolls and found that they were manuals on "nurturing the vital principle through copulation." Thereupon, Nü Ji did as follows:

[Nü] Ji secretly copied down the vital points in the texts and then set up a bedroom. She would bring in young men and have them drink her delicious liquor. Then she would have them stay overnight and practice with her the methods described in the texts. (2/14a)

Nü Ji regained her youth as a result. Later on, the immortal returned and took her away with him to instruct her further.

In the *Shenxian zhuan*, a distinctly worldy and moderately self-indulgent attitude is expressed from the mouth of Pengzu.[6] Pengzu, we are told, was 767 years old and had outlived forty-nine wives and fifty-four children. He was a master of numerous macrobiotic techniques, including the ingestion of herbs and medicines, fasting, respiratory techniques, light gymnastics, saliva swallowing, air swallowing, and sexual yoga. The text records a discourse he allegedly delivered to a female disciple named Cainü. Pengzu tells Cainü that he is different from the so-called immortals, or *xianren*, who can fly and transform themselves into birds and beasts. He derides these strange creatures who live on a diet of "primal breath" and *zhi* fungi,[7] take on strange facial appearances, grow fur on their bodies, and avoid all contact with society. In his opinion, even though they have managed to bypass death, they have lost their original integrity as human beings by shunning their natural desire for worldly pleasure and recognition. In the process, they have turned into beastlike creatures (1/4a).[8] Pengzu maintains that once one knows the proper methods for prolonging life, one should enjoy the benefits of good clothing and food, be sexually active, and participate in society as a good government official. None of life's pleasures are harmful unless pursued excessively. He specifically denounces celibate adepts as being "confused." In his opinion, people need to carry out sexual intercourse in a way that emulates heaven and earth. Heaven (*yang*) and earth (*yin*) intermingle when the sun submerges itself below the horizon. This intermingling makes the cosmos everlasting, and by extension of this principle, men and women can become immortal through sexual intercourse.

However, views of this kind were not shared by all. The proclamations attributed to Pengzu are best understood as apologetics for a faction of adepts that held a worldly and moderate outlook. The very fact that such apologetics appear in the text suggests that some adepts contrarily advocated celibacy and disdained worldly comforts and pleasures.

The *Shenxian zhuan*'s entry on Jiao Xian presents the most vivid and detailed picture of an ascetic lifestyle. Jiao Xian, we are told, was a 170-year-old man who lived in Hedong (the western part of the present-day Shanxi Province). His diet consisted of white rocks, which he somehow boiled to a consistency resembling taros. He frequently shared them with other people. Every day he went to the mountains to chop firewood, which he would bring back and secretly place at the gateways of every household in his village. Occasionally people would see him doing this. Out of gratitude, they would invite him inside to share their meal. Xian accepted these invitations, but for some reason never spoke to his hosts. Around 220 C.E., when the Han dynasty officially ended,[9] he moved to a place on the banks of the [Yellow] River. There he lived alone in a grass hut furnished with a single grass mat. His body was always covered with dirt and grime. He seldom ate. He had no contact with women and never walked on roads when he ventured outside of his hut. When his clothing wore out, he sold firewood for money to buy used clothes. He wore only a single-layered garment throughout the year, even during the coldest days of winter. Apparently due to this unusual lifestyle, the local governor regarded him as a "wise man" and came to visit him. However, Jiao Xian would not speak to him. The governor came to respect him even more for this. On one occasion, a brush fire burned down his hut when he was in it. When people went to see what had happened, they found him sitting calmly and motionlessly under the flaming ruins. After the fire had burned out and the hut had been completely reduced to ashes, he stood up. However, neither his body nor his clothing had been burnt. On another occasion, after he had built himself a new hut, the hut collapsed under a heavy snowfall with him in it. When people came to his rescue, they found him sleeping soundly beneath the snow, breathing in a relaxed manner and bearing the ruddy complexion of somebody in a drunken stupor. This convinced people that he possessed extraordinary qualities. Many people came to Jiao Xian requesting to "study the Tao" under him. But Jiao Xian always declined, saying, "I do not have the Tao." The narrative also tells us that he could transform his appearance into that of an old man or a young man at will. It ends by saying that he lived in such a way for over 200 years, until he left society entirely, never to be seen again (6/24b–25a).

Jiao Xian, we are thus told, came to be regarded as a holy man by virtue of his austere lifestyle, his reticence, and his invulnerability to fires and blizzards. These traits allegedly inspired people to seek instruction from him. Later Taoists also appear to have admired Jiao Xian's austere lifestyle. An abbreviated form of his story is found in Wang Xuanhe's *Sandong zhunang* (HY1131/TT780–782), a seventh-entury encyclopedic compilation on various aspects of the Taoist religion.[10] Jiao Xian's story is included there in a section entitled "Section on Poverty and Frugality" (*pinjian pin*).[11]

Further information on Jiao Xian is found in a passage from the *Wei lüe* (a lost text of the fourth century), quoted in Pei Songzhi's commentary to the *Sanguo zhi*.[12] There we are told that he had taken on the austere lifestyle at the end of the Han dynasty (220 C.E.), after his wife and children had been killed. The *Wei lüe*, in agreement with the *Shenxian zhuan*, tells us that he limited himself to the most meager food, clothing, and personal possessions. It also states that he avoided all contact with women and rarely spoke. However, unlike the *Shenxian zhuan*, it attributes to him no supernormal physical powers nor longevity and states that he died of illness at the age of eighty-nine. It makes no mention of his "boiling white rocks." Also, it tells us that to avoid political involvement and qualify for a daily grain allowance of five *sheng* (about one liter), he enlisted the help of an influential friend to register himself as being mentally disabled. Perhaps most interestingly, it tells us he was *derided*, particularly by the children in his community who insulted and hazed him. However, one day in 253, he correctly predicted that the Wu kingdom would defeat the Wei kingdom in battle. After this, he came to be widely acknowledged as a wise hermit.

The account of the *Wei lüe* in no way identifies Jiao Xian as an adept seeker of immortality. The author of Jiao Xian's story in the *Shenxian zhuan* may have fancifully embellished the life story of a well-known ascetic hermit in order to portray him as a Taoist adept and paragon of the ascetic ideal.

Another vivid description of an ascetic lifestyle is found in the story of Sun Deng in the *Shenxian zhuan*. There we are told that Sun Deng lived in the mountains, inside of a pit dug in the ground. There he sat day after day, playing the lute and reading the *Yijing* (Book of Changes). Like Jiao Xian, he wore a single-layered garment throughout the year. On the coldest days, he would keep himself warm by letting down his hair (which was over two meters long) and draping it over his whole body. Over the course of many years, he was sighted by people of many generations. They all viewed him as an extremely handsome man of youthful countenance. He frequently begged in the marketplaces, but gave everything he obtained to the poor. Perhaps most amazingly, the account tells us that nobody ever saw him eat (6/25a).

Begging also is mentioned in two other stories in the *Shenxian zhuan*, and one story in the *Liexian zhuan*. The *Liexian zhuan* tells the story of a certain Yin Sheng who lived under a bridge in Chang-an (present-day Xi-an) and begged daily in the marketplace. One time a person doused him with manure. Yin Sheng left, but later returned. Oddly, his clothing showed no traces of the manure. He was then arrested and bound in handcuffs and chains. But after he was released, he continued to beg. He was again arrested, then sentenced to death. But he suddenly disappeared into nowhere. Afterwards, for no clear reason, the house of the person who had doused him collapsed, killing over ten people. A ballad thus came to be sung in Chang'an that went, "If you encounter a beggar give him good liquor, so as to avoid the calamity that will destroy your family" (2/7a–b).

In the aforementioned story, the superhuman quality of Yin Sheng is reflected in his abilities to repel impurities, disappear, and bring ruin upon those who mistreat him. He seems to lack the altruistic quality attributed to Sun Deng, who generously gave what he obtained to the poor.

The *Shenxian zhuan* attributes the altruistic quality to Li A and Li Yiqi. There we are told that Li A "always begged in the marketplace of Chengdu. What he obtained he would then distribute to the poor" (2/8b). Li Yiqi, when he acquired food through begging, "would immediately hand it over to a poor person" (3/12a). In later Taoist hagiography, the holy man–beggar theme continues to be common, especially in stories about Lü Dongbin, the most popular immortal from the Song dynasty (960–1279 C.E.) onward. These stories emphasize the benefits gained by those who are kind to the beggar, more than the punishments suffered by those who mistreat him. It also is known that Wang Chongyang (1112–1170), the founder of the Quanzhen School (a large monastic Taoist school that survives to this day), required his disciples to foster their inner humility by begging for their livelihoods.[13] So far, substantial evidence from earlier periods has not been found of begging occuring as a mandatory practice for Taoist adepts. However, the presence of the holy man–beggar theme in the *Liexian zhuan* and *Shenxian zhuan* suggests that from early on, begging may have been a means of sustenance and self-discipline opted for by some immortality seekers.

Extremely common in both the *Liexian zhuan* and *Shenxian zhuan* are descriptions of immortals who lived and trained in the mountains. Mountain dwellers in the *Liexian zhuan* and *Shenxian zhuan* shun civilized, agrarian society in favor of a primitive, beastlike life in the wilderness. They eat little or nothing at all, subsisting on herbs and minerals the mountains provide. The following are a few examples from the *Liexian zhuan*:

Wo Quan was an old herb-picker of Mt. Huai.[14] He liked to eat pine seeds. On his body grew hair several *cun* (1 *cun* = 2.25 cm.) long. His eyes had become square shaped. (1/3a–b)

Qiong Shu was a Boundary Marker for the Zhou Dynasty. He was able to guide his *qi* and refine his body. He boiled stone marrow (stalactite) and ate it. He called it "congealed rock milk. . . ."[15]

When he reached the age of several hundred years he wandered about and [eventually] entered Mt. Taishi.[16] His stone bed and pillow exist there today. (1/9a)

Xiuyanggong was a man of Wei.[17] He lived in a stone grotto on Mt. Huayin.[18] In it is an overhanging stone bed that he used to sleep on. The stone is dented from erosion (because Xiuyanggong slept on it every day). He practically never ate, but would occasionally gather and eat deer bamboo (*huangjing, poligonatum sibiricum*). (1/18b)

Maonü's (Hairy Woman) style name was Yujiang. In Mt. Huayin, various hunters over many generations have sighted her. She has hair growing all over her body. She says that she was a palace attendant for the First Emperor of the Qin Dynasty. When the Qin Dynasty was overthrown, she fled and took refuge in the mountains. [There] she met the Taoist adept Gu Chun,[19] who taught her to eat pine needles. Eventually she overcame all sensation of hunger and cold. Her body felt light as though it was flying. For over 170 years, the grotto where she lives has issued forth the sounds of drums and harps. (3/7b–8a)

Interesting in the passages just cited are the strange physical traits developed by the immortals. These remind us of the aforementioned beastlike immortals disdained by Pengzu. The *Liexian zhuan* and *Shenxian zhuan* describe further such examples. The *Liexian zhuan* tells us that Mister Ning, who lived on Mt. Longmei,[20] "had a body covered with hair and had wide ears" (2/10b). Huang Yuanqiu "wore a fur coat and kept his hair let down. His ears were seven *cun* (app. 16 cm.) long and he had no teeth" (2/13b). According to the *Shenxian zhuan*, Liu Gen, who lived in a stone grotto on the steep cliffs of Mt. Songgao,[21] "went naked in winter and summer, and the hair on his body grew to a length of 1 or 2 *chi* (one *chi* = app. 22–24 cm.)" (3/10a). Hua Ziqi, after receiving the "Holy Treasure (Lingbao) Method of the Immortal Recluses" and imbibing the prescribed concoction, "shed his skin ten times in one year, just as a cicada sheds its shell" (1/5a).

The passages on Qiong Shu and Xiuyanggong suggest that Mt. Song and Mt. Hua were established early on as reputable sites for reclusive training and pilgrimage. Today, both mountains have large, active Taoist monasteries. It is common for such mountains to have sites and relics associated with famous immortals.[22] To this day, one of the peaks along the route to the summit of Mt. Hua bears the name "Maonü's Peak," in honor of the aforementioned female immortal.[23] More interestingly, a Taoist treatise of the twelfth century criticizes practitioners who rely excessively on fasting and other dietetic practices by stating, "Some people, *longing to become like Maonü* (emphasis added), ingest [various substances]. It is not that there are no more pine or arbor vitae trees. But after the northern woman (Maonü?), no one has been able to ascend the skies [by ingesting pine and/or arbor vitae tree leaves]."[24] These remarks attest to the lasting popularity of Maonü, as well as to the fact that legendary immortals were emulated by real people.

What were the motives for dietary practices such as those ascribed to adepts like Wo Quan, Qiong Shu, Xiuyanggong, and Maonü? The substances ingested by adepts were certainly often thought to have great medicinal potency. Symbolically and perhaps subconsciously, as has been suggested by Jean Levi and Kristofer Schipper,[25] the dietary practices of early adepts may have resulted from a desire to return to the lifestyle of preagrarian times when people, untainted by the evils of civilization, supposedly lived longer and happier lives.

But most important, a common goal for many adepts was to stop eating. Plant and mineral substances often were meant as aids for suppressing hunger. Highly instructive here is a passage that may have been part of Ge Hong's original *Shenxian zhuan*. This passage, which is missing from the present editions of the *Shenxian zhuan*, is found in the seventh *juan* of the *Bowuzhi*.

The *Shenxian zhuan* says, "It is a fact that food is where the 100 diseases and wicked demons gather. The less you eat, the more your mind will open up, and the longer your life span will be. The more you eat, the more your mind will be closed, and the shorter your life span will be.[26]

A possible conclusion that could have been drawn from this was that eating nothing could bring about immortality.

The substances allegedly ingested by the immortals of the *Liexian zhuan* and *Shenxian zhuan* include the following: pine seeds, pine sap, pine needles, mica, sesame seeds, peach and plum blossoms, stalactite, lychee fruit, deer bamboo (*huangjing*), *tianmendong* (*asparagus cochinchinensis*), chrysanthemum flowers, "stone grease" (a type of clay), mercury, deerhorn, chestnuts, cypress resin, sulphur, lead, the *zhu* plant (*atractylodes macrocephala*), rush and scallion roots, rape-turnip seeds, mallow (*malva verticillata*), turtle brains, limonite ("Yu's leftover food"), cinnabar, bramble roots (*rubus tephrodes*), cantalope, autumn root (*aconitum carmichaeli*), seeds of the *zhi* plant (*iris florentina*), the *changpu* plant (*acorus gramineus*), cinnamon, broom plant (*kochia scoparia*), "pine seeds that grow as parasites on mulberry trees," niter, onions and scallions, the *badou* plant (*croton tiglium*), realgar, sap of the arbor vitae tree (*biota orientalis*), flowers of the *shigui* tree (*rhaphiolus indica*), and "red flower pills" (unidentified).

While perhaps not all of these substances were considered hunger suppressants, many were taken individually or included in recipes designed to facilitate fasts.

In most cases, fasting adepts were probably permitted to drink water. The *Shenxian zhuan* tells us that a certain house servant named Chen Anshi received two pills from two immortals, who told him to never eat again. Henceforth, Chen Anshi "never ate again, only drinking water" (8/34a). If consumed in large quantities, water also could help to suppress hunger. It is plausible to speculate that some fasting adepts may have resorted to such a tactic. However, in chapter 4, we shall encounter a fasting regimen that prohibits even the taking of fluids.

Aside from ingesting small amounts of prescribed substances, fasts also were sustained through techniques of visualization, controlled breathing, breath holding, air swallowing, saliva swallowing, and talisman swallowing. These techniques usually were carried out while ingesting hunger-suppressing substances, since they were otherwise too strenuous.

The *Liexian zhuan* contains the following two passages:

The Guardian of the Pass Yin Xi was a Grand Master of the Zhou [Dynasty]. He was well versed in the esoteric studies and always imbibed the essences and efflorescences. (1/5a)

[Chixuzi ("the Master of the Red Beard")] imbibed the mists and did away with [grains].[27] (2/1a)

The term *essences and efflorescences* probably refers to celestial nutrients that were believed to issue from the sun and moon. To imbibe them, the adept would visualize the solar and lunar nutrients descending and entering his mouth. He would then swallow his air and/or saliva, which was thought to contain the celestial nutrients. "Imbibing the mists" probably describes a similar method.[28] The *Liexian zhuan* also tells us that Chixuzi ate pine seeds, an herb called *tianmendong* (*asparagus cochinchinensis*), and a type of clay called "stone grease." Yin Xi, we are told, accompanied his teacher Laozi to "the lands of the flowing sands" (foreign nations in the west) to "convert the barbarians."[29] There, Yin Xi ate sesame seeds.

The *Shenxian zhuan* similarly tells us about adepts who fasted while employing special techniques. Huang Jing of Wuling,[30] we are told, trained alone in Mt. Huo[31] for eighty years. Later, he moved to Mt. Song where he practiced "imbibing *qi* and doing away with grains (fasting)." He practiced methods of "swallowing and expelling," "womb breathing," and "internal vision." He "summoned the Six *Jia* Jade Girls by swallowing the *yin* and *yang* talismans." He visualized "a red star in front of his *dongfang* (one of the special compartments or "palaces" thought to exist inside of the head)," which would "grow larger and larger and become like a fire that enveloped the body." These methods restored him to his youth when he reached the age of 200 (*Shenxian zhuan* 10/42b).

Yuzi (Master Jade; his real name was Zhang Zhen) served the Immortal Changsangzi as a disciple, after which he founded his own school and authored hundreds of "books on the Tao." Sometimes he would hold his breath and lie motionless for extended periods. The text states, "When one tried to make him get up, he would not get up. When pushed, he would not budge. When one tried to bend him, he would not bend. When one tried to stretch him out, he would not stretch out. He would stay like this for 100 days or for several tens of days before finally rising" (*Shenxian zhuan* 8/33a).

Kong Anguo of Lu[32] practiced the "guiding of *qi*" and ingested "lead pills" (*qiandan*, perhaps better translated as "lead and cinnabar"). At the age of 200, he had the complexion of a young boy. He had hundreds of disciples with whom he lived in secrecy in Mt. Qian.[33] The text states, "Every time he entered his chamber to abstain from grains (fast), he would emerge a year and a half later more youthful than before. When he was not in his chamber, he would eat normally, in the same way as ordinary people of the world" (9/35b).

Gan Shi of Taiyuan[34] "was adept at guiding his *qi* and not drinking and eating." We also are told that "he ingested *tianmendong* (*asparagus cochinchinensis*) and practiced the affairs of the bedroom (sexual yoga)" (*Shenxian zhuan* 10/42b).

The "imbibing of *qi* "(*fuqi*) and "swallowing and expelling" (*tuntu*) ascribed to Huang Jing were methods similar to those of "imbibing the essences and efflorescences" and "imbibing the mists." Such methods were meant to satiate or prevent hunger by filling the digestive system with air and/or saliva. "Swallowing the *yin* and *yang* talismans" refers to swallowing paper talismans bearing special diagrams. Conceivably, the adept's faith in the divine efficacy of the talismans could have had the psychosomatic effect of alleviating or preventing hunger. The term *womb breathing* has been used in various ways over the years. It is hard to say exactly what it refers to in the *Shenxian zhuan*. However, "womb breathing" in most cases seems to have involved holding one's breath or slowing down one's breathing to near stoppage.

Through meditation and controlled breathing, adepts may have entered trance states where the body's metabolism slowed down drastically. Perhaps by staying in such a trance for extended periods, adepts thought they could in effect hibernate and survive without eating. Yuzi appears to be depicted doing this, as perhaps are Kong Anguo and Gan Shi, if "guiding the *qi*" can be understood as a method of breath control and internal visualization.

Even if adepts did not enter into "hibernation" states, it is possible, as Joseph Needham has pointed out, that the anoxaemia caused by breathing techniques (and aggravated high altitude conditions) led to a loss of appetite that made fasts more bearable. As Needham has also pointed out, anoxaemia could also have caused the visions and strange bodily sensations experienced by adepts.[35]

So far we have seen that the *Liexian zhuan* and *Shenxian zhuan* contain vivid portrayals of self-imposed poverty, wilderness seclusion, and fasting. Of course, celibacy is probably the practice that we most often associate with the word "ascetic." However, our two texts contain relatively few references to it.

As previously mentioned, Pengzu's criticism of celibate adepts recorded in the *Shenxian zhuan* does enable us to infer that there were celibate adepts. The *Shenxian zhuan* also tells us that Jiao Xian "had no contact with women." The text probably mentions this because Jiao Xian's celibacy was considered a trait becoming of a holy man and a reason for his longevity and indestructibility.[36] We can further cite two more episodes from our texts that bear some degree of testimony to an early celibate tradition.

The *Liexian zhuan* has a story about a flute-playing pig herder of Gaoyi[37] named Shangqiu Zixu. At the age of seventy, he "had never married and had not aged." When asked what the reason was for his perpetual youth, he would answer, "If you eat the roots of the *zhu* (*atractylodes macrocephala*) and *changpu* (*acorus gramineus*) and drink water, you will never get hungry and you will not age." For over 300 years he continued to be seen by people. However, nobody who emulated his dietetics achieved any good results because they were "lazy" and unable to persevere for even a full year. These people (who, we are told, belonged to "wealthy and noble families") would then always say, "He must possess some other secret method" (2/9b–10a).

In stating that Shangqiu Zixu "had never married and had not aged," the text may be implying a connection between sexual abstinence (or at least the avoidance of marriage) and longevity. The method of longevity explicitly cited here is an austere diet of herbs and water, and the main moral of the story appears to be that one must persevere in order to attain immortality. But could another implication be that the "other secret method" was sexual abstinence? I am not sure. This episode bears only vague testimony to a celibate tradition, if any.

However, the story of She Zheng in the *Shenxian zhuan* presents a clear example of an adept who endorsed celibacy as a macrobiotic measure. She Zheng, we are told, was a man of Badong[38] who trained somewhere in the kingdom of Wu at the end of the Han dynasty (ca. 220 C.E.).[39] He had twenty disciples whom he taught to "guide their *qi, completely refrain from [the activities of] the bedroom* (emphasis added), and ingest small pills of stone brain (stalactites)" (10/40a).

As we shall see in chapters 4 and 5, various Taoist training methods called for celibacy. Unless one was celibate, these methods were deemed futile and even dangerous. The most important purpose for celibacy was the retention of seminal fluid (referred to as *jing* or "essence"), which was considered indispensable for good health and long life. Loss of seminal fluid was thought to shorten the life span.

Still, it must be noted once again that both the *Liexian zhuan* and *Shenxian zhuan* contain many references to immortals who practiced sexual yoga (i.e., were not celibate) and do not express a critical attitude toward them. Also, many of the immortals depicted in the *Liexian zhuan* and *Shenxian zhuan* are householders. Of course, sexual yogic techniques also were designed to help the practitioner retain his *jing*, and in this sense served the same purpose as celibacy. These techniques required the male practitioner to resist ejaculation at the moment of climax during intercourse with his female partner and then send the *jing* to the brain through the spine. Practitioners of sexual yoga believed that their methods not only helped retain their *jing* but actually increased it through sexual stimulus.[40]

In sum, Taoist adepts could choose either celibacy or sexual yoga as their means for retaining their *jing*. Prior to heavy Buddhist influence, celibate monasticism did not exist as an institution among Taoists. Most Taoists probably did not believe that sexual activity was inherently immoral.

While physiological concerns dictated the practices of ascetics to a large degree, it also was considered important that they develop impeccable inner character. Most instructive in this regard is the *Shenxian zhuan*'s entry on Zhang Daoling, the semilegendary founder of the Five Pecks of Rice School (Heavenly Masters School). In it he is depicted as a master alchemist who knew how to concoct an elixir of immortality by means of the "Nine Crucibles" recipe.[41] As the story goes, he one day announced to his followers that his "Nine Crucibles" recipe would be transmitted to only two men: Wang Chang and "a man who will come from the east." When this man—who was named Zhao Sheng—arrived, he was immediately put through the following seven trials:

First trial—When Zhao Sheng arrived at Zhang Daoling's house, he was refused entry. For forty days, he stayed at the front gate, sleeping on the ground at night. To add to his difficulty, Zhang Daoling sent people to harass him with reprimands and insults. Finally, he was invited in.

Second trial—Zhao Sheng was made to camp in the fields and to guard the millet crop from wild animals. One day, at sundown, he was visited by a gorgeous woman traveler, who asked to spend the night with him before continuing on her journey the next day. He agreed, and she ended up staying for several days, since she complained of aching legs. She constantly tried to seduce him, but he managed to resist her charms till the very end.

Third trial—Zhao Sheng, while walking down the road one day, saw thirty pots of gold sitting on the ground. He left them alone.

Fourth trial—Zhao Sheng went into the mountains to gather firewood for Zhang Daoling, whereupon he was attacked by three tigers. As they devoured the clothes he wore, he remained calm and said, "I am but a Taoist adept. From my youth I have done no wrong. Therefore I came, not regarding 1000 *li* (about 415 km.) as far, to serve a divine master and seek the way of long life. Why are you doing this to me? Did the demons of the mountains not send you here to test me?" Soon, the tigers left.

Fifth trial—Zhao Sheng went to the market and bought 14 *pi* (140 m.) of silk. Even though he had paid the money, the silk merchant falsely claimed that he had not. Without protesting or getting angry, Zhao Sheng gave the merchant his own clothes as payment.

Sixth trial—When Zhao Sheng was again guarding the crops, he was visited by a beggar of loathsome appearance. His clothing was tattered, his face was covered with dirt and grime, and his smelly and filthy body was covered with festering welts. Moved to profound pity, Zhao Sheng fed him a full meal, gave him his own clothes to wear, and sent him off with a supply of his own rice.

Seventh trial—Zhang Daoling took his disciples to the top of a precipitous mountain cliff. Growing from the face of the cliff was a peach tree full of fruit. He then told his disciples that anyone who fetched a peach would be revealed profound secrets. More than 200 disciples gazed down the cliff and contemplated fetching a peach, but recoiled out of fear. Zhao Sheng alone was courageous and said, "If one has the protection of the gods, how could there be any danger? A holy master is present here. Certainly he will not allow me to die in this valley. If the master has something to teach us, then there certainly must be some way by which [the peaches] can be gotten." He then jumped off the cliff and on to the tree. He picked 202 peaches and filled the breast of his garment with them. However, the face of the cliff was steep and had no handholds or footholds. He thus threw the peaches upward, one by one. Zhang Daoling then extended his arm, took Zhao Sheng by the hand, and pulled him up. His arm stretched to a length of roughly seven meters when he did this (4/16b–17a).

After this, Zhang Daoling tested the faith and resolve of his disciples once more by jumping off of the cliff. Zhao Sheng and the aforementioned Wang Chang did the same, and landed on a ledge. There Zhang Daoling taught them the recipe for the divine elixir.

In this narrative, the greatest secrets are transmitted to Zhao Sheng only after passing all of the trials. By passing the trials, he exhibits humility, generosity, compassion, willpower, and courage. He even shows that he does not fear death itself.

The theme of trials also is found in the *Shenxian zhuan*'s entrys on Li Babai, Hugong, and Wei Boyang, which we shall now summarize.

Li Babai, an Immortal of the Shu region (present-day Sichuan), tested the character of a certain Tang Gongfang by disguising himself as one of his servants. Because he was much more hard working than the other servants, he soon won Tang's affection. Suddenly one day, the good servant fell ill. Although Tang spent exorbitant sums of money on doctors and medicines, his condition only grew worse; huge festering welts developed all over his body. When told by the good servant that the welts would heal only if somebody licked them, Tang had three maidservants lick the welts. When he requested that Tang himself lick the welts, he complied. He also asked that Tang's wife do it, so she complied as well. The good servant then had Tang bring him a tub of liquor to bathe in. After the good servant emerged from the tub with his wounds fully healed, he revealed his true identity. He then told Tang, his wife, and his three maidservants to bathe in the liquor. When they came out of the tub, they had been restored to youth. Li Babai then transmitted an alchemical scripture to Tang, who went into Mt. Yuntai, concocted the elixir, and became an immortal (2/8b).

The immortal Hugong subjected his disciple Fei Changfang to a series of trials. Fei, a wealthy government official, first had to stage his death in order to abandon his familial and occupational responsibilities.[42] Having successfully done so, he went to join Hugong.[43] Hugong left him among a horde of growling, snarling tigers. Fei was undaunted. The next day (the text does not say how he escaped the tigers), Hugong locked him inside of a stone cave. Above Fei's head was an enormous boulder suspended from the ceiling by a grass rope. As he sat under the boulder, snakes chewed on the rope. After Fei had withstood this ordeal without the least bit of fear, Hugong commended him as being "teachable" and told him to eat a pile of hideously malodorous manure containing maggots over an inch in length. Fei hesitated, and Hugong declared him unfit to acquire the "Way of the Immortals." He could only become a "master on earth" with a life span of several hundred years. Fei was thus sent back into society with a "talisman of enfeoffment," which endowed him with a wide range of thaumaturgic powers, particularly as a healer and an exorcist (5/20b–21b).

The alchemist Wei Boyang, the putative author of the alchemical classic *Zhouyi cantongqi*, entered the mountains with three disciples to concoct a "divine elixir." When the elixir was ready, Wei fed it to a dog, which died on the spot. Wei then ingested the elixir and died. One of the disciples, who refused to think that his teacher could have concocted a bad elixir, also ingested the elixir. He immediately died. The other two disciples, preferring to live out their normal life spans, left the mountain without taking the elixir. As soon as they left, Wei got up, revived the faithful disciple and the dog, and together they left the world as immortals (1/5a).

The notion clearly conveyed throughout the *Shenxian zhuan*, particularly in its stories of "trials," is that the highest form of immortality is so elusive that it can only be attained through extraordinary effort. Before one could practice the ultimate art, one had to be perfected physically and spiritually. This mentality was probably a primary factor in motivating adepts toward asceticism in its extreme forms. Adepts went through long fasts or subjected themselves to arduous and dangerous living conditions to prove to themselves, their masters, the gods, and the immortals that they possessed sufficient strength and virtue to practice the highest methods. According to the *Shenxian zhuan*, the highest method is alchemy. However, as we shall see, different schools endorsed various other types of practices as vehicles toward heavenly immortality. (By the Song period, it became standard practice to use alchemical terminology to describe training regimens centered around meditation and respiration techniques. Practitioners of these regimens—which involve no manipulation or ingestion of chemicals—are known as "internal alchemists." The claim of some internal alchemists has been that men like Wei Boyang and Ge Hong were themselves internal alchemists.)

It also can be said that immortality techniques required great courage, due to the dangers involved in carrying them out. Severe health problems and deaths may have occasionally occurred as a result of ascetic excesses. For a Taoist adept, disease and death represented failure. Such failure was understood to occur when difficult techniques were pursued incorrectly or prematurely. In theory, even the harshest austerities—those that weakened and emaciated the body—were supposed to lead to physical revival and strengthening. Even the most ardent ascetics generally did not seek to destroy the body. Yet in certain cases this may have been exactly what they were doing.

Some "immortality" methods were tantamount to suicide. The adept would poison himself to death with an "immortality potion" under the sincere belief that he would somehow proceed to an immortal existence while leaving behind a fake corpse. The *Shenxian zhuan*'s story of Wei Boyang may have issued from a faction that promoted such a method.

The *Liexian zhuan* contains stories that describe methods of self-cremation and drowning. We are told that Ningfengzi, who served the Yellow Emperor as "Supervisor of Pottery," was one day visited by a man who taught him how to manipulate fire to create five-colored smoke. Later, Ningfengzi built a fire and burned himself in it. The text states that he "ascended and descended together with the smoke." When the fire had burned out, people found his skeleton and buried it in a hill north of Ning.[44] For this reason, he was posthumously named "Ningfengzi," which means "the master enfeofed at Ning" (1/1b). This story clearly describes a method of self-cremation. Ningfengzi's alleged self-cremation also is mentioned in Tao Hongjing's (456–536) *Zhengao*, as we will see in chapter 5. Presumably, the implication of the story is that Ningfengzi had risen with the smoke to become a heavenly immortal, while leaving his skeleton (or a semblance of it) behind.

Xiaofu of Jizhou,[45] we are told, worked from his youth as a repairer of sandals in the marketplace of Xizhou.[46] After many years, he had not aged. Eventually, people took notice and came to inquire about his secrets. He refused to instruct anybody, except for a certain Liangmu,[47] to whom he transmitted "fire techniques." The text then continues with what appears to be a description (albeit obscure) of a self-cremation that brought about heavenly ascension.

As he (Xiaofu) was about to ascend beyong the "three brightnesses,[48] he took leave of Liangmu. He built fires, several tens in number, and ascended. Many people in Xiyi[49] worshipped him. (1/6b)

A possible reference to self-drowning is found in the story of Qin Gao of Zhao.[50] Qin Gao, who had "wandered about between Jizhou and Zhuo[51] jun[52] for over 200 years," one day "entered" the Zhuo River,[53] taking a seahorse with him. His disciples underwent ritual purifications, built a shrine by the river, and awaited his return. He eventually emerged from the water, mounted a red carp, and assumed his seat on the shrine altar. In the morning, 10,000 people came to see him. After over a month in the shrine he left, "entering the river" again (1/13a).[54]

The apparent self-drowning, coupled with Qin Gao's status as a sect leader and cult object, bring to mind events that transpired during the armed revolts led by Sun En, a Taoist of the Heavenly Masters School.[55] In the *Jin shu* (Official History of the Jin Dynasty), we are told that Sun En drowned himself after a devastating battle defeat in 402 C.E. His followers then declared him a Water Immortal (*shuixian*). In a shocking display of faith and loyalty, over 100 of them proceeded to drown themselves. Also, on one occasion when Sun En's faithful were forced to flee their homes for survival, the women drowned their babies in a river and proclaimed to them, "We rejoice that you are ascending to the halls of the immortals before [us]. Later we shall follow you [there]."[56]

It is difficult to say how common suicidal methods were among immortality seekers. As we shall see in chapter 5, suicidal methods were held in particularly high esteem by the Shangqing movement. However, not all Taoists viewed suicidal methods so favorably, since the highest ideal in most cases was to achieve heavenly immortality without undergoing any form of death—whether actual or feigned. Most notably, as we shall see in chapter 7, the *Yuqing jing* repeatedly denounces religious suicides.

In later years, asceticism took on many new forms and meanings. However, many of the essential traits of Taoist asceticism are conveyed in the *Liexian zhuan* and *Shenxian zhuan*. Still lacking among Taoist ascetics was any kind of organization and regulation on a large scale. Adepts of different factions appear to have had their own austerities, which they carried out for their own reasons. There was no commonly shared cosmology or ethical system that underpinned their asceticism.

What existed were various immortality techniques, many of which required isolation, fasting, or celibacy.

This situation began to change considerably in the late fourth and early fifth centuries, when the Shangqing and Lingbao movements emerged and left a strong influence on Taoism as a whole. Both movements, with their newly "revealed" scriptures, set forth comprehensive systems of doctrine and practice that gave a clearer, more universal definition to the meaning and purpose of ascetic practices. For some vivid portrayals of the lives of ascetics during the fourth through sixth centuries, we shall now turn our attention to the *Daoxue zhuan*.

CHAPTER THREE

The Lives of Taoist Ascetics (2)— Depictions in the *Daoxue zhuan*

Ma Shu's (522–581) *Daoxue zhuan* (Biographies of Learners of the Tao) is a hagiographic work that contains much valuable information on Taoist asceticism during the fourth through sixth centuries.[1] The complete text of the *Daoxue zhuan* no longer survives. However, large fragments of it have been preserved in Wang Xuanhe's (fl. seventh century) *Sandong zhunang* and *Shangqing daolei shixiang* (HY1124/TT765), as well as various other texts.[2]

An account of Ma Shu's life is preserved in two official histories. The account tells us that he was a renowned scholar—versed in "Buddhist books, the *Book of Changes* and the *Laozi*"—who attempted to live an austere, reclusive life. At the prime of his life, he went into retirement on Mt. Mao. He declined an appointment as the Minister of Revenue for the Chen dynasty. Later, he grudgingly accepted the invitation of the Prince of Poyang, but refused to live in the elegant house built for him. Instead, he chose to live in a grass hut in a bamboo grove. Members of the royalty and nobility frequently brought him gifts, but he refused these as best he could.[3] Ma Shu's apparent preference for austerity and reclusion in his personal life perhaps serves as a partial explanation for why ascetic behaviors and training methods are so frequently mentioned in the *Daoxue zhuan*. His own preferences probably dictated considerably whom he chose to depict, what he chose to mention, and how he may have embellished the information he had available.

The prominence of asceticism in the surviving *Daoxue zhuan* fragments also can be attributed to the selective preferences of Wang Xuanhe, the seventh-century compiler of the *Sandong zhunang* and *Shangqing daolei shixiang*. Wang Xuanhe appears to have held a high regard for asceticism, as is reflected in how his *Sandong zhunang* contains sections entitled "Section on Poverty and Frugality," "Section on Hiding One's Brilliance," "Section on Dietetics," and "Section on Cutting Off Grains (fasting)." Many of his quotes from the *Daoxue zhuan* are found in these sections.

The *Daoxue zhuan* consisted of twenty *juan*.[4] Fragments from entries on 106 different personages have survived, and there is no way of knowing how many more entries there originally were. None of the fragments preserve an entire entry, although some of the fragments—such as those on Fan Chai and Lu Xiujing—can be pieced together to reconstruct lengthy accounts. Unfortunately, prefatory statements stating the scope and purpose of the work do not survive. The original text in its entirety probably attempted to give a comprehensive account of the deeds of great Taoist figures from all periods, beginning from murky antiquity.[5] This can be surmised from the fact that some of the fragments record the ancient lore surrounding the mythical sage emperors Zhuanxu,[6] Yao, and Shun,[7] as well as the legend of the Lingbao Five Talismans.[8] The surviving fragments also include excerpts from entries on eighteen personages of the Han and Three Kingdoms periods. Among these personages are Han Emperor Wu, Zhang Daoling (see pp. 25–27), Jiao Xian (see pp. 17–19), She Zheng (see p. 25),[9] and Sun Deng (see p. 19). Fragments on such earlier figures are considerably outnumbered by fragments on later figures. However, this is quite likely because later authors took interest in the *Daoxue zhuan* primarily for its information on subsequent figures, since information on earlier figures could be found in previous hagiographical sources.

Ma Shu wrote not as a critical, objective historian, but as a pious Taoist intent on glorifying great Taoists and inculcating religious values. For this reason, he may have embellished or exaggerated the facts. He may have spuriously attributed certain sayings to his protagonists to make them conform to his own image of a saint. The text fragments therefore cannot be fully relied upon as being factual. We can merely speculate within the boundaries of common sense that something resembling the accounts may have taken place. The sources Ma Shu relied upon must have varied greatly. For information on earlier events and personages, it appears he relied heavily on the *Shenxian zhuan* and other books of Taoist lore available to him. For information on figures from the fourth through sixth centuries, he may have relied more on hearsay than on written sources.

However, when compared to the tales of the *Liexian zhuan* and *Shenxian zhuan*, the information in the *Daoxue zhuan* seems more credible. Many of its accounts are about people who lived in the same century as Ma Shu. While current events can certainly be exaggerated or miscommunicated, Ma Shu still would have been better informed and restrained to the facts when describing people and events known firsthand by his contemporaries. Perhaps more important, Ma Shu seems not to have been particularly interested in amazing his readers with miraculous stories (though he does record some miracles). He appears to have been much more concerned with providing moral exhortation and inspiration through living examples. For this reason, his accounts often describe deeds and traits that are in no way miraculous or sensational, but rather quite mundane. He describes such deeds and traits simply because they exemplify lofty moral virtues. While Ma Shu may well have idealized his protagonists excessively to make their life stories conform to his own values, his accounts are much more sober than those of the *Liexian zhuan* and *Shenxian zhuan*.

The *Daoxue zhuan* reflects some of the important new trends that were occuring within Taoism at the time. Perhaps most important among these was the development and proliferation of a celibate monasticism that was patterned after the Buddhist model. The *Daoxue zhuan* also provides some valuable early evidence concerning how vegetarianism came to be enforced as a Taoist monastic regulation. Also, the ascetics depicted in the *Daoxue zhuan* frequently embody the ideals of ritual piety and altruism, ideals that were vigorously endorsed by the Lingbao movement of the fifth century.

The *Daoxue zhuan*'s most vivid description of austere living is found in the story of Fan Chai. In it we are told that Fan Chai[10] lived alone, "spending entire days in silence" in a shack made from old rags and thatch. He went bare legged throughout the year, "but his legs never chapped and cracked." "He never went to sleep," but this did him no harm since "his skin was like that of a maiden and he had a beautiful face." He was respected and liked by all, and he always smiled when he entertained company.

His only possessions were an empty lunch box and a clay pot. The clay pot substituted as a pillow. Taking these belongings with him, he would wander about, begging for ten days at a time. His diet consisted entirely of rough millet and rice with vegetable stew. He avoided eating non-sticky rice, large millet, *lao* and *li* liquor (unclarified sweet wines), and tasty foods and fruits. For each ten days he limited his total food intake to about one *sheng* (0.5955 liters).

His personality, while amiable, also was eccentric. He was completely indifferent toward worldly status, recognition, and pleasure. His movements were quick, his speech rapid and nearly unintelligible. He never boasted of clairvoyant powers, nor did he speak of "spiritual omens." He refused to talk to prestigious members of the community. He never listened to music. He often sat with his eyes closed. He had the strange habit of lying down and talking to himself, uttering phrases that made little or no sense to anyone else. One of his favorite phrases was "the troops of Wang Jian have come."[11] His clothing was made from rags of different colors. He wore a hat that appeared to be several decades old. He looked filthy, yet he always smelled fragrant and clean (*Sandong zhunang* 2/1a–b).

As we can see, this man of ca. 400 C.E. lived like a vagrant and exhibited traits suggestive of insanity. While such a man might usually draw scorn and derision, the *Daoxue zhuan* portrays him as being a saint of extraordinary spirituality and virtue and says that he was respected and well liked. The understanding is that he lowered himself to vagrancy because he had transcended all feelings of pride and shame. His speech and conduct were nonsensical because his insight and spirituality eluded the comprehension of ordinary people. In describing how he avoided contact with powerful people and never boasted of any supernormal powers, the text extols his indifference toward worldly success and recognition. No clear indication is given that he practiced Taoist macrobiotics, although this is hinted at by the descriptions of his youthful complexion and his ability to live on very little food and no sleep. Fortunately, more information on him—albeit of a quite fanciful nature—is found in other sources. The *Dongxian zhuan* (*Yunji qiqian* 110) tells us

> He practiced the Non-active Way of the Taiping. When he sucked and gargled with his eyes almost fully shut, a five-colored radiance rose from his nape. (*Yunji qiqian* 110/8a–9a)

Described here is some sort of method involving the swallowing of air and/or saliva, which probably was meant to facilitate fasts.

The *Daoxue zhuan* provides one example of a married couple that opted for an austere lifestyle. We are told that Liu Ningzhi and his wife (fl. early fifth century) were both ordained priests who were "transmitted the Heavenly Master's Way of Converting the People." They used their ritual powers with great success for the benefit of others (*Sandong zhunang* 1/1b–2a). They both were uninterested in worldly wealth. Liu Ningzhi gave away his house, wealth, and the family business to his brother's household. He refused all gifts offered to him by the nobility. His wife was the daughter of a wealthy aristocrat, but whenever her father sent them lavish gifts, Liu Ningzhi gave them away to relatives. His wife was perfectly content to have him do this. The couple and their children lived in a hut "amidst the weeds" and "were able to be content amidst hardship." To earn their living they sold hay in the marketplace, charging their customers no more than they could afford. Of their earnings, they kept only what they needed for their subsistence and gave the rest to beggars. This they did even in years of famine (*Sandong zhunang* 2/2a).

The *Daoxue zhuan* also indicates that they practiced immortality techniques. One episode is recorded where Liu Ningzhi felt an excruciating pain in his forehead when meditating. When he rubbed it, nine jewels came out. The jewels shined brilliantly after he had washed them in clean water[12] (*Sandong zhunang* 5/1b). We also are told that they "lived on the south side of Mt. Heng,[13] where they gathered herbs and practiced dietetics"[14] (*Sandong zhunang* 1/1b). Eventually, Liu Ningzhi took his wife and children to live with him high up in the mountains. There they lived in a hut made of weeds. They were never to be seen again (*Sandong zhunang* 2/2a).

Another interesting and somewhat unique case is that of Kong Lingchan of Shanyin, Kuaiji.[15] We are told that he took to austerities as a direct result of his mother's death. When his mother died, he went into mourning and practiced austerities of an intensity that made him "renowned for his filial piety." He resolved to eat only porridge and vegetables, to wear only plain clothes, and to abstain completely from drinking and merriment for the rest of his life. On one occasion he went to visit his father, who upon seeing him was moved to pity by his emaciated condition. His father implored him to eat rich foods (as a filial son, Kong Lingchan could not disobey him), but oddly enough, this made him ill. He was never forced to eat rich foods again (*Sandong zhunang* 1/17b).

Perhaps the shock of his mother's death not only overcame him with grief, but also brought about a heightened awareness of death that led to religious conversion. In another fragment, we are told Kong Lingchan went on to become an eminent Taoist who "profoundly researched the essentials of the Tao." Due to his acclaim, he was invited by Emperor Ming (465–472) of the Liu-Song dynasty to reside at the newly established Huaxian Guan monastery, located next to the Tomb of Yu on Mt. Kuaiji (*Sandong zhunang* 2/7b, *Shangqing Daolei Shixiang* 1/2b–3a). In the *Nanshi* (Official History of the Southern Dynasties), we are told that he came from an extremely privileged upbringing. He had been serving as the governor of Jin'an (northeast of present-day Minhou County, Fujian Province) when he received the royal invitation (*Nanshi* 4/49, p. 1214). The *Nanshi* also tells us that shortly after the invitation, he was appointed to the post of Grand Master of Palace Leisure and became greatly renowned for his skills in astrology and numerology. It thus appears that despite his allegedly austere private lifestyle, Kong Lingchan never disengaged himself from society and politics. Also, he probably never abandoned family life, since he did have a son named Kong Gui.

While Liu Ningzhi and Kong Lingchan are exceptions, most of the ascetics depicted in the *Daoxue zhuan* were probably solitary hermits or cenobites, although in many cases no clear indication is found within the information that has survived. We are told that Zhang Ze,[16] who was reticent and indifferent to worldly matters, lived frugally and contentedly in poverty (*Sandong zhunang* 2/2b). Yu Chengxian[17] was a teacher and preacher who was well versed in the *Laozi* and *Zhuangzi*. He wore hemp cloth, rested on a straw mat, and practiced vegetarianism for forty years (*Sandong zhunang* 2/3a). Meng Daoyang[18] wore hemp cloth, ate coarse food, and owned no private possessions. We are also told that "in practicing the Tao in worship, [he] did not avoid coldness and heat" (*Sandong zhunang* 2/3a). All of these men may have been cenobites or hermits, but we have no way of ascertaining this.

Yan Jizhi clearly renounced family life, since we are told that "he abandoned his home to enter the Tao." We also are told that he ate a vegetarian diet and wore only hemp cloth (*Sandong zhunang* 2/2b).[19] It cannot be ascertained whether he pursued his religious life as a hermit or cenobite. However, as we shall see shortly, the phrase "abandoned his home" (*shejia*) closely resembles the standard phrase used to denote the act of entering a monastic order.

Deng Yuzhi (fl. 483–493)[20] fits into the category of a hermit. We are told that he lived alone in the Southern Peak Mt. Heng and wore only a tattered monk's robe throughout the year. The text also indicates that he was in mourning for some reason, hence did not wear his hair in a topknot (*Sandong zhunang* 2/3b). Another Taoist hagiographical work, Liao Xian's *Nanyue jiuzhenren zhuan* (HY452/TT201; ca. late 9th c.), offers a possible explantion. There we are told that he had previously roamed the holy mountains with an older adept named Xu Lingqi, but had been left on his own after Xu Lingqi "ascended" in the second year of the Yuanhui reign era (474).

An apparent example of a cenobite is Dongxiang Zongchao.[21] We are told that he was indifferent to worldly affairs from his early childhood. He never married or took office. His diet consisted only of hemp and wheat, and he ate just once a day at noon. Perhaps most important, we are told he lived in a "hut of self-refinement" (temple, monastery?) where "fish was never served" and his family members and disciples were all vegetarians (*Sandong zhunang* 5/7b).

Monasticism was a long-standing Buddhist tradition that some Taoists began to emulate by the fifth or sixth century. The *Daoxue zhuan* is one of the most abundant sources of evidence for this phenomenon. Dongxiang Zongchao's "hut of refinement" appears to have been something similar to a monastery, although it appears that members of his family lived there (which would not be allowed in a Buddhist monastery).

From earlier periods we can find numerous examples of Taoist adepts who left their families to live by themselves, or with a circle of fellow adepts. Vegetarianism and celibacy were not unusual. However, during the fifth and sixth centuries, it appears that celibacy, vegetarianism, and cenobitism became more common among Taoists. Buddhistic ethics came to provide much of the justification for these practices.

The standard Buddhist word used to refer to the act of joining a monastic order is *chujia*, or "leaving the family." An article on the phenomenon of "leaving the family" in Taoism has been written by Ozaki Masaharu.[22] Ozaki, based largely on information from the *Daoxue zhuan*, speculates that "leaving the family" became common among the Taoists of southern China during the sixth century. Ozaki points out that the following fourteen people are described as having "left the family": Zhang Min, Xu Mingye, Dai Sheng, Zou Rong, Xu Shizi, Zhang Yunzhi, Cheng Tongsun, Yin Faren, Zhang Yu, Chunyu Puqia, Li Lingcheng, Ji Huiyan, Song Yuxian, and Wang Daolian.[23] Interestingly enough, the last four were women.

Ozaki points out that the people described as having "left the family"—at least those for whom the period and location of their activity is indicated—[24]were active in southern China during the sixth century.[25] However, Ozaki also points out that the *Daoxue zhuan*'s entry on Lu Xiujing (406–477) strongly suggests that "family-leaving" already was taking place during the fifth century. There we are told that when he was still a government official, Lu Xiujing declared, "It would be hard to ever meet with the opportunity again." Thereupon he promptly "abandoned his wife and children" to pursue Taoist training full time[26] (*Sandong qunxian lu* 2/17a). We also are told that when he was training on Mt. Yunmeng,[27] he came down from the mountain temporarily to seek for medicines. On this occasion he stayed at his family's home for several days. While he was there, his daughter suddenly became critically ill. His family begged him to heal her, but he refused, saying, "I have left behind my wife and family and entrusted my body to the limits of the mysteries. My coming by my house now is like taking up lodging at an inn. Why should I have any feelings of attachment?" He left immediately after saying this. His daughter's disease was miraculously cured the very next day (*Sandong zhunang* 1/15b–16a).

Lu Xiujing, at least as he is depicted in the aforementioned story, believed that proper Taoist training required physical and emotional detachment from one's family. Lu Xiujing was the most eminent Taoist of his time and is particularly noted for his liturgies and his *Sandong jingshu mulu* catalog.[28] If the previously mentioned anecdotes accurately depict the lifestyle and attitude of Lu Xiujing, it seems likely—judging from his stature and authority—that a substantial portion of the Taoist clergy would have seen the need to disengage themselves from family life.

In this regard, another noteworthy figure among the protagonists of the *Daoxue zhuan* is Chu Boyu (394–479), an older contemporary of Lu Xiujing. Five different sources record the following episode about him (this particular episode is not preserved within the *Daoxue zhuan*'s surviving fragments):

> [Chu] Boyu, from a young age, had the wish to become a hermit. [He] had few cravings and desires. [When he was] 18 years old, his father made him get married. [But when] his bride [to be] entered the front gate, Boyu exited out the back gate. Thereupon he went to Shan[29] and lived on Mt. Pubu.[30] (Xiao Zixian [489–537], *Nanqi shu* [Beijing: Zhonghua Shuju, 1972], 926–927)[31]

Chu Boyu apparently believed that marriage would undermine his religious pursuits. It should be noted that Chu Boyu was one of the privileged adepts of his time who had managed to acquire authentic Shangqing manuscripts.[32] As we will see in chapter 5, the Shangqing scriptures strongly recommend celibacy for serious adepts.

The *Daoxue zhuan* indicates that the Taoist nunhood had come to exist by the sixth century. Among those mentioned as having "left the family," four were women, as we have seen. Ji Huiyan, we are told, had initially entered the Buddhist nunhood as a girl, but later switched to Taoism. Actually, whether her case actually represents evidence of Taoist monasticism is unclear; as far as it can be ascertained, her Taoist life may not have been as a celibate nun. Among the three clear accounts on Taoist nuns, the entry on Song Yuxian contains what is perhaps the most revealing episode.

> The nun (lit., "female cap-wearer") Song Yuxian was a woman of Shanyin, Kuaiji.[33] Because she had been endowed with a woman's body, she exhausted her willpower but could not become naturally devoted. When she got close to the age for wearing a hairpin (15 years old; this was considered a marriageable age), her parents married her off to the Xu

family. She secretly packed her ritual robe and boarded the carriage. After she arrived at the gate of [the house of] her husband-to-be, and the time came for the six rites (the wedding ceremony), she put on her yellow cloth skirt and hempen robe. In her hands she held a magpie tail feather and an incense burner. She did not observe the propriety of the bride. Guests and hosts at the wedding were aghast. The groom's family pressured her, but could not make her yield. Thus they gave up on her and returned her to her family. She was finally able to leave the family. (*Sandong zhunang* 4/10b)

Unfortunately, there is no indication regarding when this took place. None-theless, the aforementioned passage indicates that some female Taoists perceived a serious conflict between marriage and their religious aspirations. Also noteworthy here is how the text states that her female body made it more difficult for her to concentrate on her training. As we will see in chapter 6, the Lingbao scriptures convey a similar male chauvinistic attitude, maintaining that women are inferior to men in their capacity to seek the Tao. Based on such a view, unwavering faith and determination were the only means by which women could hope to overcome their disadvantage. Song Yuxian exhibited these virtues through her stubborn resistance of marriage.

Interestingly, the *Daoxue zhuan* contains information indicating that the government played a significant role in enforcing rules of discipline within Taoist monasteries. In one passage, Dongxiang Zongchao is lauded for his cooperation in this endeavor.

Under Liang Emperor Wu's (Wudi, r.502–550) [policy of] the "equal promotion of the Three Teachings," it was legislated that all [clergy] must be vegetarians. Even though there was this edict, few were able to obey it. [But] Yilun (Dongxiang Zongchao's style name) upheld it and carried it out. Thereupon the throngs of his monastery all became vegetarians. If anybody tried to violate the rule secretly, he expelled them. Even on occasions of feasts and festivals, no meat was eaten. People far and near praised [his monastery] for being the only one that was pure and plain. (*Sandong zhunang* 5/7b–8a)

Apparently, prior to the Emperors edict, vegetarianism was not strictly required nor observed by the Taoist clergy—nor the Buddhist clergy for that matter. Emperor Wu, in the year 504, publicly renounced Taoism and declared his faith in Buddhism. Henceforth he carried out various measures to promote Buddhism and suppress Taoism. A staunch observer of Buddhist precepts—he ate just one vegetarian meal per day and became celibate after age fifty—he was particularly intent on promoting the precept of non-killing. Buddhist sources (*Guang hongming ji, Fozu tongji*) and official histories (*Nanshi, Liang shu*[34]) attest to how he forbade the use of blood sacrifice in official rites and pressured everybody in his court to become vegetarians. He also authored a lengthy treatise (*Duan jiurou wen*),[35] forbidding the Buddhist clergy from consuming meat and alcohol and explaining the necessity for vegetarianism and sobriety.[36] The story of Dongxiang Zongchao provides an indication that this prohibition did not exclude the Taoist clergy.

Of course, a fair number of Taoist adepts in previous times probably were in effect vegetarians, since their dietary regimens called for the virtual shunning of all foods. It should also be noted, however, that their avoidance of meat served predominantly physiological purposes. In chapter 6 we will see that Lingbao scriptures of the fifth century (i.e., written prior to Emperor Wu's policies) prescribe vegetarianism for advanced adepts, and do so partially based on Buddhistic notions of *karma*. However, pressure from Emperor Wu forced Dongxiang Zongchao to demand vegetarianism for *all* of his disciples, not just the most advanced. Obedience to the Emperor's decree may have been critical for the survival of the Taoist religion. Adhering to Buddhistic principles was probably the only way for Taoists to mitigate the Emperor's hostility.

The actual extent of the suppression—for which "the equal promotion of the Three Teachings" appears to be a euphemism—remains unclear. The *Fozu tongji* of the fourteenth century tells us that in 517, Emperor Wu decreed that all Taoist monasteries must cease to operate and all Taoist clergy must be defrocked. While some have questioned whether the suppression actually ever took place, Michel Strickmann has argued that it indeed did, largely based on an incident recorded in the *Zhoushi mingtong ji* (HY302/TT152). There we are told that a thirty-five-year-old celibate "home-leaving" female Taoist[37] "married out of expediency," under pressure from the government in 504. This, of course, was the same year Emperor Wu renounced Taoism.[38] It appears that by getting married, this female Taoist was feigning her own renunciation of Taoism and return to secular life. She apparently did so to avoid some form of punishment that Taoists were suffering at the time.

While Emperor Wu clearly played an important role in enforcing discipline in Taoist monasteries, it should be noted that ethical discourses of a strongly Buddhistic tinge are found in both the Shangqing and Lingbao texts (especially the latter). Both of these corpuses pre-date Emperor Wu. The Lingbao texts provide many lists of precepts, some of which may have been written with a monastic setting in mind. There must have been a significant contingent within the Taoist fold that promoted Buddhistic ethics and eagerly emulated Buddhist forms of discipline. Ma Shu clearly favored monastic discipline, since his narrative praises Dongxiang Zongchao for his obedience to the Emperor's orders.

The *Daoxue zhuan* also lauds some of its protagonists for their ritual piety. One example is the aforementioned Meng Daoyang, who "in practicing the Tao in worship, did not avoid coldness and heat." Other examples include Zhang Min and Fang Qianzhi. Zhang Min, we are told, worshipped at the altar at the height of winter, staying awake all night while holding a candle in his bare left hand. He willingly and diligently took on menial tasks such as cleaning the ritual arena. He always deferred to others during worship by sitting away from the shade on hot days and refusing to use warm garments and quilts on cold days (*Sandong zhunang* 1/3b–4a). Fang Qianzhi is described as having "disregarded his own body in order to rescue [other living] things."[39] During liturgical rituals (referred to as *zhai* or "retreats"), he worshipped six times a day, performing a liturgy called the Confession of the Ten Directions.[40] He often worshipped by himself because nobody else possessed his endurance (*Sandong zhunang* 5/8a).

As we will see in chapter 6, liturgical "retreat" (*zhai*) rituals that lasted numerous days were emphasized by the Lingbao movement of the fifth century. Accounts such as the previous one perhaps attest more than anything else to Lingbao influence. The passage on Fang Qianzhi seems to imply that his sustained ritual piety was an altruistic act. This is probably because the liturgy he followed involved confession on behalf of all creatures—including the souls of the dead— for their deliverance and well-being.

In chapter 6 we also will see how the Lingbao movement emphasized altruism as a definitive trait of a saint, and how this probably had to do with the influence of the Bodhisattva ideal of Mahayana Buddhism. A heightened emphasis on altruism is well reflected in the *Daoxue zhuan*. One example is the aforementioned story of Liu Ningzhi and his wife, who generously gave their earnings to beggars. Meng Daoyang, we are told, always gave to the needy because he "was by nature benevolent and compassionate." During famines he cooked food and fed the starving people. Since he himself was poor, he always regretted that he did not have more to give (*Sandong zhunang* 1/4a).

However, the most poignant tale of altruism is the story of Zhang Xuanche. Zhang Xuanche worked as a tutor for a certain Zhang Guisun. One day Guisun suddenly became bedridden with palsy, whereupon Xuanche dedicated himself to caring for his illness. For three years he provided and cooked meals for him, and willingly assisted him in the use of the bedpan and urinal (*Sandong zhunang* 1/16b). Around the year 557, during the social unrest that brought the collapse of the Liang dynasty, Xuanche and Guisun fled to "the eastern fringes" (exact location unclear).[41] They barely had enough resources to stay alive. However Xuanche always cooked and shared his food with others who were hungry, even when he had next to nothing. He never ate before others had eaten their fill, and he consequently became weak and emaciated. He finally died of starvation. However, the text ends with an ambiguous sentence that reads, "But because he put himself last and others first, he eventually regained his life" (*Sandong zhunang* 1/3a–b).

What is meant by "regained his life" is unclear. The text may mean to say that his virtuous actions won him the sympathy of the gods and immortals, who miraculously resurrected him. Another possible interpretation is that he gained some form of otherworldly immortality, or perhaps reincarnation into a desirable existence. As we will see in chapter 5, the Shangqing texts express the belief that gods and immortals can intervene to favorably alter the fate of virtuous deceased persons.

The surviving fragments of the *Daoxue zhuan* include twelve passages that mention fasting.[42] Some of these passages do not specify the fasting methods that were employed, stating merely that the person "cut off grains" or "practiced dietetics." Some mention the substances the protagonists ingested. We are told Tao Dan ate noodles and jujubes (*Sandong zhunang* 3/24b), Xu Mai ate sesame seeds (*Sandong zhunang* 3/24b), Xu Mai's disciple Peng Chu ate the *shu* plant (*Sandong zhunang* 3/24b), and the female adept Xiao Zheng ate the leaves of the arbor vitae tree (*Sandong zhunang* 3/27b).[43]

Some passages mention special fasting techniques. We are told that Wang Jia,[44] as well as Xu Mai and his disciples, practiced the "imbibing of *qi*" (*Sandong zhunang* 3/24b–25a). Xu Mai also is attributed with the feat of holding his breath for "1,000 breaths" (the amount of time it normally takes to make a thousand respirations). It should further be noted that an annotation in Tao Hongjing's (456–536) *Zhengao* (13/2a) states that Xu Mai was transmitted the "Yin and Yang Lunch Box Talismans of the Six *Jia*" at the age of 23 by a Heavenly Masters School libationer (*jijiu*) named Li Dong. This probably refers to special talismans that adepts swallowed to suppress hunger. Xu Mai, significantly, was the brother of Xu Mi and the uncle of Xu Hui, two important early figures of the Shangqing movement. (Techniques very similar to those ascribed to Xu Mai will be examined in chapter 4).

The story of Zhang Min is of particular interest, in light of the new developments in Taoist soteriology that were occuring in the late Six Dynasties period. Zhang Min, we are told, fasted to the point of severe emaciation.

Thereupon [Zhang Min] abandoned his wife and children, left his family and received the Tao. He ate vegetarian food and engaged in a perpetual retreat. There was never any toil in which he would hesitate to engage his seven *chi* (168.84 cm.) of empty delusion (his body). He hid himself in a mountain in Anwu[45] and lived in silence. He did away with food for over twenty days. Bandits and vicious beasts lurked about where he was staying. His energy and life were weakening and dwindling. Friendly visitors implored him to eat, and after a while he yielded [to their requests]. After he had more or less been restored to normal [health], in the first year of the Dajian era of the Chen (569), he stopped eating again. He said, "If I protect my body, certainly my understanding will not be long-lasting and penetrating, and I will not benefit the living masses. I do not plan to stay long [in the world]. As for practicing the Tao and establishing proper conduct, why must it take place here?" [Even when] there were those who tried to persuade him [to end his fast], he refused and would not entertain [their suggestions]. (*Sandong zhunang* 5/8a–b).

As far as can be ascertained from the preceding passage, Zhang Min may have even starved himself to death. Judging from what he allegedly said when refusing food during his second fast, he appears to have been prepared to die. Taoist fasting was usually supposed to strengthen the body rather than destroy it. In the case of Zhang Min, other priorities seem to have taken over. He apparently felt his religious quest could not succeed unless he stopped clinging to life and fearing death. For some reason, he thought he could not benefit others unless he succeeded in his religious quest.

Taoist fasting methods and other longevity techniques continued to be carried out for physical strengthening and transformation. However, the story of Zhang Min reflects how the methods were increasingly being seen more as measures for eliminating desires and gaining a higher level of insight and spirituality. Buddhist influence was probably largely responsible for this phenomenon. Zhang Min appears to have emphasized spiritual cultivation lopsidedly, to the point where he was indifferent to the deterioration of his body. (Disdain for the body also can be detected in the words of Ma Shu's narrative, where the body is referred to as "seven *chi*[46] of empty delusion.") Zhang Min's desire to benefit "the living masses" through his efforts conveys the kind of altruistic sentiment that is frequently expressed in the Lingbao scriptures. As we will see in chapter 6, the Lingbao scriptures also promote the Buddhistic doctrine of transmigration and maintain that the ultimate salvation is to be gained only after a gradual process of spiritual progress that takes countless lifetimes. Zhang Min's seeming willingness to die was perhaps supported by this belief. He may have thought he could resume his religious quest in his next lifetime, in the event that he starved to death. Such seems to be what he meant when he said, "As for practicing the Tao and performing my deeds, why must it take place here?"

In sum, fasting methods continued to be practiced during the fourth through sixth centuries. In many cases, Buddhistic beliefs further justified and motivated arduous training. In the case of Zhang Min, Buddhist influence may have been at least indirectly responsible for causing him to devalue and abuse his body. The *Yuqing jing*, as we will see in chapter 7, denounces bodily neglect and abuse as heresy. Zhang Min would certainly qualify as a heretic by this standard, and the presence of Taoists like him may have prompted the attacks of the *Yuqing jing*.

CHAPTER FOUR

Taoist Methods of Fasting

Because Taoist texts frequently mention the avoidance of "grains," many modern scholars have gained the impression that Taoists held a special taboo against eating the "five grains" (rice, glutinous millet, panicled millet, wheat, and soybeans).[1] However, the fact is when Taoists spoke of avoiding "grains," they usually meant the attempt to shun all foods. The main dietary objective of Taoist adepts was to cut down drastically on the amount they ate. This certainly meant decreasing the consumption of grains (the staple food), but it also meant trying to avoid all other foods. The "avoidance of grains" was thus a much more arduous practice than the term initially implies. In the *Lunheng*, written by the Latter Han skeptic Wang Chong (23–100 C.E.), we find a passage that is highly revealing in this regard.

Some people in the world regard those who avoid grains (*bigu*) and do not eat as people who possess the techniques of the Tao. They say that people like Wang Ziqiao differed from common folk in their dietary habits, in that they did not eat grains (*gu*); [therefore] they transcend the world after a hundred years and ultimately become immortals.

This, again is false. When people are born, they are endowed with the natural impulses of eating and drinking. Therefore they have mouths and teeth on the upper parts of their bodies and orifices on the lower parts of their bodies. They eat with their mouths and teeth, and excrete through their orifices. Those who accord with these natural impulses are in accordance with the proper way of Heaven. Those who go against these natural impulses are contradicting what they are endowed with.

For a person to not eat is similar to a body wearing no clothes. You keep your skin warm with clothing and fill your belly with food. If the skin is warm and the belly is full, your spirit will be clear and vigorous. If you are hungry and yet do not fill yourself, or are cold but do not warm yourself, you will freeze and starve. How can a person who is freezing and starving live long? Also, when people live, they take *qi* from food, much as plants take *qi* from the soil. If you pull out the roots of plants from the soil, they will wither and die. If you close the mouth of a person and make him not eat, he will starve and not live long.[2]

Notice here that the terms *avoid grains* (*bigu*) and *do not eat* (*bushi*) are used alongside each other and appear to be synonymous. In saying that men like Wang Ziqiao did not eat "grains," it appears that immortality seekers really meant to say that their heroes did not eat at all, otherwise Wang Chong's rebuttal does not make sense. Wang Chong offers as his argument the commonsense observation that eating and excreting are natural functions essential to the sustenance of human life. The issue here is not any perceived harmfulness unique to rice, glutinous millet, panicled millet, wheat, or soybeans. The word "grains" in the previous passage is probably better translated as "foods." (The practice of using the name of a staple food to convey a broader meaning persists in the modern Chinese language, where the phrase "*chifan*" or "eat rice" means to eat a full meal.)

In chapters 2 and 3 we saw how Taoist hagiography makes frequent mention of fasting and the methods employed for it. In this chapter we will examine some Taoist fasting methods in detail. By doing so it is hoped that the reader will gain a vivid picture of the determination and resourcefulness of fasting adepts.

The Fasting Regimen of the *Zhonghuang jing*

The *Zhonghuang jing*[3] is a text of obscure origin and uncertain date. Its main text could date back to the fourth century or earlier. The lengthy commentary attached to the main text probably was written around 700 C.E.[4] The text is of particular interest because it describes what may be the most strenuous of all Taoist fasting regimens.

The regimen, roughly outlined, is as follows: The adept quits eating solid foods immediately and also tries not to drink fluids. He frequently swallows air through his mouth and into his esophagus, which is supposed to suppress his hunger and furthermore nourish his body with the "primal *qi*" of the cosmos. By continuing this for many days, the adept purges the defiling *qi* of ordinary foods ("grain *qi*") from his body and also exterminates its internal demons. Once this has been accomplished, the body becomes the abode of sacred deities, and its latent divine *qi* can be activated. The adept is then ready to proceed to the practice of "womb breathing" (*taixi*), which in this case denotes a rigorous technique of breath holding. The breath holding activates the divine *qi* of the five viscera (*wuzang*; the liver, heart, spleen, lungs, and kidneys), which miraculously create an immortal body for the adept. The adept carries out visualizations during the "womb breathing," and sees himself ascend to the heavenly realms of the Great Ultimate (*taiji*) and the Great Sublimity (*taiwei*). In such a way, he gains a foretaste of the realms he hopes to some day inhabit.

Let us now examine some of the major aspects of the regimen in more detail. The method of air swallowing (*fuqi*; "imbibing *qi*") is described roughly as follows in the commentary portion of the *Zhonghuang jing*'s first chapter:

At spring time, during the third month of the lunar calendar, the adept sets up a meditation chamber equipped with a desk, bed, and incense burner. He burns incense constantly. At midnight, he begins his meditation. He lies on his back, closes his eyes, and relaxes his mind. After knocking his teeth together thirty-six times, he clenches both fists tightly around the thumbs and proceeds to swallow air. During the course of breathing, the adept does not exhale the air that he has inhaled into his lungs; rather, he holds it in his mouth and swallows it, sending it through his esophagus and into his stomach. This is continued until the stomach feels full. The swallowing of air can be repeated whenever he feels hungry. During this process, the mouth and throat will inevitably begin to feel dry. The adept is thus allowed to drink certain types of fluids to quench his thirst. A recipe is given in the text for a special soup that has sesame seeds, powdered tukahoe plant (*fuling, pachyma cocos*), and small amounts of milk and honey as its ingredients. This soup, of which the adept may drink one or two cups when thirsty, "nurtures the *qi* and moistens the belly." Drinking this soup also is supposed to help keep the adept from thinking about food. The adept also can opt for a soup made with matrimony vine (*gouqi, lycium chinense*), which he may drink four times a day. But eventually he is supposed to sustain his fast without drinking fluids. As the adept continues his fast, his intestines gradually become purged of solid wastes. The adept is warned that his urine may begin to take on a yellowish-orange color (a sign of dehydration), and he may feel constant agitation or depression. However, he is not to worry; if he perseveres, he will "naturally get to understand the marvelous principles." The text states that although one can eliminate impurities from the body while drinking the aforementioned soups, higher insight can be attained only if one avoids both liquids and solid foods. As the fast is sustained for many days, the three "elixir fields" in the body begin to be "filled up." After thirty days, the lower elixir field (located in the belly in a spot behind the navel) becomes full, and the adept no longer experiences hunger. After sixty days, the middle elixir field (located in the heart) becomes full, and the *qi* permeates the entire body so the adept no longer feels fatigue and always feels light on his feet. After ninety days, the upper elixir field (in the brain) becomes full, and the adept begins to take on a visibly healthy and radiant appearance, while his mind is freed of confused thoughts. At this point, he gains insight on "right and wrong." Spiritually, the adept now resides in the sacred realm and is able to "initiate the respiration of his womb's Immortal." After 100 days, he can "see" his five viscera. After 300 days, he can see any evil spirits in his environment and is invulnerable to their deception. After 1,000 days, the adept's name is recorded in the "[divine] Emperor's registers" and his "body enters into Supreme Sublimity."

As is already evident from the preceding description, the fasting regimen is extremely arduous, and the adept must overcome many obstacles to succeed. The

Zhonghuang jing's second chapter (main text and commentary) describes the various problems and hindrances that can cause the fast to fail. The first problem addressed is the weakening of the body that occurs during the early stages of the fast. After the first couple of weeks of fasting, the body becomes free of solid wastes, and the adept begins to feel exhausted and utterly weak. However, he is told not to fear for his well-being, nor doubt that the fast can succeed. The body feels weak because "the primal *qi* has not yet reached the stomach." If the adept continues to eat air, the *qi* will penetrate and flow deeper into the body day by day. Eventually, when the lower elixir field is full, the adept will no longer experience hunger. At this point, because the *qi* has not yet permeated the flesh and skin, the adept may still feel weak. He also may become thin and bear a sickly, "yellowish" complexion. However, the adept must not be afraid, since his strength will eventually be fully restored if he perseveres in the fast. The adept is thus told, "Those who are scared by their weakness, thinness and yellow-ness cannot cultivate."

The next three problems addressed pertain to the malevolent beings in the body that are referred to as the "Three Worms" or "Three Corpses." These demons dwell in the three "elixir fields," and each work their own kind of mischief upon the adept. The commentary tells us that the Upper Worm, named Peng Ju, is white and blue in color. It causes the adept to long for delicious foods and become influenced by various other physical desires. The Middle Worm, named Peng Zhi, is white and yellow in color. It causes the adept to be greedy for wealth and easily moved toward joy or anger. The Lower Worm, named Peng Jiao, is white and black in color. It causes the adept to be fond of fancy clothing, liquor, and sex. When the adept first begins to fast, the air he swallows does not permeate sufficiently, and he is constantly subjected to the mischief of the Three Worms. This causes frequent moods of depression and anxiety. He also becomes easily tempted to indulge in sensual or culinary pleasures. He must therefore make a constant effort to resist and overcome these woes and temptations. Quoting a certain *Taishang shengxuan jing*, the commentary explains that the fast is a process during which the Three Worms are successively exterminated; the Upper Worm dies after thirty days, the Middle Worm dies after sixty days, and the Lower Worm dies after ninety days. After 100 days, the adept's body becomes healthy and strong, and his mind becomes "pure." He is no longer in danger of falling prey to his desires. When this stage is reached, the adept can see the "Five Sprouts," or the *qi* of his five viscera, which also are described as the "proper *qi* of the five agents."

The commentary to the third chapter explains that foods of the five flavors (acrid, sour, salty, sweet, and bitter) must be avoided completely if one is to produce "miraculous *qi*" from the five viscera and do away with all thoughts and desires. When the five viscera become full with air or "primal *qi*," the *qi* of each organ will turn into an internal deity. The adept will reach a higher level of spirituality and insight where he is free of worries and "understands the good and bad of the human world."

The authors and commentators of the *Zhonghuang jing* understood the inside of the body to be an elaborate network of apertures and compartments interconnected by numerous passages.[5] The commentary to the fifth chapter quotes a certain *Dongshen mingzang jing* as follows:

> Therefore if a single aperture is closed, a hundred diseases will arise. If a single vessel is blocked, the 100 passages will be in disorder. Thus if you imbibe *qi* you will have no diseases and the various vessels will naturally interpenetrate. A man of the Tao is immortal because no substances are kept in his belly. (1/11b 5th line 5th character to 7th line 9th character)

From this we can see that foods were deemed harmful because they clogged the body's apertures and passageways, creating the fundamental cause for diseases. This theory made fasting imperative. The commentary further explains that the adept must expurgate the "wicked *qi*" that is the "*qi* of grains." The body is supposed to be a residing place for innumerable gods. However, these gods refuse to live amidst impure *qi*. Only when the body is cleansed of its impurities can the gods once again return to it to take up their residence. When the body is restored to this pure, holy state, scars and moles disappear from the body's surface.

Interestingly, the commentary to the eighth chapter maintains that the sensation of hunger itself is caused by food. It explains that even after the body has completely stopped excreting solid wastes and seems to have been purged of impurities, the adept will still experience the urge to eat food because the "refined essences of grains" form a slimy membrane that covers his five viscera, six bowels, joints, muscles, and vessels. The adept is told that if he just perseveres for another twenty to thirty days, this troublesome membrane will leave the body. As this is taking place, the adept will begin to excrete blood, puss, fat deposits, and finally, the slimy membrane. He finally becomes free of impurities. The air he eats comes to permeate the entire inside of the body, which he is able to "see." Once this happens, the adept loses his desire for food. Furthermore, the mind becomes free of thoughts and worries. The adept is again told that though he may experience loneliness, emaciation, and weakness, he need not fear nor doubt. Indeed, fear and doubt themselves are his greatest enemies.

After undergoing the lengthy fast sustained by the imbibing of air, the adept obtains a stronger body and a state of mind that is detached and disdainful of worldly concerns and needs. Having thoroughly mastered the method of "imbibing *qi*," the adept can advance to the stage of "womb breathing." The method of womb breathing is roughly outlined in the main text of the twelfth chapter.

> The perfect *qi* of the five viscera are the flowers of the magic fungi.
> The liver is in charge of the east, and its color is blue.
> If you simply hold [your breath] firmly for 1,000 breaths (the amount of time it normally takes to make 1,000 respirations), blue *qi* will circulate

throughout [your body] and its color will be natural.
The heart is in charge of the south, and its color is red.
[If you] subdue[6] it for 1,000 breaths, the red color will emerge.
The lungs are in charge of the west, and their color is white.
[If you] subdue it for 1,000 breaths, its color will climax.
The spleen is in charge of the center, and its color is yellow.
[If you] subdue it for 1,000 breaths, its color will flourish.[7]
The kidneys are in charge of the north, and their color is black.
[If you] subdue it for 1,000 breaths, its color will be acquired.

The method essentially seems to consist of holding one's breath and concentrating one's mind upon a specific organ, probably while lying down. Each of the five viscera are correlated to their proper direction and color according to the scheme of five agents cosmology. While concentrating on a particular organ, the adept would probably visualize its *qi* (in its proper color) emerging from it. After holding his breath and visualizing for a very long time, the adept was supposed to actually see the colored *qi*, and the colored *qi* of the five viscera would together work to transform him into an immortal.

The commentary to the twelfth chapter quotes a certain *Taihua shoushi jing* that says, "The primal *qi* envelops the transformations. When it spreads about [the body], it becomes the six senses (sight, smell, hearing, taste, touch, cognition)." It also says, "The internal *qi* is knowledge and the womb *qi*[8] is the spirit. If you are able to practice womb breathing, you will return to infancy and become resurrected ("make your *hun* soul return")."[9] From these statements it appears that the divine, refined forms of *qi* were understood to be the entities that constituted the adept's mental and sensory capacities. It therefore follows that when divine forms of *qi* fill and permeate the body to strengthen and transform it, the adept attains great powers of insight and perception.

The commentary further indicates that the *qi* of the five viscera have a few other practical uses when activated through breath holding and visualization. The *qi* of the liver and heart can be used to cure the diseases of other people. This is done by visualizing the *qi* and then "attacking" the patient's disease with it (how the disease is "attacked" is not made clear).[10] The radiant *qi* of the lungs can be used to see through solid ground and search for buried treasures. It also can be used to "perceive the good and bad of people," meaning perhaps that the adept reads the minds of others or foresees their fortunes. By utilizing the *qi* of the spleen, the adept becomes able to go through solid surfaces.

As previously mentioned, breath holding and visualization also were used for gaining a foretaste of heavenly realms. The commentary to the eleventh chapter describes how to do this. The method is carried out in a reclining position on a bed inside a specially designated meditation chamber. The adept must have a fellow adept present to keep track of the number of respirations he makes during the night.

It thus appears that the method may have been meant to be carried out throughout the entire night. If so, sleep deprivation may have been a factor in inducing visions. One also suspects that supervision was deemed necessary because of the potential danger of self-asphyxiation.

The adept, we are told, lies with his fists firmly clenched around the thumbs and empties his mind. The text then says, "the miraculous *qi* will gradually be shut in," which perhaps means that he gradually slows down his breathing to the point of cessation. He refrains from breathing for as long as he can, for the span of up to ten, fifteen, twenty, or even a hundred "breaths."

When the adept becomes able to refrain from breathing for 100 "breaths" (and is perhaps delirious from sleep deprivation and hunger), he begins to have visions of his own three *hun* souls, and later his seven *po* souls. He now can embark on a mystical flight into the heavens, together with the three *hun* souls. While this is taking place, the seven *po* souls are left behind in the body to guard and keep it intact until the adept returns with the three *hun* souls. The *hun* souls belong to the *yang* principle and are good. The *po* souls belong to the *yin* principle and are evil. Much like the Three Worms, the *po* souls long for the body to die and therefore perform mischief to try to hasten the adept's demise. They are clad in black and carry black seals in their hands. Strangely, the seven *po* souls also are referred to as "the Dark Mother." The text then presents a chant that the adept is to recite when he sees the *po* souls.

> Dark Mother, Dark Mother, master of my corpse(s).[11] Make my bones grow, and nurture my sinews. Do not go and leave my corpse behind. Together with my *hun*-father, I will go and wander in heaven. (2/1b lines 8–9)

Having thus commanded the Dark Mother or the seven *po* souls to behave properly in his absence, the adept focuses on his three *hun* souls (his "father"). Each are clad in red and carry a red seal. They are one *shi* and five *cun* in height (about 36 cm.). Their names are Shuangling, Taiguang, and Youjing. The text, in its description of what ensues, is very vague. However, it seems that the process goes essentially as follows:

The adept exits his body together with the "more than one hundred brain gods of the Palace of the Upper Plane." Looking back down at the body, the adept sees the primal *qi* in the three elixir fields, which look like white clouds and emit a pervasive radiance. The adept then calls out the names of the three *hun* souls. Then the brain gods, commanded by the three *hun* souls, pull the adept's "primal spirit" (*yuanshen*) high up into the heavens. (The exact relationship between the primal spirit and the *hun* souls is unclear, but the understanding seems to be that the primal spirit is the entity in the adept that consciously thinks and experiences.)

As the adept exits his body, he "feels his body (an internal body equivalent to the primal spirit?) coming out from a dark room." He encounters demons and spirits of various sizes and appearances.[12] However, the adept is told not to be frightened. If he is frightened, primal *qi* will leak from his nose, making him unable to leave his body. This, explains the text, is "because the primal *qi* corresponds above with the *hun* spirits." The implication of this is perhaps that the adept's ability to retain his breath directly affects the ability of the *hun* souls to propel his primal spirit upward.

Throughout the evening, the practitioner monitoring the adept must keep track of the number of respirations he makes. Presumably, this is so the adept can gauge his progress.

The thirteenth through fifteenth chapters of the *Zhonghuang jing* describe the splendor of the heavenly realms of the Great Ultimate and the Great Sublimity. The commentary elaborates on the theme of heavenly splendor by contrasting the divine realm with the ordinary world. The commentary to the thirteenth chapter states that "the palaces and mansions of the upper realm are produced from the obscure darkness" and that "they are all formed from *qi* of five colors." This five-colored *qi*, we may note, is the same material the adept activates in his five viscera. On the other hand, "the land of the lower realm all came to exist due to the arbitrary congealing of watery *qi*." The "upper realm" is further described as a place where there is an "unmoving force that is self-so," where "nobody gives rise to the labors of moving and functioning." Unlike the moon and sun of the "lower realm," which are the "pure *qi* of *yin* and *yang*," those of the upper realm are "the subtle *qi* of the seven rare treasures." Time moves more slowly in the upper realm, where one day lasts as long as a full year in the lower realm.

Because the adept does not eat the food of the lower realm, he can partake in the splendors of the upper realm. The commentary quotes a passage that reads, "If you do not eat the essences of the soil, you will live on and reside in the City of the Great One."[13] The commentary then explains, "This means that both the body and the mind get to go." This would seem to indicate that the entire body of the adept was supposed to become immortal and ascend to the heavens. However, there is some ambiguity as to whether such was the case.

The first sentence in the main text of the first chapter reads, "[In order to] internally nurture your body (*xing*; form) and spirit [you must] eliminate your cravings and desires." The commentary elaborates by stating that the adept is to nourish his "true body (form) that is without appearance." Apparently quoting the Taoist mystical philosophical classic, the *Xisheng jing*,[14] it says, "The true Way is to nurture the spirit and the false way is to nurture the [physical] body." It then states that one is to nurture one's "primal spirit of the numinous valley" within one's own "heavenly valley"; one of the body's "39 passages."[15] From these statements it would appear that the "body" to be nurtured is a formless internal entity that is equivalent to the "spirit." However, the main text on its own does not clearly say that this is the case.

In the eleventh and fourteenth chapters, the main text refers to how the adept, as he ascends to heavenly immortality, is clad in a resplendent five-colored garment adorned with wings. The commentary to the eleventh chapter quotes a certain *Zhongtian yujing*, which says the wings will resemble those of a cicada. The commentary then draws an interesting analogy between the cicada and the transformed adept.

The cicada grows wings because it drinks dew and eats *qi* (air). Thus it can be known that people imbibe the primal *qi* and the heavenly garment congeals upon the body.

The cicada larva, when it metamorphoses, casts off its shell and flies off. If one carries the aforementioned analogy further, one could say that the adept, with his new internal body, casts off his ordinary body and proceeds to heavenly immortality. This could be what the commentator meant to imply. Whatever the case, the main text and commentary were probably written several centuries apart from each other. It could be that the author of the main text envisioned the immortality of the actual physical body, while the commentator believed in the survival of an inner, formless body.

The Fasting Regimens of the *Daoji tuna jing* and *Tuna jing*

As we have seen, the *Zhonghuang jing* maintains that an adept can fast to the point of severe weakening and emaciation, yet fully recover by simply continuing to fast. The same assertion is made in fragments that have survived from the *Daoji tuna jing* and the *Tuna jing*.

Daoji tuna jing

The *Daoji tuna jing* (*The Scripture of the Foundation of the Tao on Expelling and Taking In*) is a lost text of uncertain date. Fragments of it survive as quotes in the *Sandong zhunang*, which means that it had been in circulation at least by the seventh century. Its title indicates that it was a manual of respiratory practices. The word "tu" (to expel from the mouth, to spit, to exhale) probably describes how the adept expels the old, impure *qi* from his mouth. "Na" (to take in, to put in) probably describes the taking in of fresh, clean air to cleanse and nourish the body. This explanation is mere guesswork, since the portions of the text that described the actual exercises have not survived. However, the passage translated next makes it clear that the exercises were designed to facilitate a rigorous fast similar to that described in the *Zhonghuang jing*.

When a Taoist adept has cultivated his body and fasted by means of expelling and taking in for 10 days (one *xun*), his vital energy (*jingqi*)[16] will feel slightly feverish, and his complexion will become haggard and yellowish. After 20 days, he will feel dizzy and will be clumsy in his movements, and his joints will ache. His large bowel movements will become somewhat difficult and his urine will take on a reddish-yellowish color. Sometimes, he will have bowel movements that are muddy at first and firm afterwards.[17] After 30 days, his body will be emaciated and thin and [he will feel] heavy and weary when he walks.

After 40 days, his facial complexion will become cheerful (ruddy, healthy) and his mind will be at ease. After 50 days, the five viscera will be harmoniously regulated and the vital energy will be nurtured within. After 60 days, the body will have been restored to its former strength (that it had prior to the fast), and its functions will be well regulated. After 70 days, his heart will dislike boisterousness, and his [only] aspiration will be to fly up on high. After 80 days, he will be peacefully content, and will be in serene solitude. He will believe and understand the techniques and methods. After 90 days, [his skin] will have the smooth luster of glory and elegance, and sounds will be clearly heard. After 100 days, the vital energy will all arrive, and the efficacy will increase day by day.

If he practices this without ceasing, his life span will naturally be extended. After three years, his burns and scars will disappear, and his facial complexion will have a radiance. After practicing for six years, his bone marrow will be abundant and his brain will be filled. He will have clairvoyant knowledge regarding matters of existing and perishing. After nine years have elapsed, he will employ and command demons and spirits, and will take on the title of Perfected Man. Above he will assist the Supreme August One. His life span will equal that of Heaven and his radiance will merge with the sun. If you transmit [this lesson] to an unworthy person, you will suffer a calamity. (*Sandong zhunang* 3/23a–b)

Tuna jing

The *Tuna jing* (*The Scripture on Expelling and Taking In*) also is a lost scripture that was written before or during the seventh century. Fragments of it are preserved in the *Sandong zhunang* and the *Taiping yulan* (a government-sponsored encyclopedia compiled in 983). The passage translated next is found in the *Sandong zhunang* (4/1a–b). The length of the fasting process described in it is much more feasible than that described in the *Zhonghuang jing* and *Daoji tuna jing*. For this reason, it probably provides a more authentic picture of the duration of fasts carried out by real adepts.

To do away with grains and not eat is the Way of the Primal Spirit. After the first one or two days, the grain *qi* will not yet have been subdued, and your facial appearance will be morose and yellowish. After three days, the grain *qi* will leave, and the vital energy will arrive. After four or five days, the *yin* and *yang* of your vital energy will be harmoniously regulated. After six days, your subtle spirit will be stable and you will have clear vision and hearing. Walking about will become easier as you become stronger by the day. After seven days, you will constantly be on the verge of levitation. Thanks to the Ultimate Tao, you will be in communication up above with the gods when dreaming and when awake. After eight days, your spirit will travel about in the eight limits.[18] You will be able to do so silently. Always [when you do this] your mouth will naturally taste sweet. Your will and your bones (mind and body) will naturally become strong. After nine days, the subtle spirit will be in order. If your body is weak, it will become strong. Your spirit and *qi* (or perhaps, "divine *qi*") will be solidified day by day. Without going, you will naturally be far away. Without coming, you will naturally be near. Your facial appearance will daily become more joyful. After ten days, the various gods will arrive at your gates which are all closed. Jade Girls will attend you on your right and left. You will rise up lightly like a swallow that flutters amidst the clouds. The Tao will thus be acquired.

Imbibing the Five *Qi*

Immortality seekers believed benevolent deities lived in remote heavenly realms, and in the sun, moon, stars, and planets. They believed these deities would generously nourish them with wonderful life-giving *qi* if invoked properly. Various methods were devised for bringing this about, and perhaps the most widely employed among such methods was the method of Imbibing the Five *Qi*. The "Five *Qi*"—also known as the "Five Sprouts" or the "Cloud Sprouts"—are the *qi* of the five agents (wood, fire, earth, metal, and water) that issue from the five directions (east, south, center, west, and north). Based on the scheme of five agents cosmology, the Five *Qi* are further correlated to the five colors (blue, red, yellow, white, and black), the five planets (Jupiter, Mars, Saturn, Venus, and Mercury), and the five viscera (liver, heart, spleen, lungs, and kidneys).

While nourishing and transforming their bodies with the power of the celestial Five *Qi*, adepts would engage in fasts. The intensity and duration of the fasts probably varied among adepts over the centuries. It seems logical to think that the fasts were usually not as intense as what is prescribed in the *Zhonghuang jing*. While adepts were ideally supposed to make the celestial Five *Qi* their sole source of nutrition, they were fully aware of the dangers of trying to do so. For this reason, adepts were usually advised to supplement their diet with special substances and potions. While the best adepts may have attempted to fast and imbibe the celestial Five *Qi* on a permanent basis, most adepts probably did so just temporarily and periodically while observing a more moderate diet on normal occasions.

The earliest and most basic method for imbibing the Five *Qi* that survives today for our scrutiny is found in a text called the *Taishang lingbao wufu xu* (HY388/TT183). This text, which shall be referred to as the *Wufu xu* from here on, describes macrobiotic techniques of various kinds and provides illustrations of various thaumaturgic and protective talismans. It also contains myth narratives and a short liturgy. Most of the methods in the *Wufu xu* probably originated from diverse factions of Latter Han dynasty (25–220 C.E.) immortality seekers. These factions each promoted beliefs and practices of their own. However, one thing they appear to have had in common was that they were connected in some way with the *mileu* of magicians (*fangshi*) who propagated the *wei* ("weft") apocrypha.[19] The methods of the *Wufu xu* were written down and assembled together in various stages, and the text was completed in its present form some time around 410 C.E.[20]

According to the *Wufu xu* (1/11b–14b), the Five *Qi* issue from the lofty heavenly realms of the five directions. The eastern heaven is the "Heaven of the Nine *Qi* of the Green Sprouts." Its *qi* has the color of the "first sprouts of spring grass." The eastern heaven is as radiant as the sun. It contains palaces where the Jade Girl of the Blue Waist and the Most High True King dwell. These two deities ride about the universe, mounted upon divine beasts.[21] They fortify the world's *yin* and *yang* ethers with the "*qi* of the Nine Heavens" and the "flowing fragrance of the Nine Springs." The text follows with similar descriptions of the heavens of the other four directions. The details of these descriptions can be summarized as follows:

(South)—Name: Heaven of the Three *Qi* of Vermilion Cinnabar.
Qi: Vermilion, "like the crimson clouds that cover the sun."
Deities: Jade Girl of Great Cinnabar, Elder of the Primal *Qi*.
(Center)—Name: The Mountain of the Grand Emperor of the Primal
        Cavern.
Qi: Yellow
Deity: Grand Emperor[22]
(West)—Name: Heaven of the Seven *Qi* of the Bright Stones.
Qi: White, "like the moon that drops down amidst the radiant clouds."
Deities: Plain Girl of the Most High, Grand Master of the Primal *Qi*.
(North)—Name: Heaven of the Five *Qi* of the Black Delicacies.
Qi: "Like when gale winds blow over a burning forest (black as smoke)."
Deity: Jade Girl of Nocturnal Radiance.

As is the case with the eastern heaven, the *qi* and the deities of the other four heavens are described as roaming about and permeating the universe with their nourishment.

The method for imbibing the Five *Qi* is to be carried out at dawn "when the rooster cries." The adept silently recites five short chants that are directed at each of the five directions. The chants go as follows:

(East) In the east are the green sprouts.
I eat the green sprouts,
And drink from the morning flowers.
(South) In the south is the vermilion cinnabar.
I eat the vermilion cinnabar,
And drink from the cinnabar pond.
(Center) In the center *wuji*,
Is the magnificent Mt. Tai.
I eat its subtle *qi*,
And drink from its sweet springs.
(West) In the west are the bright rocks.
I eat the bright rocks,
And drink the miraculous fluid.
(North) In the north are the black delicacies.
I eat the black delicacies,
And drink the jade syrup. (3/21a–b)

After each chant, he stimulates the salivary glands by rubbing various parts of
the mouth with his tongue and swallows the saliva three times.

The method for picking the green sprouts [is to be practiced] when the
rooster cries. After reciting the chant, use your tongue to rub the surface
of your upper teeth, lick your lips, rinse your mouth [with saliva] and
swallow it three times. After reciting the Vermilion Cinnabar chant, use
your tongue to rub the surface of your lower teeth, lick your lips, rinse
your mouth [with saliva] and swallow it three times. After reciting the
chant of the *wuji* in the center, stick your tongue upwards and use it to
stab the *xuanying*,[23] lick your lips and swallow it (the saliva) three
times. After reciting the Bright Stones chant, use your tongue to rub the
surface of your teeth, lick your lips, rinse your mouth [with saliva] and
swallow it three times. [After] each swallowing, knock your teeth
together 2 × 7 (fourteen) times. After reciting the Black Delicacies
chant, use your tongue to rub beneath the tongue. While holding your
breath inside with your nose, swallow it (the saliva) three times. This is
called, 'drinking and eating in a self-so manner' [and] 'the Way of
Womb-breathing.' For each swallowing, make the Jade Water (saliva)
fill the mouth. (3/16a)

The preceding passage seems to suggest that the adept is to hold his breath
only during the swallowing of the northern *qi*. However, elsewhere, the text states,
"When finished [with the chanting and swallowing], the breath held in your nose
will have come to a limit, so gradually release it. If you make [the holding of breaths]
surpass five or more [chantings and swallowings] the true way will be completed"

(3/21b). Provided the translation is accurate, it appears that the adept tries to hold his breath throughout the entire procedure.

The saliva the adept drinks is understood to be nourishment from the heavens. The culminative effects of drinking it are described as follows:

> Always drink from the spring (swallow saliva), knocking [together] the jade [pieces] (the teeth) and doing away with food. [If you do so] you will revert to a youthful visage. The 100 evils will avoid you from a distance, and you will command and control the throngs of spirits. You will have long life and perpetual vision; your life span will extend to hundreds of thousands of years. Your eyes will become square-shaped with penetrating vision, and your intestines will transform into muscles. (3/17a)

The constant saliva swallowing transforms the adept into an immortal, superhuman being with no digestive system. The digestive system becomes obsolete because he no longer eats food.

The Shangqing movement of the fourth century and the Lingbao movement of the fifth century later devised their own methods for imbibing the Five *Qi*, based largely upon the model provided by the *Wufu xu*.[24]

Imbibing the Essences of the Sun and Moon

Although Taoists devised methods for feeding off various heavenly bodies, methods for feeding off the sun and moon were especially common. Two of the earliest methods for feeding off the sun and moon are described in the *Wufu xu* and the *Laozi zhongjing* (a text probably written in the late second or early third century C.E.[25]).

According to the *Wufu xu*, the solar essence is to be eaten between sunrise and high noon on the first, third, fifth, seventh, ninth, and fifteenth days of the month. The method is carried out as follows:

The adept first visualizes the sun inside of his heart. Inside of the sun is a black canopy, and under the canopy is a small red child. Red vapor permeates and surrounds the adept's body. The vapor then rises from his head and wraps itself around the sun up in the sky. The adept addresses the sun with the words, "Lord Sun, the Primal *Yang*, return to my Crimson Palace (heart) and combine your virtue with me. Together [we shall] nurture the small child" (1/25b). He then visualizes the essence of the sun descending down into his nostrils and mouth, and swallows it twenty-seven times. The solar essence fills his heart. From this point, three deities dwell in the heart, seated on a couch of gold and jade. The Father of the Great One sits on the left, the Mother of Black Radiance sits on the right, and the Baby Child sits in the middle. They (or just the Baby Child?) dine on "the divine liquor of jade efflorescences and the heavenly fungi and herbs." By visualizing thus, the adept enables himself to "never hunger nor thirst, and to have long life."

The lunar essence is eaten at midnight on the fifteenth of the month (the night of the full moon). The adept faces the moon[26] and chants, "Lord Moon, the Primal *Yin*, return to the Elixir Field and combine your virtue with me. Together [we shall] nurture the small child" (1/25b). He visualizes the "white vapor and yellow essence of the moon" coming into his nose and mouth, and swallows it twenty-one times. Thus, "the lunar essence lodges in the kidneys and [the adept] obtains long life" (1/26a).

In addition to feeding off the sun and moon, the *Wufu xu* also advises the adept to eat the essence of the north pole star. This is to be done at sunrise, noon, sunset, and midnight, although the days on which to do this are not specified. The adept visualizes the "Great August Star of the Northern Extreme" and chants the words "Supreme Emperor of August Heaven, the Most High Lord of the Tao; [I], your descendant, the insignificant common man *so-and-so* (the adept says his name here) am fond of the Tao and wish to obtain long life." He visualizes the stellar essence coming down to the space between his eyebrows, after which it flows into his nostrils and mouth. He swallows it fifteen times and visualizes it filling his heart, gallbladder and spleen. In the spleen he sees the "Mother of the Tao," who is "in charge of feeding and nurturing the baby." Again, the text states that if the adept practices this method he will obtain long life and never be thirsty nor hungry.

It is not specified how rapidly the adept should decrease his dietary intake, nor for that matter is it clearly indicated that the adept is supposed to try to fast. But these visualizations probably were conducted during fasts, since they purported to eliminate hunger and thirst. Through the numerous swallowings, the adept would fill his stomach with air and/or saliva (the text does not clearly specify), and this would hopefully help subdue his hunger.

The *Laozi zhongjing*'s method involves similar visualizations that pertain to feeding an internal "baby." However, the "sun" and "moon" that nourish the baby exist inside the body.

> Always visualize the sun and moon beneath your nipples. Inside the sun and moon are yellow essence and red *qi*. [The yellow essence and red *qi*] enter the Crimson Palace (heart), and then [enter] the Purple Chamber of the Yellow Court. The yellow essence and red *qi* fill up the Great Store-house (stomach). The baby, seated in the passageway of the stomach and facing directly towards the south, drinks and eats the yellow essence and red *qi*. Thereby he is satiated. The 100 diseases will be eliminated and the 10,000 calamities will not afflict you. If you always visualize this, you will ascend and become a Perfected Being. (*Yunji qiqian* 18/7a–b)

Prior to the aforementioned passage, the text states that the baby in the stomach is "my own body." Later on, in the twelfth section, it states, "Visualize your own body in the passage of the stomach" (*Yunji qiqian* 18/7b). Apparently, the adept identifies with the baby because the baby personifies the core of his inner nature and physical vitality. The internal solar and lunar nutrients are sent to the baby through visualization alone; the adept does not swallow air or saliva. So if this method did indeed help suppress hunger, it was perhaps due to a psychosomatic effect made possible by the adept's faith.

Many other methods for imbibing solar and lunar essences were devised over the centuries. They are far too numerous to cover here. Both the Shangqing and Lingbao movements strongly endorsed such methods.[27]

Talisman Swallowing

As mentioned in chapter 2 (p. 23), the *Shenxian zhuan* tells us that Huang Jing "summoned the Six *Jia* Jade Girls by swallowing the *yin* and *yang* talismans." A detailed description of what may be this very same method is found in a text of unknown date called the *Shenxian shiqi jingui miaolu* (The Marvelous Record in the Golden Box on the Imbibing of *Qi* of the Divine Immortals, HY835/TT571). The description occurs in a section entitled, "The Method of Imbibing the *Yin* and *Yang* Talismans and Summoning the Six *Jia* Jade Girls." There it states that the method is performed while "avoiding grains," in the event that the adept has become "worried that his five [visceral] spirits may wander out of the body and evil delusions might afflict and agitate him" (1a).

At sunrise, the adept stands facing the east, holding a paper talisman in his left hand and a cup of water in his right. He recites the words, "[I], so and so am fond of the true Tao and [I] eat the *qi* of Central Harmony. Chengyi, Jade Girl of Great Obscurity of the *jiazi* day (of the sexegenary cycle); [I implore you to] serve me and attend me with a lunch box so that wherever I may be, my methods will be [successfully] accomplished, and I will acquire whatever it is I seek. Do not allow me to thirst and hunger. [Bring enough food so that] an army of any size, or people of any number can have their hunger satisfied" (1a–b). After reciting these words, he swallows the talisman and washes it down with the water. The ritual is continued for sixty days, divided into six ten-day segments during which six different Jade Girls are addressed. On odd numbered days of the sexegenary cycle, the *yang* talisman is eaten. On even numbered days, the *yin* talisman is eaten.

Another talisman swallowing method designed to subdue hunger is described in a fragment from a late third century scripture called the *Sanhuang wen* (Writs of the Three Emperors).[28] It is preserved in the *Wushang biyao* (HY1130/TT768–779), a Taoist encyclopedia commissioned by Emperor Wu of the Northern Zhou dynasty (Wudi, r. 561–578). It describes how to use a certain "Talisman of the Blue Womb of the Vermilion Official."

> This [talisman] was received by the Father and Mother of the Nine Heavens from the Queen Mother of the West. On mornings of long months, swallow [one of these talismans] written in red. On mornings of

short months, swallow one written in black. Always burn incense and pay your respects [to the gods] all night long for one night before swallowing it. This allows a person to not hunger. It also replenishes his *jing* and supplements his brain. It makes the body light and gives it a beautiful complexion. It extends the life span limitlessly. If a Taoist adept does not see this text, his swallowing of *qi* and practice of the Tao will be but futile hardships. (25/7b–8a)

Evidently, the talisman was to be used by fasting adepts who practiced methods of air swallowing. If talismans did indeed help suppress hunger, this may have been because a psychosomatic effect was brought about by the adept's faith in the talisman.

Sucking on a Seed

In the *Wufu xu* a method is found called "Yue Zichang's Method of Holding a Jujube Seed in the Mouth." The method consists simply of sucking on the seed of a jujube, and thereby drinking one's own saliva.

The way to long life is to always hold a jujube seed in your mouth [and suck on it] in the same way a baby suckles. After a long while, saliva will fill the mouth. Swallow two-thirds of it and then swallow the remainder together with air. This is called "recycling the *jing*." [The *jing*] circulates and returns to the beginning [in a route that is] like a jade ring. While you are doing away with grains, you will come to a minor crisis after five days and your head will feel dizzy. After a while, [the dizziness] will stop. After 14 days, your head will feel dizzy again, [but] the dizziness will stop after a while. After 21 days, your *qi* will be stable. If you want to eat, you can eat, and if you do not want to eat, [your eating] will naturally cease. While you are doing away with grains, you must not engage in sexual intercourse. You may eat small amounts of jujubes and dried meats. Drink no more than one *sheng* (200 ml.) of liquor. The method is the same for both men and women. (2/36a–b)

By drinking his saliva, the adept feeds off of his recycled *jing*. The word *jing*, in certain contexts, can denote the "essences" or nutrients in foods. In the previous passage, it seems to denote the body's internal nutrients that are essential for the fasting adept's survival. The underlying assumption seems to be that semen (also referred to as *jing*) is a valuable internal source of nutrition, and this is probably why sexual activity is forbidden during the fast. The adept starves himself to where the body shows clear signs of stress. However, the fast is only mandatory for twenty-one days, during which some solid foods (dried meats and jujubes) can be eaten in small quantities.

Drug Recipes

Although the ideal for Taoist adepts was to eat nothing, this was unfeasible in most or all cases. For this reason, Taoists ingested various substances—preferably in small amounts—to stave off hunger and sustain the body through its travails. Also, in most cases, the substances were ascribed salubrious, life-extending properties of their own that made them desirable. The most abundant collection of early hunger-suppressing drug recipes is found in the *Wufu xu*. Many have also been preserved in the writings of the Shangqing movement of the fourth century.

Recipes in the *Wufu xu*

The ingredients found most commonly in the recipes of the *Wufu xu* are sesame seeds, poke root, deer bamboo, and grains. We shall now examine a few samples of the recipes that feature these ingredients.

One recipe that features sesame seeds as the main ingredient is "The Perfected Man's Method for Abstaining Completely from Grains." The recipe is given in the text as follows:

> Take two *dou* (about 4 liters) of sesame seeds and five *sheng* (about 1 liter) of fagara (Chinese pepper, *zanthoxylum planispinum*). First remove the black skins (of the sesame seeds). Pound the two ingredients together and sift. At first eat five *ge* (about 100 grams) [of the mixture] three times a day. If you have no water (to drink with it), you can use honey to [mix into the powder to] make pills. Take one pill the size of a chicken egg four times per day. Naturally, you will not hunger. During years of famine you can eat this medicine by itself and abstain completely from grains. If thirsty, drink only water. Do not eat anything else. If you eat anything else you will become hungry. [This medicine] gives you 100 times your normal energy. Coldness and heat will no longer afflict you. [The medicine] can cure the 100 diseases. Divine Immortal-hood will naturally be brought about.[29] (2/5b–6a)

This method purports to enable the adept to survive on nothing else but water and the prescribed potion. It is clear that the author had the shunning of all ordinary foods in mind when he spoke of "avoiding grains." The passage also is interesting in that it recommends the potion as a means for surviving famines. This concern with famines seems to bear a strong connection to certain beliefs conveyed frequently in the *Wufu xu*; beliefs that anticipated regular and inevitable cycles of cosmic strife, devastation, and restoration.

Poke root (*zhanglu, phytolacca acinosa*) is a toxic[30] plant commonly used as a diuretic. Its toxicity may have been what made it an effective hunger suppressant. This is the impression one gets from the following recipe:

Add one *dou* (about 2 liters) of *tianmendong* (*asparagus cochinchinensis*) powder to ten *jin* (about 2 kilograms) of yeast and 3 *dou* (about 6 liters) of rice. Let the poke roots sit [in the mixture] for six days. Thereupon begin to eat them while observing ritual prohibitions. In five days your food intake will start to decrease. After 20 days, grains will be eliminated and your intestines will be so fat that they can only hold air. The various worms (the Three Worms?) will all leave. Your ears and eyes will hear and see clearly. All of your moles and scars will disappear. When the moon rests in the *yugui* constellation and the day reaches the *ding* hour (2 A.M.), gather the poke root plant. Eat a piece the size of a jujube three times per day. Taoist adepts always grow this plant in a garden by their meditation chambers. It allows a person to communicate with the gods. (2/11a)

The poke root's poison affected the body rapidly and drastically. Apparently it made the adept eat less because the poison caused an inflammation in the intestines. The statement "your intestines will be so fat that they can only hold air" suggests that adepts who ingested poke root were expected to practice air swallowing. The phrase "it allows a person to communicate with the gods" suggests that poke root may have also had a hallucinatory effect on adepts. As we can see, poke root also was thought to help exterminate the Three Worms, and it seems likely that it was ascribed this capacity simply because it is poisonous.

Further on, the text gives a recipe for poke root pills that are meant specifically for killing the Three Worms.[31] It then states that if the adept takes three of the pills daily, the Three Worms will come out decomposed in his stool. The Lower Corpse comes out after thirty days, the Middle Corpse after sixty days, and the Upper Corpse after 100 days. The Upper Corpse is black and shaped like a hand. The Middle Corpse is blue and shaped like a foot. The Lower Corpse is white and shaped like an egg. The text then goes on to describe how the worms do their evil deeds and how they must be expelled for any immortality technique to be effective. Once they are expelled, the adept "never again feels hungry nor thirsty, and his heart is calm and free of thoughts" (2/24b). It also says that poke root brings about the same results when made into a powder and taken by itself. Berries of the pagoda tree (*huai*, *sophora japonica*) also can be eaten to serve the same purpose. However, the text then goes on to indicate that the quickest way to expel the Three Worms is by imbibing the Five *Qi*.

Those who can adeptly imbibe *qi* need not use these recipes. Furthermore, the perfect *qi* are the green sprouts, the essences of the five directions. If a Taoist adept imbibes them (the *qi* of the five directions), the Three Worms will run out in 21 days. (2/24b)

However, imbibing the Five *Qi* alone would have been too strenuous for most adepts. Therefore, they were given the alternative of expelling the Three

Worms and overcoming hunger more gradually through the ingestion of prescribed substances.

Deer bamboo (*polygonatum sibiricum*) is a nontoxic plant. Its Chinese name is *huangjing*, which translated literally means "yellow essence." The *Wufu xu* states that deer bamboo is the "essence of the sun" that congeals in the "nine heavens," drifts about and disperses among the mountains. Nourished by the clouds and rain, it transforms and grows into an herb. The ingestion of deer bamboo is in this sense a technique for imbibing solar essences. We also are told that deer bamboo grows on the slopes of the Taihang mountain range[32] and is yellow in color and sweet in flavor (2/18a–b).

Deer bamboo can be eaten in small quantities if one simply wants to benefit from its medicinal qualities. It also can be eaten in larger quantities to substitute for food. It can be prepared and eaten in various ways. Its roots can be steamed, dried, and made into a powder, of which a spoonful is to be ingested each day. Its berries can be soaked in drinking water to make juice. The roots can be boiled and mixed with soybean powder, then made into small cakes. The adept also can drink the water in which the roots have been boiled. The stem and the leaves can be mixed into porridge and eaten. The wonderful effects of deer bamboo are to be brought about not only by preparing and ingesting it properly, but by observing an austere and unworldly lifestyle. One passage states that for the drug to confer longevity, the adept must "abandon glory and elegance." For the drug to confer immortality, he must "abandon the secular world" and live alone in the mountains (2/19a).

The following recipe can be used for making deer bamboo pills:

> During the second and eighth months take the roots and shave off the fuzz. Wash thoroughly and cut into fine pieces. Boil one *hu* (about 20 liters) [of the deer bamboo pieces] in six *dou* (about 12 liters) of water, using a fire of moderate strength from morning till evening. When the medicine has cooked thoroughly, remove it [from the fire] and cool it. Press and crush it with your hands. Strain out the fluid with a wine press to make pills. Remove the impurities and dry it out to make a powder. Keep it in a kettle. If you [use the powder] to make pills (perhaps by mixing with honey?) the size of chicken eggs and ingest three per day, you can avoid grains and stop eating. You will feel neither coldness nor heat, and your going about will be swift as a galloping horse. If a person is able to abstain from [the activities of] the bedroom (sexual intercourse), he will not age, his life span will have no limit and he will become an immortal. If he does not abstain from the activities of the bedroom, the longest he can live is 200 years. (2/21a–b)

As we can see, deer bamboo was thought to have maximum efficacy when the adept fasted and remained celibate. Although it was deemed effective even without austerities, a thoroughgoing asceticism involving solitude, fasting, and celibacy was deemed necessary for its maximum effect to be gained. On the other hand, deer bamboo was thought to be completely ineffective if one's lifestyle was blatantly contrary to such standards. The text thus states that Sun Quan (182–252 C.E.), the king of the Three Kingdoms Wu state, ate deer bamboo. However, no positive effects came about because he "did not abstain from [the activities of] the bedroom and did various uncalm things." "Uncalm things" probably refers to his military pursuits and decadent lifestyle (22a–b).

Deer bamboo was meant to serve as survival food during times of crisis—self-imposed or otherwise. The text says that when one ingests deer bamboo, "he need not avoid tigers and wolves nor fear military upheaval." It also says, "When you go about in the mountains you can [pick it and] eat it raw to your mouth's satisfaction, and drink [only] water when thirsty." Deer bamboo, we are told, is sometimes referred to as "food for alleviating the plight of the poor." This is because "in a year of famine it can be given to old people and children who can eat it while not eating grains" (2/22a).

Some of the hunger-suppressing recipes in the *Wufu xu* include grains as their main ingredients. From this it again seems clear that the reduction of the overall dietary intake was the primary concern of Taoist dietetics, rather than a taboo on grains. Two examples of hunger-suppressing recipes that include grains follow:

"The Divine Immortal's Method of Eating Blue Millet"
Take one *dou* (about 2 liters) of blue millet (a type of large-grained millet with a bluish color). Wash and steep in some high-quality liquor for three days. [Then] steam without letting anything leak out. Steam 100 times and let it sit out in the open 100 times. It is preferable to not expose it to sunlight. Store it in a soft leather sack. Thereby, when you want to enter the mountains and travel long distances, you can eat [the millet] once (amount to be eaten is not specified), and it will sustain you for ten days as you go without eating. If you eat it again after the ten days, you can go without eating for 49 days. If you eat it again after the 49 days, you will be able to make 490 years your interval [between meals]. There is a variant recipe that says to use black millet. Yet another recipe says to use three *dou*. (2/34b)

"Method for Abstaining from Grains"
Use five *ge* (100 ml.) each of non-glutinous rice, millet, wheat, soybeans and hemp seed. Fry the beans before grinding them into powder. Mix the ingredients together with one *jin* of honey. Put over a flame and bring to a boil 100 times. Then put it into cold water [to cool it off] and make into pills the size of plum pits. Take one pill per dose (how often the pill is to be taken is not specified). You will be able to go for the rest of your life without getting hungry. Each ingredient is to be treated (ground?). Only the beans need to be fried. (2/36a)

Recipes in the Shangqing Texts

As we will see in chapter 5, the Shangqing texts strongly endorse fasting and make it a prerequisite for receiving and studying the holiest scriptures. They thus contain numerous descriptions of fasting techniques. Although the Shangqing movement emerged during the latter half of the fourth century, the recipes themselves are probably earlier in their origins. Here we shall examine two of their most important drug recipes; *xunfan* and "white rocks."

The two main ingredients used for preparing *xunfan* are rice and the leaves of a shrub called the *nanzhu* (*vaccinium bracteatum*).[33] *Nanzhu* leaves on their own were thought to have hunger-alleviating qualities. A surviving fragment of the *Dengzhen yinjue* (an important collection of Shangqing writings) states that they can be used to relieve hunger during times of famine or extreme poverty.[34] It logically followed that *nanzhu* leaves could be used by an adept who was voluntarily decreasing his dietary intake.

The most detailed discussion on *xunfan* that we have available is a section in the *Yunji qiqian* (74/1a–7b) entitled *Taiji zhenren qingjing ganshi xunfan shangxian lingfang*,[35] which we shall refer to from here on as the *Xunfan lingfang*. There we are told that the adept should gradually reduce his food intake while ingesting *xunfan*. At first, the adept should limit himself to a quota of 2.5 *sheng* (about 0.5 liters) of food per day. After a year, he should reduce the daily quota to two *sheng*. After three years, he should reduce it to one *sheng*. After four years, he should reduce it to 0.5 *sheng*, and he should stop eating food entirely by the end of five years. At this point, the adept will become "light and bright" and gain "great effects." He becomes able to "eat nine meals in one day or go without eating throughout the year." An annotation to the text adds that the reduction of the food intake will proceed more easily if the adept's diet consists of wheat noodles (*Yunji qiqian* 74/6b–7a).

According to the *Xunfan lingfang*, one *hu* and five *dou* (app. 30 liters) of nonglutinous rice are used to concoct a single batch of *xunfan*. Five *jin* (about 1.1 kg.) of *nanzhu* leaves—three *jin* if they are dried—are boiled to produce a dark reddish-blue fluid, which is left to cool. After it has cooled, the adept uses the fluid to wash and cook the rice. The cooked rice is then left to dry out completely.

The adept eats two *sheng* of the *xunfan* (the dried rice) per day and is not allowed to eat any meats, except dried ones. Also, he is not to engage in any sexual activity, because if he does, "impurity will spread about and the medicine will be ineffective" (*Yunji qiqian* 74/3a). If the adept wants to accelerate and enhance the efficacy of the *xunfan*, he can grind seven *liang* (about 97 grams)[36] of hollow azurite (*kongqing*), one *jin* (222.73 grams)[37] of cinnabar (mercuric sulfide, *dansha*), two *jin* of tukahoe, and five *liang* (about 7 grams) of *jing* (*vitex negundo*) tree leaves to a very fine texture. He then mixes these ground ingredients into the fluid for washing and cooking the rice. The text also describes the effects of hollow azurite and cinnabar and the prohibitions involved in their ingestion.

Hollow azurite, we are told, satiates the stomach, improves the eyesight, strengthens the sinews, supplements the fluids, increases the *jing*, and makes the face youthful. However, if the person ingesting hollow azurite engages in sexual intercourse ("bedroom activities"), his (or her?) "*qi* will be defiled" and his "spirit will perish." The consequence is immediate death (*Yunji qiqian* 74/4a).

Cinnabar, we are told, fills the bones, increases the blood, strengthens the will, supplements the brain, increases the *qi*, and "regulates" the lungs. It enhances the circulation and "harmonizes" the joints. However, people who ingest cinnabar must not eat meat, "tread upon impurity," or engage in sexual activity. If they violate these injunctions, they will suffer from coughing, abdominal ailments, and "chronic bone-withering diseases"[38] (*Yunji qiqian* 74/4a–b).

As can be seen, the dietary and sexual prohibitions become stricter and much more emphatic when hollow azurite and cinnabar are taken. Hollow azurite is mildly toxic and cinnabar is highly toxic. Even though the ancient Chinese were well aware of their toxicity, both were commonly employed to treat bodily ailments.[39] While both minerals are undoubtedly included in the *xunfan* recipe because of their ascribed medicinal benefits, their toxicity in itself may also have been a desired quality, due to the need to exterminate the Three Worms.

A passage in the *Zhengao*, an important collection of Shangqing writings, recommends adepts to "boil and eat white rocks" when they "avoid grains and enter the mountains." The text then states that an immortal named Baishizi (Master of the White Rocks) had invented this method for eating white rocks, after having received his inspiration from a passage in a certain *Taisu zhuan*[40] that read, "White rocks have *jing*" (5/14a–b).

Another version of the story of Baishizi is found in the *Shenxian zhuan*.[41] As may be recalled, the *Shenxian zhuan*'s entry on Jiao Xian also mentions the boiling of white rocks. So what specifically were "white rocks"? Apparently, they were pieces of white quartz. Various Shangqing writings describe a method for boiling white quartz pieces, and the claim seems to have been that this was the very same method mastered by Baishizi. It is described in detail in three different sources[42] and mentioned frequently in the *Sandong zhunang*.[43][44] In our brief examination of the method, we will primarily follow the text of *Yunji qiqian* 74/7b–13a ("Taishang jushengyu zhu wushiying fa" [The Most High Method for Boiling Five Quartz Pieces in Sesame Oil]).

The recipe calls for 10 *jin* (one *jin* = 222.73 g.) of shallots, 1.5 *hu* (one *hu* = 20.23 l) of black sesame seed oil, 5 *dou* (one *dou* = 2.023 l) of honey, 26 *hu* of mountain spring water, and 5 unscratched, unblemished pieces of white quartz. The adept first polishes the quartz pieces on a whetstone until they become shaped like tiny sparrow eggs. He then carries out a retreat of thirty to sixty days. Then, on the ninth day of the ninth month, he sets up an earthen hearth and places a large iron kettle on it. At the hour of *you* (6 P.M.), the adept, facing east, kneels in front of the kettle and tosses the quartz pieces one by one into the kettle, reciting a verse and holding his breath for "five breaths" before each toss. The verses mention the names of the each of the "five rocks," along with the bodily organs they purport to sustain. Each chant invokes the protection of specific gods.

The adept then stands up and puts the shallots, honey, and sesame oil into the kettle, one by one. He adds water and covers the kettle with a wooden lid. The next morning, he lights a weak fire under the kettle. As the water evaporates, he keeps adding water until it is all used up. After all of the water has evaporated, the kettle is left to cool for five days. Then, at dawn, the adept swallows the five quartz pieces one by one with the sauce they were cooked in, and washes them down with water. The chants are repeated before swallowing each rock. In the days following this, the adept continues to eat two *ge* (one *ge* = 0.2023 l) of the sauce per day, together with liquor, until it is all gone. The adept may then make a whole new batch if he so wishes. A passage from the *Dengzhen yinjue* states that this method enables adepts to transform their bodies to where they become able to eat enormous quantities of food ("nine meals in one day") if they so wish, without hindering the flow of *qi* in their bodies. However, at the same time, they also become able to survive without food. The passage further states, "They can also go the entire year without getting hungry, reversing their aging process and returning to youthfulness." Thus, the method for eating white quartz pieces is claimed to be one of the best methods for "cutting off grains."[45]

Curiously, however, the text of the *Yunji qiqian* does not mention this capacity to transform the digestive system. This is perhaps because it was taken for granted that the method would have such an effect. Rather, emphasis is put upon the capacity of the "five rocks" to preserve and protect the five viscera and subsequently bring about a truly miraculous phenomenon. This amazing property is described most vividly in a passage from the *Dengzhen yinjue*, preserved in the *Sandong zhunang* (3/7a–b). This passage claims that the "five rocks" work their marvelous effects after the adept dies. They "protect and settle the five viscera," and this in turn causes the *hun* and *po* souls, and an entity called the Great Spirit (*dashen*), to remain with the corpse after death. Even though the skin and flesh decompose, the five viscera, the bowels, the Three Origins (elixir fields?), the brain, the skeleton, and the bone marrow remain intact. After an interval that ranges from between three to forty years, the Great Spirit—preserved in a cranial compartment known as the Dongfang—miraculously regenerates the flesh, blood, and other bodily fluids. The adept thereby becomes resurrected with a body superior to that which he had prior to his death.

Because this capacity to bring about resurrection is the point of emphasis, the recipe in the *Yunji qiqian* is prefaced by a narrative[46] about a certain Zhao Chengzi. Zhao Chengzi, we are told, boiled and ingested the "five rocks," and later on died. The narrative then tells of a how a certain man, while strolling along in the mountains, discovered the body of Zhao Chengzi. All that remained of the body were the dried bones and the five viscera, preserved in perfect condition. White quartz pieces glimmered from within each viscus. The man, reasoning that he must have happened upon the corpse of a Taoist adept who had failed his trials, decided to take and then eat the quartz pieces for his own benefit. However, after he had done this, the "five rocks" flew right out of his mouth and returned to Zhao Chengzi's five viscera. Later, Zhao Chengzi was resurrected. The man who stole the quartz pieces was less fortunate; he and his entire family died of leprosy.

Final Comments

Taoist adepts went to great pains and resorted to a seemingly limitless variety of measures in their endeavor to stop eating. The material we examined from the *Zhonghuang jing* in particular gives us an understanding of some of the basic physiological theories that dictated fasting. The *Wufu xu*, on the other hand, does not carry out detailed discussions on physiology. Rather, in that text we find a strong preoccupation with the need to survive famines. This preoccupation seems to have resulted from the belief that the world was doomed to undergo regular and inevitable cycles of strife, devastation, and restoration.

Several of the fasting methods just examined require celibacy. This is understandable in light of the fact that fasting adepts were trying as much as possible to sustain themselves on the precious vital forces of their own bodies. No bodily fluid was more cherished than *jing* (semen). Taoists reasoned that if semen (*jing*) could create a new life when administered outwardly in sexual intercourse, it would certainly exercise the same life-bestowing property if retained within.[47] Furthermore, as was mentioned (see p. 59), the word *jing* can sometimes denote the "essences" or nutrients in foods, and the understanding may have been that semen (*jing*) is an internal nutrient. When trying to shun all nutrients from without, one could not afford to deplete one's nutrients from within.

It also appears that in some cases fasting adepts practiced celibacy to gain the support of divine beings and to experience visions of them. As may be recalled, the *Tuna jing* says that the fasting adept will be attended by Jade Girls after ten days (see p. 53). When carrying out the talisman-swallowing method of the *Shenxian shiqi jingui miuolu*, the adept implores the Six *Jia* Jade Girls to bring him "lunchboxes" (see p. 58). It was believed that Jade Girls could come to the aid of fasting adepts. Adepts also desired to "see" the Jade Girls and thereby gain assurance of their support. Most interestingly, celibacy was considered a prerequisite for getting to see them. Evidence for this is given in the following fragment from the *Sanhuang wen*:

> If you want to ascend as an Immortal, you must abstain completely from the *yin* and *yang* (sexual intercourse). You will thereby be able to see Jade Girls. Those who are unable to seek ascension as immortals and are

unable to abstain from the *yin* and *yang*, can only beckon Plain Girls. (*Wushang biyao* 25/1b)

By cutting off his this-worldly sexual relations and passions, the adept gains encounters with beautiful divine women. The idea seems to be that the Jade Girls provide the adept with feminine companionship as well as nourishment. Thus, in his trance visions, the adept is to be compensated for the culinary and sexual pleasures he has sacrificed. The visions, when they did occur, probably resulted partly from the sublimation of desires.

CHAPTER FIVE

Asceticism in the Shangqing Texts

The biographical section of the *Nanshi* (Official History of the Southern Dynasties) records the story of a certain Deng Yu, the Master of the Southern Peak. In it we are told that Deng Yu shunned government service and lived in a tiny wooden shack on Mt. Heng. He never came down from the mountain. For over thirty years he "cut off grains" and lived on mica powder and stream water. He recited "the scripture(s) of the *Dadong*" day and night. Emperor Wu of the Liang dynasty admired him greatly. One time, Deng Yu prepared an elixir for the Emperor, who for some reason "did not dare take it." Instead, he stored it in a tower and worshipped it regularly on Taoist festival days (presumably, this took place before Emperor Wu's renunciation of Taoism in 504). One day, Deng Yu was visited by the Divine Immortal Lady Wei and an entourage of thirty youthful female immortals. After a lengthy conversation, the immortals proclaimed to him that he was predestined to attain immortality and that they had been watching over him for a long time. In the fourteenth year of the Tianjian reign era (515 C.E.), he saw two large blue birds frolicking before him. After the birds had left, he proclaimed to his disciples, "Seeking it has been very arduous, but having attained it, I am very relaxed. The blue birds just came, and [thus] the time has come." He died a few days later "with no illness," and the entire mountain was filled with fragrant air that was "unlike anything that ever existed in the world."[1]

The story of Deng Yu provides us with a good example of an ascetic who followed the beliefs and embodied the ideals of the Shangqing movement. The "scripture(s) of the *Dadong*" most likely refers to the Shangqing scriptures. Another possibility is that it refers specifically to the *Dadong zhenjing*, which was considered the holiest of all the Shangqing scriptures. The "Divine Immortal Lady Wei" refers to Wei Huacun, a female adept who allegedly attained immortality and acted as the primary preceptress in the revelations that inspired the Shangqing scriptures. Deng Yu's vision of beautiful young women bears a similarity to the visions experienced by Yang Xi, the recipient of the so-called revelations. Highly intriguing here is Emperor Wu's reluctance to ingest Deng Yu's elixir. One wonders whether the elixir was toxic, particularly because toxic potions are endorsed in the Shangqing texts.

The original Shangqing texts were authored by the visionary mystic Yang Xi (330–?) in the town of Jurong (in present-day Jiangsu Province) between 364 and 370 C.E. The contents of the texts were allegedly revealed to him by divine beings in visions. Yang Xi passed the texts on to Xu Mi (303–373, a court official) and Xu Hui (341–370, Xu Mi's son). Xu Hui eventually left the secular world to devote himself to the scriptures and their prescribed methods on Mt. Mao.[2]

Isabelle Robinet emphasizes that Yang Xi was a mystic or a visionary, as opposed to a medium. As she explains, a medium acts as a simple, unsophisticated mouthpiece for the god or spirit that possesses him or her. The information brought forth by a medium typically consists of fragmentary responses to the concerns of specific situations. Yang Xi, on the other hand, produced a full-fledged religious system with a comprehensive scheme of cosmology, soteriology and praxis. Also, unlike a typical medium, Yang Xi was highly cultured. His writings reflect a deep familiarity with the Confucian classics and most other forms of intellectual literature available at his time. He also was a first-rate calligrapher, and the excellence of his calligraphy later came to be the standard by which the great Taoist scholar Tao Hongjing distinguished his authentic manuscripts from forgeries manufactured by other hands.[3]

Yang Xi produced a religious literature that fit the tastes of the religiously inclined segment of the educated elite. More specifically, as has been pointed out by Miyakawa Hisayuki and Michel Strickmann,[4] Shangqing doctrines served the agenda of the elite clans who had migrated southward and established themselves in the Wu region after the fall of the Han dynasty. Later, when the Western Jin capital of Luoyang was conquered in 311 by non-Chinese peoples,[5] these southern clans became relegated to a subservient role under the imperial family and northern aristocrats who had fled southward and established a new capital at Jiankang (present-day Nanjing). Power struggles between the northern and southern aristocrats existed in the sphere of religion as well as in politics. Many of the northerners belonged to the Heavenly Masters School, which had set out to win converts in the south and destroy the temples of local popular cults. The Xu family (beginning with Xu Mi's father and uncle) had chosen to collaborate with the new elite by serving as officials under their regime and converting to the Heavenly Masters School. While subservience on the secular plane was irreversible, the appearance of the Shangqing scriptures elevated the Xus to a privileged position in the religious sphere. By owning Shangqing text manuscripts, the Xus believed they possessed the sole means by which a mortal could communicate with the holiest divine beings and attain the highest levels of immortality. Their beliefs and claims were soon to be shared by a limited circle of kinfolk and fellow southern aristocrats who gained access to the texts. The immortality to which they claimed exclusive access was supposedly far superior to that which could be gained through the practices of the

Heavenly Masters School and the older southern macrobiotic traditions. While the first Shangqing proponents did not deny the legitimacy of such earlier movements, they relegated their practices to the status of "minor methods" (*xiaofa*). "Minor methods" were methods that were thought to prolong life and help qualify an adept to learn "superior methods." The "superior methods" consisted primarily of the incantations and visual meditations of the Shangqing texts, among which the *Dadong zhenjing* was considered the holiest. Thus the proponents of the Shangqing texts became the custodians of a what they believed was the highest religious path.

Robinet states that the significance of the Shangqing texts does not lie so much in their originality,[6] but rather in how they synthesize various earlier beliefs and practices and blend them into a comprehensive religious system. Robinet points out that the development and eventual proliferation of this religious system represented a crucial juncture in Taoist history. Taoist immortality seeking was previously "a young system in perpetual gestation," which emphasized the experience and inspiration of the individual. The Shangqing movement turned it into a fixed system that could provide a basis for an established school. The Shangqing texts purported to be the product of a single, all-important revelation. Rather than gain one's own unique religious illumination, it now became important to learn the message revealed to Yang Xi and to somehow relive his experience. This meant being initiated into the school and gaining access to the all-important scriptures.[7]

The earliest Shangqing proponents were few in number. They lacked a formal, independent organization of their own. But eventually the fame and acclaim of the scriptures began to grow as they were transmitted to more people. This growing acclaim provoked the activity of imitators who produced their own texts. Most important among such texts were the Lingbao scriptures. The success of the Lingbao scriptures in turn inspired the writing of newer, apocryphal Shangqing texts that incorporated Lingbao doctrines. It soon became very difficult to identify the original Shangqing texts, as the original set of manuscripts had become divided among different hands and sets of copied manuscripts had been infiltrated with apocryphal material.[8]

During the second half of the fifth century, certain erudite Taoists made efforts to identify the original Shangqing texts. The first such effort was initiated by Gu Huan. Shortly before the year 465, Gu Huan, who had transcribed the original manuscripts in the custody of a certain Ma family, met in the Shan mountains (in eastern Zhejiang) with Du Jingchan and Zhu Sengbiao. Du possessed original manuscripts that he had inherited from his father, and Zhu had received original manuscripts from his mentor Chu Boyu. The three men examined the texts they had in hand and produced the *Zhenji* (Traces of the Perfected), an anthology of writings that they had determined were authentic products of the revelations. Regrettably, this compilation has been lost.[9]

A similar endeavor was later carried out by Tao Hongjing (456–536). Born to a clan allied by marriage to the Xus, he was an initiated Taoist adept and esteemed official of the Qi dynasty. He saw his first authentic Yang Xi manuscript during his Taoist apprenticeship under Sun Youyue (a pupil of Lu Xiujing).[10] He was so impressed by its literary style and calligraphy that he was immediately convinced of its divine inspiration. He became increasingly preoccupied with gathering and studying Shangqing manuscripts, and he eventually retired from his government post in 492 to study the texts full time on Mt. Mao. The fruits of his studies were the *Zhengao* (Proclamations of the Perfected, HY1010/TT537–640) and the *Dengzhen yinjue* (Secret Lessons for the Ascent to Perfection, HY421/TT193).[11]

The *Zhengao*, which survives as a complete work, contains mostly writings by Yang Xi that purport to convey the teachings revealed to him in his visions. However, some passages appear to be excerpts from certain texts Yang Xi had in his possession. The *Zhengao* also preserves some private correspondences between Yang Xi and the two Xus. Alongside these materials are found annotations by Tao Hongjing. Tao Hongjing also added a postface that narrates the history of the revelation and transmission of the Shangqing texts.

The *Dengzhen yinjue* is an annotated collection of methods and rituals from Yang Xi's writings. Unfortunately, most of it has been lost. What survives is found in a short edition that preserves only a small portion of the original,[12] and in fragments quoted in various sources such as the *Sandong zhunang* and *Taiping yulan*.

Needless to say, we are greatly indebted to Tao Hongjing for enabling us to know much of what we can about the Shangqing movement. Furthermore, he was responsible for establishing a formal Shangqing School on Mt. Mao. Thanks to his personal prestige and connections, his school managed to curry the favor of Liang Emperor Wu, an ardent Buddhist who denounced and suppressed Taoism (see pp. 38–39).[13] The Shangqing School (also known as the Mao Shan School) flourished throughout the remainder of the Six Dynasties and Tang periods as one of the foremost schools of Taoism.

The Shangqing movement perpetuated and reinforced the ascetic spirit of single-minded striving. In doing so it partially drew upon Buddhist teachings. However, the movement drew much more heavily from the physiological theories and mysticism of its indigenous Taoist predecessors and promoted asceticism as a means of maintaining the body and gaining the sympathy of gods and immortals. It inherited and further developed many of the ascetic practices (especially fasting methods) from previous years and made them into prerequisites for the transmission of the holiest Shangqing scriptures.[14]

The Buddhist Influence

Erik Zürcher and Isabelle Robinet have pointed out that the impact of Buddhist beliefs on the Shangqing texts is superficial, particularly when compared to the impact that Buddhism left on the Lingbao texts. The Buddhist elements in the

Shangqing texts usually amount to little more than terms and phrases taken out of context and changed or obscured in their meaning.[15] However, a more profound level of Buddhist influence can be identified in a group of passages found in the *Zhengao* (6/6a–12a, 9/6a–b, and 9/19b–20a). Modern scholarship has revealed that these passages were taken and adapted from a Buddhist sutra called the *Sishi'erzhang jing*[16] (The Forty-two Chapter Sutra; this sutra was alleged to be the first Buddhist sutra ever to be translated into Chinese[17]). In the *Zhengao*, the borrowed passages are imbedded within discourses that were allegedly revealed by Taoist immortals. The passages express some fundamental Buddhist beliefs and attitudes and betray the fact that Taoists had begun to take a few Buddhist tenets to heart. By their nature, these tenets encouraged single-minded, painstaking effort, while proclaiming the futility of a mundane life bound with desires and familial attachments.

Perhaps the most fundamental tenet of Buddhism is that the essence of all existence is suffering (the first of the Buddha's Four Noble Truths). One passage in the *Zhengao* draws this very tenet from the *Sishi-er zhang jing* and utilizes it to exhort Taoist adepts toward painstaking religious training.

The Blue Boy of Fangzhu appeared and proclaimed, *"For a person to practice the Tao is also to suffer, but to not practice the Tao is also to suffer. People from their birth reach old age, and from old age reach [the stage of] illness.* Protecting their bodies *they reach [the point of] death.*[18] *Their suffering is limitless. In their minds they worry and they accumulate transgressions. With their births and deaths unending, their suffering is difficult to [accurately and sufficiently] describe* (emphasis added). Even more so it is because many do not live to their old age ordained by Heaven! [By saying that] to practice the Tao is also to suffer, I mean that to maintain the Perfect purely and immaculately, to guard the mysterious and long for the miraculous, to search for a teacher while struggling, to undergo hundreds of trials, to keep your heart diligent without failure, to exert your determination firmly and clearly; these are also the utmost in suffering." (*Zhengao* 6/6a)[19]
(The italicized portions of this passage were borrowed from the thirty-fifth chapter of the *Sishi'erzhang jing*.)

The aforementioned passage asserts that the process of training entails much suffering. Yet one should not shy away from it, since the essence of life under any circumstance is suffering. It also is noteworthy that the passage mentions an endless cycle of births and deaths. The doctrine of reincarnation was apparently accepted by the early Shangqing movement, even though few other references to it can be found in the Shangqing texts.

When Taoists accepted the doctrine of reincarnation, they came to believe that they had gained their status as Taoist adepts (and as humans) by accumulating great merit over countless past incarnations. This created a sense of urgency to make good on their elusive privilege by striving hard to gain immortality. Failure meant undergoing countless further rebirths before the privilege could be regained. While this attitude is conveyed most frequently and forcefully in the Lingbao scriptures (as we shall see in chapter 6), it is also expressed in the following words of Tao Hongjing, found within his annotations to the *Dengzhen yinjue*:

> "Over 10,000 *kalpas* you formed your causes and now you have this life. Once you lose this life, it will likely be another 10,000 *kalpas* [before you get another rebirth as privileged as this]. How can you not bravely and fiercely devote your labors to hereby from this [existence] pursue eternal life?" (2/18b)

Another pertinent theme found in the *Zhengao*'s borrowings from the *Sishi'erzhang jing* is the elimination of desires. One borrowed passage compares the process of eliminating desires to that of picking up pearls. It states that the pearls will eventually all be gathered if picked up one by one, and desires can be completely eliminated by removing them one by one.[20] The passage goes on to describe how a fatigued and heavily burdened ox, when trudging through thick mud, wishes only to get out of the mud to gain some measure of ease. A Taoist adept, it tells us, must yearn to be free from his emotions and desires even more than the ox yearns to leave the mud. Only if he contemplates the Tao with this single-minded yearning can he escape suffering and "acquire the Tao" (*Zhengao* 6/6a–b). Another passage compares a person who desires wealth and sex to an ignorant child who wants to lick sweet honey off the sharp blade of a sword. The child will not be fully satisfied even if he licks the honey and furthermore runs the risk of having his tongue severed. Similarly, one who craves wealth and sex is never satisfied when he indulges himself and does himself great harm in the process (*Zhengao* 6/8b).[21]

Perhaps most significantly, the *Zhengao*'s borrowings from the *Sishi'er zhang jing* single out sexual desire as the worst kind of desire and explicitly enjoin the reader to avoid marriage.

One borrowed passage states, "As for what is great among longings and desires, nothing is greater than lust. The guilt it brings on has no limit, and it is a matter that cannot be forgiven." The passage goes on to surmise that if there existed any other form of desire as harmful as lust, nobody would be capable of practicing the Tao (*Zhengao* 6/9b).[22]

Yet another passage borrowed from the *Sishi'erzhang jing* urges its reader to avoid or abandon married life, claiming that it is a misfortune greater than incarceration and bondage. It goes on to state that a prisoner still possesses some hope of release, but a married man does not, since he willingly binds himself to his predicament out of his affection for his wife and children. Furthermore, the harm wrought by the the emotions and desires involved in marriage is comparable to that of a tiger's bite (*Zhengao* 6/8b–9a).[23]

The Buddhist solution to the aforementioned problem has always been to enter a monastic community. As mentioned in chapter 3, celibate monasticism based on the Buddhist model appears to have come into practice among some Taoists by the sixth century. Although the earliest recipients and proponents of the Shangqing scriptures did not belong to monastic institutions, the truly serious among them were probably celibate. It is recorded that Xu Hui, when he retired from public life to train on Mt. Mao, divorced his wife and returned her to her original family.[24] It also is known that Tao Hongjing never married. No indication is given in any source about whether Yang Xi was married, but he presumably would have practiced celibacy if he desired to follow the teachings of his texts.

Non-Buddhistic Reasons for Celibacy

Taoists have always had their own reasons for preferring celibacy, even prior to significant Buddhist influence. These reasons were primarily physiological rather than ethical, and their continued importance is well reflected in the Shangqing texts.

A passage in *Zhengao* 10/23b–24a states, "If a Taoist adept seeks to become an immortal, he must not copulate with women. Each time you copulate, you nullify a full year's medicinal strength. If you ingest nothing and engage in bedroom activities, you will lose thirty years off your life span."

The meaning of "medicinal strength" (*yaoli*) is unclear. It probably refers to the salubrious effects accumulated through the regular ingestion of prescribed medicines. It also may refer to the good effects of training in general, if "medicine" is meant figuratively. Whatever it means, the idea is that sexual activity counteracts the "medicinal strength," especially if one "ingests nothing." Apparently, special medicines were supposed to be taken to supplement the *jing* if one could not manage to be celibate.

Found in *Zhengao* 10/18b–19a is "The Oral Lesson of Feng Yanshou, the Perfected Man of Supreme Purity." There it is stated that adepts must "pacify their hearts and nurture their spirits, practice dietetics and cure their diseases, make the Palace of the Brain full and abundant, and not use up their primal *jing*." It then warns against depleting the body's vitality through sexual intercourse and ejaculation, and speaks of how sexual intercourse nullifies one's "medicinal strength."

> If a person who studies [the perpetuation of] life copulates once, he will nullify a single year's medicinal strength. If he copulates twice, he will nullify two year's medicinal strength. If he exceeds three copulations, the medicine that he nullifies [will be so much that it will be] all gone from the body.

It also states that sexual intercourse is so detrimental to the pursuit of immortality that it can even cause "those who have been mysteriously selected (lit., "pulled out"), whose names have been written in gold upon the Jade Registers in the Great Ultimate,"[25] to be susceptible to "non-life" (*Zhengao* 10/18b–19a).[26] This probably means that even those predestined to immortality by virtue of their heredity and past merits can fall victim to death as a result of the evils of sexual activity.

"The Oral Lesson of the Female Immortal, the wife of Liu Gang" (*Zhengao* 10/25a–b) says flatly, "Those who seek immortality must not associate with women." This injunction is particularly important on the ninth day of the third month, the second day of the sixth month, the sixth day of the ninth month, and the third day of the twelfth month. On these days, adepts are told to remain in their rooms and make sure not to look at women. The explanation for this is as follows:

> If the Six Corpses (the Three Corpses of the adept himself and of the woman that he looks at?) cause chaos, the blood in your viscera will be disturbed and aroused, your three *hun* souls will be unguarded, your spirit will weaken and your *qi* will leave. All of these [factors] will accumulate, and bring about death. As for why you avoid [women] on these days, it is not only to block off lasciviousness. It is [also] to pacify the female palaces. The female palaces[27] are in the *shen*[28] and the male palaces are in the *yin*.[29] *Yin* and *shen* punish each other. Both execute each other.[30] On these days the Three Corpses of men and women come out from the pupils of the eyes. Female Corpses beckon the male, and male Corpses beckon the female. Misfortune and harm pass back and forth, making the spirit perish and thus blemishing your rectitude. Even if a person does not notice it, his body is exposed and has already been harmed because the Three Corpses fight within the eyes, while blood is shed within the Niwan (a compartment in the brain). On these days, even if it is a girl who you are extremely fond of, or a wife of a close friend, you absolutely must not look them face to face. My predecessor and teacher became an Immortal by simply practicing this method. The [proscription] does not apply to [your] closest of relatives to whom you have no thoughts [of sexual attraction]. (*Zhengao* 10/25a–b)

While some of the details in the previous explanation are hard to comprehend, the gist is that the demonic forces in the bodies of men and women lust and mingle with each other, regardless of the conscious intentions of those they inhabit.

Zhengao 10/21b–22a describes a method designed to eliminate lustful impulses by controlling the *hun* and *po* souls and exterminating the "evil corpses." On prescribed days,[31] the adept observes a retreat of purification—preferably abstaining from sleep—and paints a red dot under his left eye and a yellow dot under his right nostril. He knocks his teeth together, recites a chant, knocks his teeth together again, swallows saliva three times, and presses the dots seven times each. The text explains that the left eye and right nostril are the routes through which evil spirits exit and enter. The red and yellow dots represent the hot rays of the sun and moon that burn the internal demons to death. After carrying this out faithfully for three years, the adept is supposed to lose all sexual desire.

Certain training methods endorsed in the Shangqing texts required celibacy for their full effectiveness, as well as for safety. One particular meditation technique called the "Way of the Black and White" (*xuanbai zhi dao*)—described in both the *Zhengao* and the *Dengzhen yinjue*—bears a particularly strong injunction. The method is to be carried out from sunrise till noon. The adept visualizes black *qi* in the Niwan (in the brain), white *qi* in the heart, and yellow *qi* inside the belly. The three *qi* emerge from the body and envelop it, transforming into fire and making the adept "interpenetrate and perceive the body as though inside and outside were one." The adept then swallows air 120 times. After describing the method, the text warns

> The meat of the six varieties of livestock, along with food that has the five acrid flavors, is absolutely prohibited. You must separate your place of sleeping [from that of your spouse] and contemplate amid stillness. The affairs of the bedroom are absolutely prohibited. *If you engage in the affairs of the bedroom, you will immediately die* (emphasis added). This method is similar to the Guarding of the One, but it is a shortcut that abbreviates [the complicated details]. Its injunction against sex is stricter than that of the Guarding of the One. The injunction entailed in the Guarding of the One only requires moderation of it (sexual activity). (*Zhengao* 10/2a–b, *Dengzhen yinjue* 2/21a–b)

As we can see, the importance of celibacy varied according to the method. When practicing the Way of the Black and White, complete celibacy was imperative for one's very survival. The Guarding of the One required only moderation in sexual activity. However, the method thought to work faster with less bothersome details was the method of the Black and White. Celibacy was thought to enable adepts to pursue the better of the two methods.

At the time of the Shangqing revelations, a method of sexual yoga called the "Method of the Red Realm of the Yellow Book" was being practiced within the Heavenly Masters School. In the *Zhengao*, we find two discourses—attributed respectively to Perfected Man Qingxu and Lady Ziwei—that assess the benefits and drawbacks of this method. While acknowledging its efficacy to a very slight degree, these discourses ultimately deem it a minor method, the dangers of which far outweigh the benefits.

The discourse of Perfected Man Qingxu (Wang Bao) starts by claiming that the first Heavenly Master Zhang Daoling "merely used it as a method for sowing seeds in receiving the teachings and carrying out evangelism." The exact meaning of this is unclear, but it perhaps means that after being entrusted by Taishang Laojun (the deified Laozi) with the task of indoctrinating the masses, the Heavenly Master used the method to "sow seeds" of faith and open the gateway to salvation for those of lesser spiritual caliber. "Perfected Man Qingxu" goes on to state that the method is not something that a Perfected Man (or an adept aspiring to become one) concerns himself with. He further states that he has never seen the method succeed, even though he has repeatedly seen it fail and lead to divine punishment. Even if one defies the odds of ten million to one and succeeds at it, the best possible result is "non-death" (i.e., mere earthbound immortality). Zhang Daoling's heavenly ascension was certainly not achieved through it. Finally, he states that the method should not even be spoken of, and that those who practice the superior methods while harboring lustful thoughts will be interrogated and punished by the Three Officials (the judges of the netherworld).[32] He describes the actions of such adepts figuratively as "carrying jade and walking into a fire" or "burying a dog in a golden coffin" (*Zhengao* 2/1a–b).

The discourse of Lady Ziwei describes the Way of the Red Realm of the Yellow Book as an inferior method that confers longevity and nothing more, and states that the method is too vulgar to even be discussed by celestial Perfected Beings. "Lady Ziwei" also warns against the dangers of practicing the superior Shangqing methods while harboring lecherous thoughts. She states that the punishments for this include menial labor under the Three Officials and disqualification from election as a heavenly immortal. Posthumous rites of expiation then become the only hope for salvation, but such rites do not confer the higher forms of salvation. Finally, she declares, "Put succinctly, if you are chaste, spirits will descend [to your midst]. If you are devoted, you can command gods" (*Zhengao* 2/1b).

Gaining direct encounters with immortals and gods was indeed one of the main reasons for maintaining celibacy and eliminating lust. A passage in *Zhengao* 6/14a proclaims

> Those who are perfect have no feelings of [erotic] passion and desire, nor any thoughts of man and woman. If [thoughts of] red and white exist in one's bosom,[33] the sympathy of Perfected beings will not come about as a response, and Divine Women and Superior Worthies will not descend [before you]. (*Zhengao* 6/14a)

At the end of chapter 4 it was suggested that the repression and sublimation of sexual desires may have induced visions of attractive female immortals. Such appears to have been the case with early Shangqing adepts. In fact, some adepts compensated for the sacrifice of worldly romance by entering into divine "partnerships" with immortals of the opposite sex. The *Zhengao* indicates that Yang Xi was "betrothed" by his immortal preceptress Wei Huacun to a Perfected Woman named Jiuhua Zhenfei (Perfected Princess of the Nine Flowers), who bore the appearance of a thirteen- or fourteen-year-old girl. She was to frequently visit him in his visions and was scheduled to become his companion in the celestial realms.[34] Xu Mi was promised a similar liaison with Lady Wang Youying of the Cloudy Forest. In *Zhengao* 2/16b–21a numerous poems are found that are ascribed to Lady Wang and addressed to Xu Mi. These inform him of their betrothal and urge him to train more diligently to expedite their union. These unions, however, were to be completely spiritual and platonic, devoid of sexual contact and passion.[35] In one of her messages to Xu Mi, "Lady Wang" explains as follows why their union could not yet be realized:

> However, your polluted thoughts have not yet been purged, and your vulgar greed is firm within you. Your lustful thoughts have not yet been cut off,[36] and your holy pond (mind?) is not yet clear. We cannot yet discuss with each other the time of the inside and outside (?), and revel in the mingling of [our] two forms. (*Zhengao* 2/17b–18a)

Another interesting manifestation of this mysticism of sublimated sexuality is to be found in one of the many fasting methods endorsed by the Shangqing movement. The method is preserved in two texts; the *Yupei jindang jing*[37] and the *Mingtang yuanzhen jingjue*.[38] To carry it out, the adept visualizes a red sun with nine purple rays in the daytime and a yellow moon with ten white rays at night. The sun/moon hovers a few meters away from his face, and its rays enter his mouth. In the center of the sun/moon he sees the Jade Woman of the Cinnabar Aurora of the Highest Mysteries of the Greatest Mystery, who spews red *qi* from her mouth. This red *qi* enters the adept's mouth and is swallowed ninety times. After this, he visualizes the sun/moon, with the Jade Woman inside it, approaching his face. The text then tells the adept to "command that the Jade Woman's mouth press a kiss upon your own mouth, causing the liquor of the pneuma to come down into the mouth."[39] The adept then swallows this "liquor of the pneuma" (his saliva) ninety times. The text then says that the adept should visualize the sun and the moon with equal frequency as often as he can. The text finally states that after five years of practicing the method, the adept will actually be visited by the Jade Woman of the Great Mystery. This Jade Woman can turn into several tens of Jade Girls, who the adept will have under his command.

Gaining Divine Sympathy

The Shangqing texts describe mystical encounters of various kinds. For bringing these about, ascetic discipline in general—not just celibacy—was deemed essential. Through ascetic discipline and inner devotion, adepts hoped to win the sympathy of gods and immortals who could sustain them with their divine powers and reveal secret immortality methods to them.

One of the most compelling passages in the *Zhengao* is a poem about an anonymous adept who overcame crushing feelings of despair, homesickness, and loneliness to pursue meditation alone in the wilderness.

> The master entrusted himself to his spirit and *qi*,
> Throwing his [bodily] form into the eastern forest.

He bathed himself amidst the desolate hill,
Separating himself from [persons of] like heart.
Whenever he gazed eastward toward the Canghai,[40]
He sighed at the quickness of his going (the imminence of his eventual
    death).
When looking westward at the limits of the clouds,
Despair arose from within him.
Vaguely envisioning his home village,
His feelings of melancholy piled up.
As he longed to head on his way home,
He simply redirected his feet and restrained himself.
Hereby he stabilized his mind and thought of one thing.
Secluded, he put his trust in the miraculous void.
Climbing up onto steep and precarious cliffs,
He looked up to the Mysterious (the Tao) in anxious anticipation.
While darkening his aspirations within his dwelling,
He wandered amid the clouds and rose to Perfection.
[Thus] for the first time he felt like his [bodily] form was not his own
    substance.
Finally he lost his body and followed his spirit.
With his mind wandering beyond the raging winds,
The road to the world was forever cut off.
His feet were happy in the desolate forests,
As his external hazards were all blocked off.
He exerted his willpower without tiring,
And was devoted and sincere without relent.
He finally encountered an enlightened master,
And received a strange technique.
In purity he discussed the new marvels [with his master],
As sounds of jade resonated secretly.
He expelled and took in [*qi*] with a peaceful expression,
Refining his soul and protecting his bones.
With harmonious *qi* [his mind] was pacified and eradicated [of thoughts],
And no longer was there an inside and outside. (*Zhengao* 18/10a)

The adept's efforts, we are told, resulted in an encounter with an "enlightened master" who conferred special techniques upon him. After this, he meditated and apparently fasted (if "expelled and taking in" refers to a fasting technique), bringing about an ecstatic wandering outside of the body and a dissolving of the distinction between "inside" and "outside." If the previous account is in any way based on actual events, the adept may have encountered his "master" in visions resembling those of Yang Xi, and fasting may have helped induce his trances.

The Shangqing texts convey a fervent faith in sympathetic and supportive divine beings. Such faith encouraged adepts to subject themselves to lonely, miserable, and dangerous circumstances. One passage ascribed to a certain Lady Zhonghou refers to diligent adepts as "those who leave their lives in the hands of the Superior Perfected Beings and entrust their bodies and *qi* to the management of the gods" (*Zhengao* 8/9b). Eventually, it was hoped that by exhibiting devotion and sincerity to the immortals and gods, an encounter would be earned, whether in a vision or in person. During such encounters, divine beings were thought to confer methods that could bring about immortality.

The importance of sheer devotion and earnestness is reflected in a story presented as a proclamation by the immortal Dinglujun.[41] In it we are told that there was a man who wished to seek the Tao but did not know how. All he could do was worship a withered tree morning and evening and proclaim, "I beg for long life." He did this relentlessly for twenty-eight years, after which flowers bloomed from the tree one morning. A person (a Perfected Being?) then came before him and told him to eat their honeylike nectar. After doing as told, he became an immortal (*Zhengao* 12/12b–13a, *Wushang Biyao* 65/1b).

The aforementioned story is followed in the text by two more stories that bear the same moral. One is about a man named Liu Shaoweng who was bestowed the Way of Immortality by the Elder of the Western Peak, after training in Mt. Hua and worshipping the mountain for twenty years. The other story is about a man who worshipped the Yellow River for ten years and earned an encounter with the Marquis of the Yellow River and the Earl of the Yellow River. These deities taught him methods for walking on water without drowning. Later, this man "acquired the Tao" and was sighted on the Central Peak Mt. Song.

Sympathetic divine intervention also was thought to occur after death. Found in *Zhengao* 16/6b–7a is an autobiographical poem ascribed to a certain Xin Xuanzi, the son of the high official Xin Yin who served under Han Emperor Ming (Mingdi, r. 58–75 C.E.). In the poem, Xin Xuanzi starts out by describing how he had been "fond of the Tao" from his youth and had pursued "bitter training." He "observed the doctrines and precepts" and ate just one vegetarian meal per day (a possible implication here is that Xin Xuanzi also was a practicing Buddhist). He cut off his worldly attachments and wandered about in the mountains and forests. However, he did not realize that his ancestors had committed many transgressions and that he had inherited their guilt. As a result, Xin Xuanzi died prematurely (apparently by drowning).[42] However, by virtue of his "bitter training," he had gained the sympathy of two deities, the Queen Mother of the West and the Northern Emperor of Fengdu (the underworld). The latter commanded his subordinate underworld deities to transform Xin Xuanzi into a "miracle-working god." At the end of the poem, Xin Xuanzi states that this all took place "200 years ago," and that he is presently awaiting the time when he will proceed to the Southern Palace of Zhuling to become transformed into an immortal (*Zhengao* 16/6b–7a).[43]

The concept of hereditary guilt had been embraced by Taoists since at least the second century.[44] Even after the doctrine of reincarnation was accepted, Taoists continued to believe that one could be tormented or blessed by the consequences of the demerits or merits of one's ancestors.[45] The Shangqing texts in various places convey a belief in the fiery Southern Palace of Zhuling, where the dead can be sent to be transformed into immortals by the holy flames.[46] The Shangqing texts also claim that their advanced methods can transform an adept's ancestors in the fires of the Southern Palace and make them immortal, thus freeing the adept of his hereditary guilt.[47]

A truly ambitious Shangqing adept sought access to the greatest secrets to avoid physical death altogether and achieve direct ascension to the highest heavens. For this to become possible, it was thought that the adept had to constantly prove his worth to the gods and immortals. Thus the theme of trials, so prominent in the *Shenxian zhuan* (see pp. 25–28), also appears in the Shangqing texts. The *Zhengao* 5/2a–10a deals extensively with trials and is presented in the form of discourses proclaimed by a certain "Lord" (*jun*).[48] The "Lord" first presents a list of scriptures and methods (2a–4b) and states that if one receives and masters these, one will become a Perfected Man of the Nine Palaces,[49] a status superior to that of a mere Immortal (4a).[50] The "Lord" then states that he will transmit the Tao, but warns that the recipient—this presumably refers to Yang Xi and/or the two Xus—must undergo trials administered by his own mentor, the Pine Master of the Southern Peak.[51] The "Lord" then states, "If one passes all of the twelve trials of the Way of Immortality, one can be transmitted these scriptures. These twelve trials are great trials. All [of them] are overseen by the Perfected Men of the Great Ultimate. Can you not be careful?(5b)"

Sometimes the trials were thought to be too difficult for even the best adepts. In *Zhengao* 5/5b–6a, "the Lord" tells the story of Qingwugong who trained in Mt. Hua for 471 years,[52] but failed three of the twelve trials. Later, when he succeeded in concocting and drinking the "golden liquid," he was conferred only the status of Immortal (*xianren*) and did not become a Perfected Man (*zhenren*).

Another story of failure is that of Liu Fenglin, a man of the Zhou period (ca. 1100–256 B.C.E.). He first trained on Mt. Songgao for 400 years, during which he attempted to concoct a "divine elixir" three times, only to be foiled by "wicked creatures." He then moved to Mt. Weiyu[53] where, we are told, he is still living. He is able to hold his breath for three days without breathing and is over 1,000 years old. He gained his earthbound immortality by ingesting golden thread (*huanglian* or *coptis chinensis*). However, he has not ascended as a heavenly immortal because he has failed many trials (*Zhengao* 5/9b).

A success story, on the other hand, is that of Huangguanzi. Interestingly, the text tells us that "from his youth he was fond of the Tao, and his family revered the way of the Buddha." Every morning for forty-nine years, Huangguanzi kowtowed, worshipped, and "begged for long life." Eventually, he began to practice dietetics on Mt. Jiao,⁵⁴ where he passed all 140 trials administered by a Perfected Man of the Great Ultimate. Because of this, he was able to ingest the "golden elixir" (*jindan*)⁵⁵ and recite the *Dadong zhenjing*. He was conferred the lofty rank of "Immortal Chamberlain of the Left of the Great Ultimate."⁵⁶

"The Lord" also tells stories that describe the types of trials that took place. The first such story (5/5b) is about Liu Weidao of Zhongshan,⁵⁷ who had been training in Mt. Bozhong⁵⁸ for twelve years when an immortal came to administer trials. The immortal made him lie under a boulder 100,000 *jin* (about 20,000 kg.) in weight, suspended from a single white hair. Liu lay there for twelve years without showing any signs of fright. After passing numerous other trials, he "ascended to heaven in broad daylight."

Another story (5/7b) is about a certain Mr. Fu, who in his youth trained in a stone grotto in Mt. Jiao. After seven years, he was visited by Lord Lao of the Great Ultimate. Lord Lao handed him a wooden awl and told him that he could obtain the Tao if he drilled a hole through a stone slab five *chi* (about 1 m.) thick. Mr. Fu spent forty-seven years pursuing this task day and night without ceasing, until he finally drilled a hole all the way through the slab. He then obtained a "divine elixir," ascended into the heaven of Taiqing, and became the Perfected Man of the Southern Peak.

Other passages in the Shangqing texts convey the belief that trials can occur at unexpected moments in any situation. A passage in the *Zhengao* 8/2a–b—ascribed to the Lady of the Yixian Palace⁵⁹ (the deceased mother of Xu Hui) and addressed to Xu Hui—states, "For a person to study the Tao is like traveling 10,000 *li* (over 4000 km.). Wherever he goes he undergoes everything, whether it be coldness, heat, good, bad, grass, trees, water or earth; and there he finds trials" (*Zhengao* 8/2a–b). Provided my interpretation is correct, the passage is stating that trials confront Taoist adepts at all times and situations. Thus, an adept always had to be prepared.

In the *Zhengao* 5/7a, "the Lord" describes how Perfected Beings can assume disguises when administering their trials.

> Perfected Men conceal their Tao-marvels and manifest themselves in ugly forms. Sometimes they will be wearing tattered [garments], their bodies will be emaciated, or they will have the appearances of idiots. When a person wants to study the Tao, [Perfected Beings] administer these trials, but people are invariably unable to recognize them. When they do not recognize them, they will have failed the trials. You must always be careful about this. (*Zhengao* 5/7a)

As mentioned in chapter 2, stories of the Song period onward describe how the Perfected Man Lü Dongbin assumes the guise of a beggar to test the character of people. Shangqing proponents ascribed similar tactics to their immortals. To pass such a trial, an adept needed the attentiveness, perceptiveness, and humility to identify the saint among the vagrants and to bow to him for instruction. Any arrogant compulsion to be derisive or condescending toward the underprivileged had to be overcome.

This same moral is conveyed in an incident described in the "esoteric biography" (*neizhuan*) of Peijun, one of the many ancient immortals revered within the Shangqing tradition.[60] In it we are told that Peijun was born in 178 B.C.E. to a Buddhist family in Xiayang, Fufeng (this is clearly an anachronism).[61] He was a very religious youth. At the age of ten, he acquired the habit of meditating and reading scriptures day and night without sleeping. His first trial occurred when he was traveling to a Buddhist temple with his two friends Zhao Kangzi and Hao Jicheng to celebrate the Buddha's birthday on the eighth day of the fourth month.

> It was a cloudy and rainy day. There suddenly appeared a pauper clad in an old single-layered garment and yellow turban, who followed the Lord's (Peijun's) carriage from behind and begged to be given a ride. The Lord (Peijun) paid his respects [to the pauper] and asked him [who he was], but did not receive an answer. The Lord got off the carriage and let him get on. Kangzi and Jicheng got very angry and asked [Peijun] why he was allowing such a person into their carriage. But they finally consented to let [the pauper] ride with them at the Lord's urging. The Lord himself followed [the carriage] from behind on foot with no change in expression. The man given a ride also acted naturally, and showed no signs of shame. Just as they were about to reach the temple, [the pauper] said, "My house is near here," and got off the carriage. Suddenly, they lost him. (*Yunji qiqian* 105/1a–b)

The hagiography goes on to describe how Peijun met other divine beings and was conferred various methods and scriptures. Does the aforementioned story intend to imply that the pauper was the Buddha himself? This is highly possible.

In sum, the Shangqing texts assert that divine beings always observe the progress of adepts and are prepared to help them if they possess good character and show sufficient effort. When Shangqing adherents engaged in asceticism, they must have found encouragement in this belief.

Evils in the Worldly Environment

The Shangqing texts also convey the grim feeling that manifold evils lurk within the world. The fervent yearning for divine sympathy and assistance is highly understandable in light of this. Antiworldly sentiments undoubtedly strengthened the resolve of adepts to escape the world through heavenly immortal ascension.

The tragic story of Lü Chengzi described in the *Zhengao* lucidly conveys the belief that adepts are surrounded by demons who wish only to ruin them. Lü Chengzi, we are told, had been fond of practicing macrobiotics and studying the

Tao from his youth. When he was in his forties, he went into training on Mt. Jing.[62] One day, when he was over seventy years old, he "underwent a trial at the hands of the mountain spirit of Mt. Jing." The text is obscure regarding what exactly the trial was, but apparently the mountain spirit deceived Lü Chengzi by disguising itself as a Perfected Being. The text states, "Chengzi, mistaking it for a Perfected Being, worshipped it." He then got bitten by a giant snake (the text probably means to say that the mountain spirit transformed into the giant snake and bit Lü Chengzi). His wound was nearly fatal, but he survived the crisis by visualizing the "Most High One" (a deity) and meditating upon the "seven stars" (the Ursa Major). Later, he lost his left eye to the trickery of yet other demons (how exactly this happened is not specified). Sadly, the story concludes with the statement, "In the end he never acquired the Tao, and he died in the mountains." The text then warns its readers to be careful not to suffer the same fate, and explains that Lü Chengzi's failure was caused by his "wicked thoughts," which made him lack true devotion and single-mindedness (*Zhengao* 5/9a).

The basic message here is that the life of the Taoist adept is extremely hazardous, since he is in constant peril at the hands of evil forces. Nonetheless, his survival can be guaranteed if he can evoke the protection of divine beings by keeping his mind pure and by remaining diligent in his training. Based on such a view, it would be conceivable that demons could render adepts vulnerable by planting wicked thoughts in their minds. As we have seen, lust was regarded as the most damaging of wicked thoughts. Not surprisingly then, we are told in *Zhengao* 5/13b that demons exploit the sexual desires of adepts.

> The Lord said, "In the world there are evil and powerful demons of the lower earth. Many of them turn themselves into women in order to tempt and test people." (*Zhengao* 5/13b)

The text goes on to say that if an adept encounters a woman who he thinks may be a demon, he should hold his breath and visualize the *heng* and *fu* stars of the Ursa Major while composing his mind and body. He should then look at the "pearls within the circles" (the pupils of the woman?). If they have a murky appearance, she is a demon. If they have a radiance in them, she is a "person of the Tao of Immortal-hood." Encounters of this kind most likely occured in visions such as those experienced by Yang Xi. Here we seem to have instructions that were intended for those who partook in mystical experiences. As speculated before, the encounters that ascetics had with female immortals likely resulted from the repression and sublimation of sexual desires. If so, we find indication here that ascetics were in frequent conflict with their sexual desires, which confronted them in the form of tempting visions. Our text, however, attributes such tempting visions to the work of demons.

In ordinary everyday experience, demonic trials were thought to come in the form of diseases. One particular Shangqing scripture, the *Xiaomo jing*, provides us with interesting information about how the Shangqing movement understood diseases.[63] This text features long lists (1/6a–14a) of divine medicines that are not available in this world. Adepts, when they fell ill, were supposed to be able to cure their diseases by merely reciting the names of these medicines. The text also contains a short narrative that describes how the immortal Chisongzi,[64] prior to "attaining the Tao," overcame illness. According to the narrative, he became ill when training on Mt. Jinhua.[65] His illness remained serious for sixteen years, even though he continued to "contemplate Perfection and preserve his *jing*." Amid this suffering, Chisongzi pursued the Tao more single-mindedly than ever and obtained an inner peace. He no longer grieved over his illness nor worried whether he was going to die. Still, "the so-called spirits and demons of the Six Heavens"[66] continued to hinder his training by afflicting him with diseases. In some cases, the demons did so at the request of "Superior Beings," who wished to test Chisongzi's fortitude. However, Chisongzi proceeded to observe a retreat of purification (*qingzhai*), recite "the [section on] Wisdom," and sing "[the section on] Eliminating the Devils" 3,000 times (this apparently means to say that he recited the names of the celestial medicines). Once he had done so, all of his ailments were healed, his heart "opened up," and he felt a joy surpassing any joy he had felt prior to his illness (*Xiaomo jing* 1/2a).

The narrative is followed by an explanation of the "purpose" of diseases. The first purpose of diseases, we are told, is to "test the sincerity of the heart." The second purpose is to expurgate the Three Corpses and other impure forces in the body. The third purpose is to "eliminate what is improper" (from the mind?). The fourth purpose is to refine what is "dusty and impure" (the body?). The text then states that those who are single-minded in their religious quest can be quickly cured of illnesses. Those who are sincere and diligent, yet prone to distraction and confusion, will also be cured, albeit not as quickly (*Xiaomo jing* 1/2a–b).

Diseases were generally thought to be caused by demons with entirely malicious motives. However, as we can see, the *Xiaomo jing* maintains that they also serve good purposes, and for this reason they sometimes occur under the approval of benevolent divine beings. Through diseases, divine beings could gauge and facilitate the progress of adepts. The *Xiaomo jing* even claims that diseases can be beneficial to the body, since they help purge it of malignant forces. One is reminded here of how the *Zhonghuang jing*, *Tuna jing*, and *Daoji tuna jing* ascribe the same effect to the self-imposed ordeal of fasting (see pp. 44–53).

The grim worldview of the Shangqing movement was underpinned by beliefs concerning cyclical cosmic eras, or *kalpas*. The word "*kalpa*" (transliterated into Chinese as *jie*) was one of the first Buddhist terms borrowed and used by Taoists. In a Buddhist context, it means "a period of time"; generally a very long period of time during which worlds undergo the process of creation, maturation, decline, and destruction. The word was borrowed and used by Taoists to explain their own beliefs. The earliest Chinese theories on cosmic eras were developed well before the Shangqing movement, and traces of these theories can be found in very early texts such as the *Han shu*,[67] the *Wufu xu*, and the *Laozi zhongjing*.[68] Several different Shangqing texts provide us with expositions concerning cosmic eras.[69] Although these expositions do not always agree in their details, they do concur in their general outlines. They all speak in terms of recurring cycles of great and small *kalpas*. A Great *Kalpa* constitutes a lengthy period of time that elapses between the world's creation and devastation. Small *Kalpas* are smaller divisions of time that together make up the sum total of time contained within a Great *Kalpa*. Calamities occur at the end of both great and small *kalpas*. However, the calamities at the close of the Great *Kalpas* are much more severe. At the end of a Small *Kalpa*, political unrest and natural disasters kill off the evil people, allowing only the righteous to survive. At the end of a Great *Kalpa*, the world is completely destroyed. A "Sacred Lord" then arrives on the scene to select the righteous who will survive and dwell in the utopia that he will establish.

Sadly, early Shangqing proponents believed that the world was rapidly approaching the end of a Great *Kalpa*. They believed the forces of evil and destruction pervaded it more than ever. This view is well reflected in *Zhengao* 8/8b, in a passage allegedly proclaimed by the immortal Lord Baoming toward Xu Mi during a time of illness.

> Right now, when [the spirits and demons] of the Six Heavens (the mundane realm)[70] are everywhere, and the [traces of] the Great Peace are weak, [living] souls are unable to cooperate with and obey [the Tao], and are only able to bring about the various forms of wickedness. Therefore, the spiritual light is remote, and wickedness takes advantage of its proper duty.[71] You are advanced in age and have been without virtue for a long time. The chaos and confusions of demonic accusations have piled up [and caused your illness]. (*Zhengao* 8/8b)

Xu Mi is thus told that he is a victim not only of his old age and past transgressions, but also of the era in which he lives. It is a time when the primitive bliss (Great Peace) has been long lost and has yet to be restored. On the verge of the apocalypse, the world is overrun by evil spirits who are eager to exploit the weaknesses and shortcomings of human beings.

The Shangqing texts bemoan and disdain the evil ways of worldly people at the end of the age. Inherent here was the danger that this hatred of human evil could degenerate into hatred toward the people themselves. To what extent this danger materialized is difficult to say. However, one passage found in the *Zhengao* 10/24b is somewhat disturbing in this regard.

> The Oral Lesson of Chen Anshi:[72] As for a Taoist adept's tying and combing his hair, his eating and drinking, and his handling of his footwear and bedding, he must not let those who are not Taoist adepts see

his grooming, interfere with his dining, move his footwear, or use his bedding. [This is because] the demons that reside within the *po*-bodies[73] of those worldly corpses will come and invade your own spirit(s). The reason why Taoist adepts live in the mountains and forests to conceal themselves is because they want to distance themselves from the clamor and filth, and detach themselves from the duties of the human realm. This is for fear that the 100-odd external objects will violate their nature and life-destiny. Be discreet about it (your training). (*Zhengao* 10/24b)

The disdain for people expressed here borders on the pathological. Ordinary people not engaged in Taoist training are called "worldly corpses." The evil forces that infest their bodies are deemed capable of infecting the adept.

Of course, we also are told that even when adepts detached themselves from evil people, they still had to contend with demons. Theories of demonology are articulated in two scriptures that we shall refer to as *Yuqing yinshu* 1[74] and *Yuqing yinshu* 2[75] (*Yuqing yinshu* translates into *The Hidden Book of [the Realm of] Jade Purity*). According to Robinet, these texts are early Shangqing apocrypha (texts written by Shangqing proponents after the initial revelations to Yang Xi). The methods described in them were meant to complement the recitation of the *Dadong zhenjing*.[76]

Yuqing yinshu 1 (16b–17a), in a passage ascribed to a deity called the King of the Divine Empyrean of the Jade Purity, explains why demons are allowed to flourish in the world. It describes how "demons and devils" (*guimo*) employ various clever tactics and disguises to wreak havoc in the mundane world ("the Six Heavens"[77]). They do so, however, under the approval of the benevolent divine beings of the "Three Heavens." The text states that the "wicked abominations" of the demons and devils "accord with the cycles of the Six Heavens." This apparently means that the demons and devils orchestrate the strife and calamities that are preordained to occur at the end of the cosmic cycle. Their deeds are punishments for the evil populace of a decrepit age, whose impure hearts are filled with a conniving cleverness and a recalcitrance to the moral standards of the gods and immortals. For this reason, the "High and Superior Beings" allow the demons and devils to inflict suffering upon people so they might repent. The passage ends by saying that when the cosmic cycle comes to an end, the demons will have no purpose to serve and will hence cease to exist. This is because the surviving populace will be pure of heart and naturally fit to attain immortality (16b–17a).

Both *Yuqing yinshu* 1 and *Yuqing yinshu* 2 describe methods by which the adept can utilize the power of good gods to protect himself from demons. Although adepts had to live in cautious fear of demons, they could find solace in the belief that demons were ultimately inferior and subservient to the forces of good. *Yuqing yinshu* 2 provides adepts with a further sense of security by describing how the Demon–Kings, the chieftains of the demonic hordes, can be rendered powerless beneath the might of the Great King of Jade Purity who Eliminates Devils (Yuqing Xiaomo Dawang).

Yuqing yinshu 2 tells us that the Northern Monarch Great Demon–King and his demonic throngs dwell in palaces perched on the gigantic Mt. Luofeng. The Great Demon–King constantly seeks to undermine the strivings of adepts because "he dislikes it when people attain immortality." This is because he realizes that they will surpass him in power and status if they succeed at becoming immortals. In other words, the Grand Demon–King is motivated by vain feelings of envy. Hoping to confuse adepts, he rides about in the sky in a chariot, singing "the folk ballad in 3,000 lyrics." Sadly, we are told, many adepts fall prey to his tactics (3a).

However, while living in the self-delusion of being "King," the Great Demon–King is subservient to the Great King who Eliminates Devils. Consequently, the Great Demon–King eventually has to perform a duty that completely contradicts his own wishes.

> When students of later ages attain Immortal-hood, the Great King who Eliminates Devils always orders the Grand Demon–King to protect and elevate [the adept] and testify [on his behalf]. Thereupon [the adept] can fly about in [the Heaven of] Upper Purity. (2b)

To avoid performing this task, the Demon–King tries hard to prevent the adept from succeeding. *Yuqing yinshu* 2 provides the adept with various means to overcome the trials set forth by the Great Demon–King. These include knowing the many names of the Great Demon–King and his palace, knowing the lyrics to the folk ballad sung by the Great Demon–King, and reciting the "incantations of the 100 Gods of the King who Eliminates Devils." The text then states, "When the demonic trials have been extinguished, Perfect Spirits will be able to descend [into your midst] and you can see their Perfect Forms. In broad daylight you will fly up to the Palace of Jade Purity" (3a).

Yuqing yinshu 2 goes on to describe a set of eight Demon–Kings of the Eight Directions, who on the days of the eight seasonal transitions (*bajie*)[78] take turns flying about and imposing trials upon adepts. The text provides the adept with lengthy chants to recite on these days. If these chants are recited without fail for a designated number of years, the adept becomes able to directly encounter the good gods of each respective direction, to whom the Demon–Kings are completely subservient.

As we will see in chapter 6, this concept of Demon–Kings also can be found in the Lingbao scriptures. The Lingbao scriptures contain references to the malicious Demon–Kings of the Five Directions, who are powerless before the Five Monarchs (or Five Venerables). In both Shangqing and Lingbao doctrine, it is recognized that the most precarious trials and temptations occur at the advanced stages of training. At these stages, adepts carried out a high degree of self-denial while attempting to commune with the divine. They taxed the resources of their minds and bodies to the point of peril and suppressed their most basic and powerful desires. Doing so probably made them highly vulnerable to disease, depression, fear, and delusion. The Demon–Kings seem to personify these difficulties and dangers.

The Place of Asceticism in the Hierarchy of Spiritual Progress

The hope for divine sympathy and intervention encouraged adepts to persevere in austerities. However, it also is conceivable that such an emphasis on divine grace could have undermined the importance of ascetic personal effort. If salvation is credited to the work of divine beings, the conclusion could be drawn that one should entrust oneself entirely to their grace and abandon strenuous personal effort. To a certain degree, this was what happened in the Shangqing movement. Prior ascetic training methods were devalued in a certain sense; on their own, they were no longer considered capable of conferring the highest forms of immortality. Rather, the combined practice of various such methods was deemed useful for eliminating desires and conditioning the body. Such an effort was believed to evoke divine sympathy and help qualify the adept for access to the holy scriptures. Also, it must be noted that certain Shangqing theories about the afterlife tended to vindicate less austere forms of religiosity. Avenues toward salvation were conceived for those who showed certain moral virtues, without undergoing rigorous training. For example, a fragment of the *Baojian jing* (The Scripture of the Precious Sword)[79] cited in *Zhengao* 16/10a1–12a7 states, "people of utmost filial piety and/or utmost loyalty" could become *dixia zhuzhe* or Masters in the Underground, minor officials in the underworld of Mt. Fengdu (also known as Mt. Luofeng) where the dead were judged and sentenced.[80] After 140 years they were to be conferred teachings that would enable them to become "minor Immortals." Similar processes of slow advancement are described for those who "have the virtue of superior sages."[81] People who exhibited righteousness, integrity, frugality, and chastity could become "pure demons" or "good and luminous demons." "Pure demons" and "good and luminous demons" were to be promoted to the rank of Master in the Underground after 280 years and 400 years, respectively, and from there were to eventually get the opportunity for further advancement. One's fate also could be determined by the deeds of ancestors. As we have seen in the story of Xin Xuanzi, hereditary guilt was thought to undermine the efforts of sincere ascetics. Contrarily, if one had virtuous ancestors, one could attain immortality or a more privileged reincarnation as the result of *their* merit, as indicated in the following passage from the *Baojian jing*:

> If your ancestors have merit with the Three Officials, [the merit] will flow down to their descendants. Sometimes the refinement and trans-formation [into an immortal] will be passed on from one generation to another. Or one may get reborn into a different family. These things are

caused by the hidden merit of the seven generations of ancestors. Roots and leaves connect with each other. (*Zhengao* 16/12a, *Daodian lun* 2/12a)

However, Shangqing doctrines ultimately affirmed the need for ascetic personal effort. The slower and lower forms of salvation available to nonascetics were not to be desired by serious adepts. Ascetic training was still indispensable if one wanted to qualify to receive the holy scriptures. Once one received the scriptures, one would recite them and carry out their prescribed visual meditations.[82] The maximum effect of this was not to be gained without the simultaneous observance of rigorous self-discipline.

As has been mentioned, the holiest Shangqing scripture was the *Dadong zhenjing*. The *Ciyi jing* contains methods that were to be carried out in preparation for receiving the *Dadong zhenjing*. The extant edition of the *Ciyi jing* (*Dongzhen gaoshang yudi dadong ciyi yujian wulao baojing*; HY1302/TT1025) discusses the rules for the transmission of the *Dadong zhenjing*. On pages 1b–2a we find the following passage:

If you possess this scripture, you must practice [the methods included in] the text. You must always hide yourself quietly in a secluded room, scatter fragrances (sprinkle perfume, burn incense?) and sweep away the dust. [Make your] spirit reside in the dark forests. Avoid and distance yourself from the human realm. [Live in] lonesome serenity and abandon [worldly] affairs. Get rid of your [worldly] burdens and bring in Perfection. Make your heart vast and forget about competing. Entrust yourself to and accord with the roots of the profound. Live alone in the dark room. Cut off grains and do away with spices. The blandly flavored skies above will spew forth their liquids and harmonize your fluids. With your solitary form, do away with your companion. In the darkness gaze at your three *hun* souls. Undergo bitter training (*kuxing*) for a long time. Do not eat after the noon hour. Engage in a bitter retreat for three years, and then you can receive and read the *Dadong zhenjing*.

Thus, according to the *Ciyi jing*, an adept aspiring to the highest form of salvation had to leave social and family life to engage in a secluded retreat of "bitter training" (*kuxing*) for three years. As is clearly described, this purification requires "cutting off grains" (which probably meant to limit the intake of all foods) and complete fasting after the noon hour. This latter requirement—which also is emphasized in Lingbao texts—was customary among Buddhist monks and is likely a result of Buddhist influence. The ideal form of nourishment during this three-year retreat is the "liquid" from the heavens, which presumably means that the adept is to "nourish" himself with techniques of saliva swallowing. The phrase "with your solitary form do away with your companion" suggests that celibacy also was required. The *Ciyi jing* states too that retreats of a shorter length are required for the transmission of other holy texts.

As has been pointed out by Robinet, the *Ciyi jing* is not one of the original Shangqing scriptures. It is a collection of discourses and methods, some of which came from Yang Xi's hand, but also others which are apocryphal. The first nineteen pages—which include the passage quoted earlier—were most certainly authored after the revelations, since they reflect some influence from Lingbao doctrines.[83] Therefore, we cannot, based on the aforementioned quoted passage, conclude that the austerities referred to in it were required for the transmission of the *Dadong zhenjing* during the earliest years of the Shangqing movement. There is, however, clearer evidence that the "avoidance of grains" was always a requirement. In the fifth *juan* of the *Zhengao* we find a passage that states

> When studying [the way of long] life amidst humans, you should eat medicines only. *If you do not cut off grains, you will be unable to hear the [teachings of the] Dadong* (emphasis added). As for the methods for cutting off grains, there are methods in the world. (*Zhengao* 5/15b)[84]

The precise meaning of "the *Dadong*" is difficult to determine. It may refer specifically to the *Dadong zhenjing*, or more generally to the holy scriptures and advanced methods of the Shangqing movement.[85] Whatever the case, we can see that the Shangqing movement made fasting mandatory for its most ambitious adepts.

The Glorification of Suicidal Methods

Certain methods tantamount to religious suicide were promoted by the Shangqing movement.[86] Michel Strickmann has suggested the possibility that Xu Hui, who died in his late twenties, had himself employed such a method. He also has speculated that Tao Hongjing's adolescent disciple Zhou Ziliang had done the same. Of course, suicidal methods actually purported to be immortality techniques, since in theory the adept would only seem to die, while actually proceeding to a new, eternal life.

The *Zhengao* 10/5a contains a very explicit description of a suicidal method. There it states that if an adept ingests a spoonful of the "White Powder of the Perfected of the Great Ultimate for Abandoning the Waistband,"[87] he will feel a sharp, stabbing pain in the heart. After three days he will become thirsty and drink a *hu* (about 20 liters) of water, after which he dies—or so it seems. The corpse later disappears, leaving only the clothes. At this point, the adept becomes an "immortal released in broad daylight."[88]

In the *Zhengao* we also find passages eulogizing men who "staged" their deaths, some in a very gruesome manner. Lupigong,[89] we are told, "swallowed jade flowers (highest-quality jade)," after which "flowing worms came out from the door [of his house]." Chou Jizi[90] swallowed "golden liquid," after which the stench of his decaying body could be smelled as far as 100 *li* away. The Yellow Emperor concocted the Elixir of the Nine Cauldrons at Mt. Jing and was buried at Qiaoling.[91] Sima Jizhu[92] ingested the "Cloud Powder," after which he "sank and ascended," and had his head and legs buried in different locations. Mo Qiu swallowed the rainbow elixir and drowned himself. Master Ning ingested paraffin and walked into a fire.[93] Wu Guang picked leeks and entered into a pure and cool pool.[94] Bocheng retained his *qi*, and his intestines and stomach "rotted three times"[95] (*Zhengao* 4/15a–b). The reference to Bocheng is particularly interesting in that it seems to say that he "pretended" to die of starvation by practicing a technique of breath holding or air swallowing.

Elsewhere, the *Zhengao* explains that such men actually attained immortality, but in doing so feigned their deaths through the "liberation from the corpse" (*shijie*). They did so because they "wanted to cut off the feelings about life and death, and show the people that there is a limit [to life]," and because they "wanted to cut themselves off from men of the world, and block off the [worldly] yearnings of secular folk." Their alleged death is completely different from that of ordinary people, "whose corpses rot in the Great Yin (netherworld), and whose flesh feeds the mole-crickets and ants" (*Zhengao* 14/17a–b).

Suicidal methods are thus justified and lauded as serving a didactic purpose. Noteworthy here is the paradoxical notion, conveyed also in the *Shenxian zhuan*, that one had to stop fearing death and grasping for life, if one was to gain eternal life. One could perhaps say that the suicidal methods were the consummate expression of the Shangqing movement's world-denying spirit. However, it could also be said that suicide is a cowardly act; a quick and easy way out. It would seem that the virtues of devotion, courage, and strength were better embodied by adepts who trained long and hard without cutting their lives short.

In this regard, it would be interesting to know exactly *how* highly the Shangqing movement regarded the suicidal techniques. From the evidence available, it is difficult to determine whether the rank of immortality gained through suicidal methods was thought to be as high as that gained by reciting and carrying out the visualizations of the *Dadong zhenjing*. It should be noted that the *Wufu xu* (pre-Shangqing in its content) describes a suicidal method, but states that the method is "a path taken by lower-level immortals."[96] Based on this precedent, it would seem doubtful that the Shangqing movement would have attributed the highest efficacy to suicidal methods. But if so, why would Xu Hui commit religious suicide? We may never know.

CHAPTER SIX

Asceticism in the Lingbao Scriptures

The Lingbao scriptures[1] were written some time between 420 and 471 C.E., probably by more than one author.[2] While we do not know exactly who the authors and earliest proponents of the texts were, it appears most likely that they included some members of the Ge clan. The Ge clan was a prominent southern aristocratic clan that had previously produced two very famous figures in the history of Taoism; a much fabled third-century adept named Ge Xuan, and his nephew Ge Hong, the great alchemical writer. The former, as we shall see, is frequently depicted in the Lingbao scriptures as being an ideal saint. Interestingly enough, the Ge clan was intermarried with the Xu clan that had received and propagated the Shangqing texts.[3] Not surprisingly, the impact of Shangqing doctrines can be identified in some of the Lingbao scriptures. The earliest Lingbao proponents also were connected in some way with the Heavenly Masters School. This is apparent from how some Lingbao texts express a high regard for the first Heavenly Master Zhang Daoling and promote ritual practices and ethical precepts that betray Heavenly Masters School influence.

The Lingbao corpus expounds a syncretic doctrinal system that combines old and new elements. The most prominent trait of the Lingbao scriptures is that they present their form of Taoism as *the* greatest religious path and assert this claim through elaborate myths. These myths claim that the greatest of all gods, the Primordial Heavenly Worthy (the Tao personified), reveals the Lingbao scriptures to the world at various junctures within the cosmic cycles. He does this to bring about happiness and salvation to all living beings. The myths also claim that the most sacred of all writings, the Lingbao Five Perfect Writs,[4] originated as primordial cosmic prototypes formed from celestial radiances and ethers, and that these prototypes emit the force that creates and sustains the cosmos. The soteriological vision of the Lingbao texts is much more universal than that of the Shangqing texts. The Lingbao movement asserted its claim to exclusive truth much more forcefully and aimed to save all living beings, however wretched. For this reason, the Lingbao movement claimed to be the Great Vehicle (*dasheng*, Mahayana), compared to which all other religious paths are but the Small Vehicle (*xiaosheng*, Hinayana). In making this claim, the Lingbao movement most certainly imitated Mahayana Buddhism. As a whole, the system accommodates the religious needs of less sophisticated believers to a much greater degree than the Shangqing system by emphasizing rudimentary moral indoctrination and communal festivals.

As we shall see, the ideal of universal salvation and the doctrine of reincarnation both had a profound impact upon the form and meaning that asceticism took in the Lingbao movement. The Lingbao scriptures strongly endorse ascetic practices of the kind pursued by Taoists in previous years. In doing so, they also assert that adepts must be thoroughly altruistic in their endeavors and must conform to specific standards of personal discipline and ritual piety. (Short descriptions of the Lingbao scriptures cited in the discussion that follows are provided in the appendix.)

The New Saintly Ideal

The Lingbao scriptures, much like the Shangqing scriptures, claim to contain truths revealed from divine realms. The scriptures frequently take the form of narratives wherein intricate discussions occur between great teachers (gods, immortals, or great adepts) and their students. The famous adept Ge Xuan appears frequently, sometimes as the teacher and sometimes as the student. He also is depicted as the blessed recipient of Lingbao scriptures. In all instances, he represents the paragon of saintliness.

The *Zhenyi quanjie falun miaojing* is the prologue to a set of three scriptures putatively transmitted to Ge Xuan by three different "Perfected Men of the Mysterious One" named Yuluoqiao, Guangmiaoyin, and Zhendingguang. According to this text, the "old texts" of the three scriptures existed prior to the creation of the present world, were stored in the Dark Terrace of the Six Directions of the Most High, and were guarded by Jade Girls and Jade Boys. They are transmitted to humans once every 40,000 *kalpas*. The text states that it was determined that Ge Xuan would become their blessed recipient. It then describes the events that led directly to the transmission.

> The Immortal Duke on the Left of the Great Ultimate (Ge Xuan), on Mt. Tiantai, engaged in a silent retreat and expiated his transgressions. Burning incense, he confessed and repented. He contemplated upon the Perfect and kept his mind upon the Tao. Within 100 days a divine light appeared faintly atop the empty darkness. The cloudy luster flickered on and off, sometimes dispersing and sometimes concentrating, illuminating the hall of retreat in a winding fashion. The Immortal Duke himself realized that his thoroughgoing [self-imposed] suffering had distantly moved the Heavenly Perfected Beings. Hereupon he trained and contemplated upon his *karma* from the obscure past with extraordinary diligence and vigor.

Within a year of engaging in the retreat, he finally brought about a communication with the Superior Saints. (1b)

Here Ge Xuan is portrayed engaging in a religious regimen that involves suffering (*ku*). This suffering is directly responsible for bringing him into contact with the Perfected Beings, who reveal the scriptures. Also noteworthy is that this self-imposed suffering takes the form of a lengthy retreat (*zhai*) of worship, confession, and contemplation.

The *Zhenyi quanjie falun miaojing* continues with a description of how the three Perfected Men of Obscure Unity descended upon Ge Xuan's meditation chamber in full divine splendor, mounted on radiant jade carriages and attended by tens of thousands of Jade Boys and Jade Girls. The three Perfected Men took turns commending Ge Xuan for his virtues that had qualified him for the blessed transmission. They extolled him repeatedly for the compassionate good deeds and rigorous training that he had carried out over many *kalpas*. He had harmed his body in order to rescue living beings. He had opened up the way to salvation for many. He had shown mercy to all living species down to even the grasses and trees. He had rejected the wealth and glory of government office to pursue Taoist training in the desolate hills. He had served his teachers humbly and reverently. He had contemplated the Tao constantly amid bitter suffering. He did not desire a coat when cold. He did not give pleasure to his mouth when hungry. He had controlled his emotions and withstood his lust. Furthermore, he had inherited the merits of his ancestors, who had shared their food with the poor and exhibited benevolence towards the birds and beasts. His merits, both personal and hereditary, had transformed his body to where his "purple viscera" contained "the Perfect" and his head emitted a strange radiance (2b–3b).

The *Benxing yinyuan jing* (The Scripture on Causation from Past Deeds) asserts that Ge Xuan's altruism was what made him clearly superior to ordinary Taoist ascetics.[5] There it is indicated that he had attained the lofty rank of Left Immortal Duke of the Great Ultimate. While he was still a human being dwelling in the ordinary world, he had been able to visit the Jade Capital in the highest heavenly realm[6] and gain an audience with "the Peerless Emperor of the Void." The text records an incident that allegedly took place on the first day of the first month in the third year of the Chiwu reign era (240 C.E.). Ge Xuan had climbed Mt. Laocheng to contemplate the Tao in a "silent retreat" (*jingzhai*). There he was visited by thirty-three earthbound immortals and Taoist adepts. One of the earthbound immortals, apparently jealous of Ge Xuan, asked him why he alone had managed to gain his lofty grade of Immortal-hood. While asking this, the earthbound immortal pointed out that he and his fellow "lower officials" (lowranking immortals) had been studying the Tao in the mountain forests for as many as "600 *jiazi*"(this could be interpreted as meaning 600 years, or as meaning 600 sexegenary cycles [36,000 years]) (1a).

To this, Ge Xuan promptly responded. He first explained that during the primitive age that directly followed the creation of heaven and earth, there had existed no discrepancies among human beings in terms of their worthiness or their life spans. People spontaneously accorded with the Tao and did not even need to observe religious practices to properly do so. But eventually, human beings lost this capacity. The ways of people came to deviate from the Tao in various degrees, and discrepancies consequently arose among them. Ge Xuan then pointed out to his visitors what they had done wrong. Even though they had studied the Tao and received scriptures, they had performed few good deeds. They were concerned only with gaining salvation for themselves, and they did not even think about saving others. They did not put their faith in the "Great Scriptures" (this probably means the Lingbao scriptures). They did not carry out the retreats, nor did they obey the precepts. They did not respect the proper teachers ("the Doctrinal Masters of the Three Caverns"). In sum, they "took pleasure in the Small Vehicle," and for this reason attained no more than earthbound immortality. To gain a higher status that would enable them to be summoned to the highest divine realms, they needed to accumulate merit by rescuing people from calamities and diseases. Ge Xuan then pointed out that for this reason, "Pengzu who is 800 years old, Anqisheng[7] who is 1,000 years old, and Baishisheng who is 3,000 years old still wander among people." These immortals also had practiced mere minor methods and performed few meritorious deeds. Furthermore, Ge Xuan pointed out, some immortals have been unable to gain ascension even after 10,000 years. On the other hand, there have actually been many adepts who have quietly accumulated merit, after which they have successfully ascended to the heavens or undergone the "liberation from the corpse." However, most of them have done so secretly, and hence remain unknown (1b–2a).

Probably most noteworthy here is how Ge Xuan criticizes his visitors for practicing the "Small Vehicle." The Small Vehicle (or Hinayana) is a Buddhist term commonly used by adherents of the Mahayana (Great Vehicle) schools. It refers derisively to the Theravada schools whose doctrines and practices serve only the good of the individual (that is, in the opinion of Mahayanists). Mahayana Buddhism claims to bring salvation to all, which theoretically makes its doctrines greater in their capacity as a vehicle for salvation. Ge Xuan, in the previous passage, makes a similar claim on behalf of the Lingbao movement. According to him, the earthbound immortals had shunned the Great Vehicle of Taoism in favor of its Small Vehicle by neglecting to follow the doctrines and practices of the Lingbao.

Ge Xuan's main advice to the earthbound immortals is that they should establish their merit by striving to alleviate the plight of the world. The earthbound immortals and Ge Xuan personify the basic differences between the classic Taoist immortal and a new type of Taoist saint. Ge Xuan distinguishes himself primarily through his compassion and altruism, and in this sense resembles a Bodhisattva. A Bodhisattva is the ideal saint of Mahayana Buddhism, an enlightened being who postpones his or her entry into *nirvana* for the sake of helping and guiding the unenlightened. The Lingbao movement, which clearly imitated Mahayana Buddhism in its claim to being the "Great Vehicle," also appears to have been influenced by the concept of the Bodhisattva.

The necessity of helping those in need also is articulated in the *Benyuan dajie jing* (*The Scripture of the Great Precepts of the Original Vow*).[8] This scripture, which is presented as a lesson to Ge Xuan by his principle teacher, the Perfected Man of the Great Ultimate Xu Laile, includes the following passage:

> In studying the way of immortal ascension, when you establish 1,200 good merits, you will in the end never receive your retribution.[9] If you establish 3,000 merits you will ascend to heaven in broad daylight. [These merits] all [pertain to] rescuing people from the hazards which put them on the brink of death. Administering grace to those people is the best. In studying the Tao you must make all your deeds comply with the doctrines, [thereby] broadly establishing your field of merits and giving rise to your heart of great compassion. In motion and in stillness always give rise to the intentions of the Tao. If one is able to be like this and [thereupon] expel and take in, ingest medicines, wear talismans, read scriptures and meditate diligently for an entire life without tiring, how can there be anyone [like this] who will not attain immortality? People take medicines, wear talismans, read scriptures and observe retreats and precepts without this [compassionate virtue], and therefore for their whole lives they achieve no [positive] results. Students [of the Tao] should reflect clearly upon these essential words. (8b)

While the value of personal training was affirmed, the adept was first and foremost required to carry out good deeds for the benefit of other living beings. Without good deeds, personal training was futile.

Presumably, an altruistic ascetic would willingly suffer harm for the benefit of others. Such an ideal is conveyed in how the *Zhenyi quanjie falun miaojing* states that Ge Xuan "harmed his body in order to rescue [living beings]." Perhaps the most extreme expression of the altruistic ideal is found in the *Shangpin jie jing* (*Scripture of the Upper Section Precepts*). This scripture takes the form of a sermon delivered by the Primordial Heavenly Worthy to an assembly of divine beings. In it we are told that the "Heavenly Girls of Resolute Mind" and the "Immortals Who Withstand Humiliation" came to the assembly and uttered their ten Superior Vows.

1. I wish to give the flesh of my body as food for the starving birds and beasts.
2. I wish for the eight fats of my body to become fuel for the lamps, so that they can continue to shine.
3. I wish to lend my strength to relieve those who toil, and to rescue people by carrying their burdens.

4. If I see poor people naked, I wish to give them food and clothing.
5. If I happen upon an ill person, I wish to give him medicine.
6. When I recognize a need among people, I wish to help by providing what is needed.
7. [As for] those people who despair and suffer, [I wish to] bring them joy in accord with their situations.
8. As for those prisoners who are executed and have their [slain] bodies put on display, I wish to bear their punishment for them.
9. I wish that all pregnant women will quickly give birth.
10. I wish that all frontier regions will be subdued and returned [to the rule of the legitimate Chinese empire]. (2a)

The altruism expressed here is particularly poignant in that the beneficiaries of the life sacrifice include birds, beasts, and criminals. Certainly this extreme altruism was not expected of all believers. However, it represented an ideal to be admired by all and aspired to by the very best Taoists.

It also is relevant to mention that martyrdom is prescribed in the *Taishang dongxuan lingbao jieye benxing shangpin miaojing* (HY345/TT177),[10] a somewhat later text of the Lingbao movement. There the reader is told to uphold his religious principles under all circumstances. When his life is threatened by the violence of wicked people, he is told *not* to defend himself. The reassurance given is that he will thus become transformed into a Perfected Being, while his assailants suffer divine punishment.[11]

Faithful sacrifice of one's life also is promoted in the *Taishang zhutian lingshu duming jing* (The Most High Miraculous Book of the Various Heavens, the Scripture on the Deliverance of Lives [HY23/TT26]). This scripture narrates fundamental cosmological and soteriological legends. It starts out by describing at great length how the Primordial Heavenly Worthy established five "lands of the blessed" in the Five Directions,[12] starting from the central land, the "Land of the Hall of Great Blessings"(*da futang guo*). After this, he returned to the "Lodge of Perpetual Enjoyment" (*changle she*) in the central land, where entire nations of people from outlying regions visited him in the hope of obtaining salvation. The [Primordial] Heavenly Worthy thereupon tested their resolve. He shut off the radiance of the sun, moon, and stars, enveloping the cosmos in darkness for three days and three nights. He gathered firewood and built a huge bonfire, upon which he then sat. His burning form could be seen throughout the cosmos, but there appeared to be no way by which the faithful could approach him to receive instruction. He then proclaimed, "If you want to obtain long life, you must enter the fire so that you can receive the doctrines from me." Upon hearing this, 72,450 people gathered up the courage to enter the flames. The Primordodial Heavenly Worthy immediately conferred the scriptures and doctrines upon them, whereupon they "obtained deliverance" and vanished from sight. Looking on upon this scene were 400,000 people, who returned to their homelands in fear, assuming that the courageous faithful had burned to death. Upon their return, they were met by their fellow country folk who had entered the flames. They immediately regretted their own lack of faith. All who had entered the flames lived for 30,000 years, never undergoing pain, suffering nor aging (11a–b).

While the aforementioned story may have been believed literally by believers, it also serves as a parable illustrating how one should be willing to risk his or her life to seek salvation. It illustrates as well how the vast majority of humanity wants to gain salvation but shrinks from the opportunity due to the sacrifices involved. Intriguing here is how the story depicts the greatest god of the religion inflicting apparent harm upon himself for the salvation of human beings. It probably is the closest Taoist parallel to the Christian crucifixion narrative, although the Primordial Heavenly Worthy does not experience agony, death, and resurrection.

Finally, while on the subject of life sacrifice, it is worth mentioning a story found in the *Chishu yujue* (*Jade Lessons on the Red Writing* 2/1b–4a).[13] The story is about a sixteen-year-old girl named Aqiu Zeng. As has been pointed out by Stephen Bokenkamp,[14] this story conveys the male chauvinistic view that only men are capable of directly achieving immortality. Bokenkamp further points out that the story is a direct adaptation of a parable found in the Buddhist *Longshi nü jing*,[15] translated by the eminent monk Zhiqian.

According to the story, Aqiu Zeng saw a golden light one day while bathing. When she went outside to get a better look, she saw the resplendent countenance of the "Perfect God of the Tao." That day she vowed to observe the retreats and precepts in order to receive scriptures. She hoped to thus erase her bad *karma* and achieve rebirth as a man, whereupon she would train to become a Flying Immortal. Unfortunately, this vow did not go unnoticed by the Five Monarch Demon–Kings. As has been mentioned in chapter 5, Demon–Kings were thought to envy and resent adepts who sought to escape the profane realm and ascend to an exalted status superior to their own. Thus, the story goes, these five Demon–Kings disguised themselves as the holy Five Monarchs in the hope of deceiving Aqiu Zeng. They appeared before her and told her to abandon her religious pursuits. They told her that her father had already made plans for her marriage,[16] and proclaimed that principles of filial piety ordained that she obey him. However, Aqiu Zeng could not be persuaded. After the Demon–Kings had given up and left, she built a bonfire in which to cremate herself alive, hoping her ashes would be blown away by the wind and "settle down in the Tao's midst." She then climbed a wall directly above the blazing fire and jumped down. At this very moment, the Primordial Heavenly Worthy rescued her from the flames and transformed her into a man. He then entrusted her/him to the Worthy God of the Southern Extreme as a disciple.

The story just cited illustrates the ideal of pious life sacrifice. But perhaps even more interestingly, it presents marriage and Taoist training as being conflicting priorities for a woman. This suggests that there were female Taoist adepts who made celibacy a very serious priority. It seems possible that Taoist nunhood already existed in the fifth century.

Turning our attention back to Ge Xuan, it may be recalled how he was commended for accumulating great merit over numerous incarnations. Also, we find Ge Xuan criticizing the earthbound immortals for not accumulating sufficient merit in past lives. Throughout the Lingbao scriptures, we find exhortations grounded on the fundamental Buddhistic notions of *karma* and reincarnation. The main body of the *Benxing yinyuan jing* is a discourse ascribed to Ge Xuan himself, directed at the earthbound immortals. It describes some of the incarnations he underwent before achieving his saintly status (the total number of his incarnations is said to have been countless). The discourse skillfully demonstrates the principle of cause and effect in a way that serves a didactic purpose for believers at all levels.

The discourse tells of how he was born into a wealthy family, but mistreated his servants. Consequently, he became reborn as a messenger and suffered frequent beatings at the hands of those he served. To better his fate, he gave his personal belongings to the poor and served a Taoist priest as a lay disciple. This earned him a rebirth as an aristocrat. However, because he enjoyed fishing and hunting, he died and went to hell. There he was made to walk amidst "sword mountains and double-edged sword trees." He was also "boiled in hot water and made to swallow fire." He then underwent successive rebirths as a pig and a goat. He was then reborn as a lowly man of evil character who frequently defrauded people of their money. This caused him to be reborn as an ox. After being slain and eaten, he was rewarded— perhaps because he had fed and nourished others—with rebirth as a man of moderate social standing. In the rebirths that ensued, Ge Xuan came to participate more and more in the Taoist religion, thus bringing about a marked improvement in his fate. In one of these lives he finally became a Taoist adept. However, because he was so busy with his duties as a teacher and ritual expert, he proclaimed the wish to be reborn as a woman so he could enjoy himself in silent nonaction. During his subsequent life as a woman, he/she carried out retreats, read scriptures, and proclaimed the wish to be born as a king who could act as a powerful patron of the Taoist religion. He was thus reborn into a royal household, and when still crown prince, proclaimed the wish to be a hermit.[17] Eventually, in what was to become the next to the last of his incarnations, Ge Xuan became a Taoist master who "aspired to the deeds of the Great Vehicle." He went to a master of the doctrines (*fashi*) to receive the Great Scriptures of the Three Caverns. He lived in constant worship and observance of retreats and precepts while practicing dietetics and methods of "expelling and taking in" (*tuna*). But because he had not yet eliminated his causes (*yinyuan*) for rebirth, he died and was reborn into a Taoist household. Once again he grew up to be a Taoist adept and resumed the practices of his preceding life. This time he succeeded in capturing the attention of the Superior Saints (*shangsheng*) and became the recipient of revealed texts.

The basic message here is that the highest immortality can be attained only after a virtually limitless amount of "toil and suffering" over countless lifetimes. The well-intentioned strivings of an adept are never futile. Even if they fail to immediately confer immortality, they still bring about an auspicious rebirth into a setting conducive to Taoist training. In the discourse, Ge Xuan describes not only his lives as a religious man, but also his immoral lives that had brought forth bad retributions. The law of cause and effect is thus demonstrated in a way that encourages moral goodness in all people. It is shown how faith and moral goodness of any kind always has its rewards, while unethical conduct inevitably leads to punishment. Also, by describing the sequence of his rebirths at such length, the discourse conveys the elusiveness of the final goal, the attainment of which can be severely delayed by lapses in spirituality and conduct. The adept is thus exhorted to strive hard in his present life, since incarnation as an adept is a hard-earned privilege that is much too valuable to waste.

Near the end of the *Benxing yinyuan jing*, one of the earthbound immortals tells Ge Xuan about how he had once encountered the first Heavenly Master Zhang Daoling on Mt. Kunlun,[18] who appeared before him in full divine splendor with divine throngs in attendance. The earthbound immortal asks Ge Xuan how Zhang Daoling had achieved his exalted status. To this, Ge Xuan replies that the Heavenly Master had "toiled and suffered" through many cosmic eras just as he had. He had studied scriptures, observed retreats and precepts, and saved the masses through his evangelism. In fact, the Heavenly Master's merits in these respects surpassed even his own (7a).

This homage paid to Zhang Daoling reinforces the text's basic message and indicates that the Lingbao movement by no means intended to undermine the authority of the Heavenly Masters School. While the nature of the relationship between the Lingbao movement and the Heavenly Masters School cannot be fully ascertained, it does not seem to have been antagonistic.

The *Xuanyi quanjie falun miaojing* (The [Perfected Man of the] Mysterious One's Marvelous Scripture of the Wheel of the Doctrines of Encouragement and Admonishment) describes the proper lifestyles and training regimens to be observed by three categories of "gentlemen." An examination of these descriptions provides further evidence for the emphasis placed upon asceticism and altruism. At the same time, the descriptions seem to attest to a certain form of elitism that could have been justified by the principles of *karma*.

"Upper gentlemen," we are told, work to vastly propagate the religion and assist the king of the nation in carrying out good government. They generously aid those in need. They give away their food to the poor, and "go naked in order to clothe those who are cold." They extend their benevolence to all living beings, including the birds and beasts. Their generosity reaches out to all living beings. They diligently obey their religious teachers and uphold their doctrines. They engage in "perpetual retreats," during which they "bitterly contemplate" and "polish [their insight into] the Dongxuan (Lingbao scriptures)." They "expel and take in *qi* and fluids, with their minds like ashes and their wills diligent." They "cut off and abandon the burdens of lust."[19] They eliminate the "myriad thoughts" from their minds. As a result, after "one death and one life," they become Superior Immortals. Their bodies ascend to the Great Ultimate, and they attain the rank of Immortal Chamberlain (*xianqing*) (1a).

"Intermediate gentlemen" similarly devote themselves to the well-being and salvation of all, and thereby gain great merit. They are loyal to their rulers and filial to their parents. They train and worship diligently. "From sunrise till evening" (or perhaps, "at sunrise and in the evening") they "cultivate and polish [themselves]." They "savor the holy volumes" with their mouths as they burn incense and scatter flowers. In eating, they "do not wish to be filled." In clothing themselves, they "do not mind being cold." They are not demoralized by suffering, nor do they rejoice in pleasures. In toiling, they do not slacken, and when weary, they work even harder. As a result, after "three deaths and three lives," they become able to "fly and wander about in the [Realm of] Taiqing."[20] They receive the rank of Perfected Man of the Nine Palaces (1a–b).

"Lower gentlemen" cultivate their moral character by cutting off their emotions and withstanding their sexual desires. They nurture their spirits by "ingesting (*fuyu*)." They distance themselves from glory and elegance by dwelling in desolate forests. They "cut off grains and refrain from eating." They observe a "perpetual retreat" and contemplate the Tao. They do not eat after the noon hour. They respect-fully obey their teachers and make the birds and beasts their companions. They live alone in mountain caves, feeling no despair and harboring no desire to return to society. They feed off arbor vitae trees. Their visages show signs of starvation, but their sincere devotion remains unchanged. They always bear relaxed expressions in spite of their difficulties. They courageously face their trials. They thus evoke the sympathy of the Emperor of the Void (*xuhuang*). They "transform" after "nine deaths and nine lives." Mounting upon empty space, they "fly and wander about amidst the Five Peaks" and "freely wander in the Great Non-being." Ultimately, they gain the rank of High Immortal (1b–2a).

When comparing the traits attributed to the three levels of "gentlemen," it is difficult to discern the distinctions that determine the disparities in their ultimate rank and the speed of their progress. They all practice a similar degree of asceticism. If anything, the asceticism of the lower gentlemen is the most severe. The prime distinction, rather, seems to lie in the performance of altruistic deeds of evangelism and charity. Superior and intermediate gentlemen are both described as proficient in this respect, while lower gentlemen are not. In this sense, the lower gentlemen appear similar to those earthbound immortals in the *Benxing yinyuan jing*, whom Ge Xuan criticizes for practicing the "Small Vehicle." Yet the similarity is only partial in that the lower gentlemen, unlike the earthbound immortals, revere their teachers ("Master–Treasure," which probably designates teachers of the

Lingbao movement) and engage in "perpetual retreats." In this sense they adhere to the Great Vehicle. The term *lower gentlemen* seems to designate the reclusive wilderness-dwelling ascetics somehow affiliated with the Lingbao movement.

It seems valid to speculate that the lower gentlemen were people of lowly status in both the religious and social hierarchy. This, along with their reclusion, would have made them less capable of meritorious social action. The term *upper gentlemen* seems to describe the highest-ranking clergy who could exercise influence over the political elite and leave a benevolent impact upon the entire nation. "Intermediate gentlemen," then, would also describe people of significant clerical and social standing, capable of propagating the religion and administering charity effectively. This capacity to benefit the religion and the nation may also have had to do with personal affluence. However, there is considerable doubt as to whether a full-time adept was allowed to retain personal wealth. As we will see later, precepts promoted by the Lingbao movement require that an advanced adept leave behind the wealthy aristocratic life.

Nonetheless, one's placement within the three categories was probably largely determined by upbringing and social status, since these quite likely determined their place within the clerical hierarchy. If such elitism existed, it could have been rationalized on doctrinal grounds, since the principle of cause and effect clearly attributes high social standing to merits from past lives. A logical inference would be that an aristocrat has more past merit than a peasant, meaning that he is fewer rebirths away from heavenly immortality. This is, of course, if he is willing to "toil and suffer" in the religious life. Another hint indicating that the three categories are based on social background is that the description of lower gentlemen makes no mention of scriptural study and recitation. In contrast, we are told that intermediate gentlemen "savor the holy volumes" and upper gentlemen "polish [their insight into] the Dongxuan (Lingbao scriptures)." In other words, the term *lower gentlemen* may refer to those who were illiterate, due to a lowly upbringing. Since the holy scriptures were of paramount importance, it is understandable that the inability to study them would have been seen as a serious disadvantage that could set back one's progess by six to eight incarnations.[21]

Precepts and Retreats

An essential element of the Lingbao doctrinal system is its mythology. A brief version of its basic cosmic myth is found in the *Zuigen dajie jing* (*The Scripture on the Roots of Sins and the Great Precepts*, 1/2a–3b).[22] The narrative describes a cyclical cosmic process that occurs over an inconceivably long period of time. Long periods of primal darkness and chaos are interspersed between intermittent eras where worlds populated by living beings are created and destroyed. Each time a world is created, the Primordial Heavenly Worthy manifests himself—bearing a different title each time—to expound the proper path to happiness and long life. He brings forth the cosmic prototypes of the Lingbao Five Writs, which let forth the creative, life-sustaining force of the universe. Those who receive and obey his teachings live long, while the faithless and disobedient die young and accumulate transgressions. After he leaves, people increasingly fall victim to their own greed, avarice, and hypocrisy, and the world declines toward its eventual destruction. People suffer damnation and bad rebirths as retribution for their transgressions. The final part of the narrative indicates that the world is presently in just such a decrepit state and issues the following advice to human beings:

> Hereby you shall know and accept my (the Primordial Heavenly Worthy's) teachings. Be careful in your actions, without forgetting. Evangelize extensively and open up [the way to] salvation. Reveal it to all gods and humans. Make all men and women entrust themselves to the Gates of the Doctrines. [They must] *obey the precepts and carry out the retreats* (emphasis added), distancing themselves from the various sources of evil. Make them joyful and peaceful in their lives and deaths, [so that they can] obtain the Tao spontaneously.

Precepts and retreats were considered the foundation of proper religious life, and their observance is enjoined here as part of the fundamental solution to human plight. Precepts and retreats of numerous varieties and levels of intensity are described throughout the Lingbao scriptures. Asceticism was to typically manifest itself in the form of highly intensified precepts and retreats.

Precepts

The most advanced precepts endorsed by the Lingbao movement were the 300 Great Precepts for Monitoring the Body (*guanshen dajie*). These precepts are preserved today in the *Shangqing dongzhen zhihui guanshen dajie wen* (HY1353/TT1039) and the *Wushang biyao* 45/1a–17b. They are not enumerated in any of the extant Lingbao scriptures.[23] However, Lingbao adherents were apparently familiar with them and regarded them as guidelines for the very best adepts. The *Zuigen dajie jing* contains a clear allusion to these precepts. It states, "The Primordial [Heavenly King's][24] wisdom regulations in three categories have been formulated into the Great Precepts for Monitoring the Body, consisting of 300 entries in total." It then points out that these precepts can be properly observed by only the very best adepts. Their demands elude the capabilities of most people, particularly due to the general moral laxity of the decrepit age. The *Zuigen dajie jing* thus sets forth an alternative, less demanding set of ten precepts, in the hope that those less capable can "enter the Gates of the Doctrines" (1/5b).

> 1. Do not envy those who excel you. [Do not] persecute those who are worthy and enlightened.

2. Do not drink liquor in reckless abandon, defiling and disturbing your Three Palaces (Elixir Fields).
3. Do not commit adultery with another man's wife, out of your greed for the delicate and smooth [touch of a woman].
4. Do not abandon and neglect the aged, ill, poor and lowly.
5. Do not insult righteous people nor verbally attack your fellow students [of the Tao].
6. Do not greedily accumulate valuable treasures without being willing to give alms.
7. Do not kill living beings [as offerings in order to] worship the demons and spirits of the Six Heavens (profane realm).
8. Do not criticize and discuss the scriptures, making them out to be fallacious.
9. Do not turn your back upon your obligation to your teacher by deceiving and tricking new students.
10. Be impartial with your entire heart, exercising benevolence and filiality towards all. (1/6a–b)

A similar set of ten rudimentary precepts is found in the *Dingzhi tongwei jing*. As Stephen Bokenkamp has pointed out, the first five of these were almost certainly inspired by the five lay Buddhist precepts that proscribe killing, stealing, adultery, deception, and alchohol consumption.[25] (The *Dingzhi tongwei jing* differs slightly by proscribing *drunkenness*, thus condoning moderate alcohol consumption.) Precepts 6 through 8 are positive enjoiners directing believers to be friendly and supportive in their relationships with others. Precept 9 admonishes believers to bear no thoughts of revenge toward those who "defeat" them (do them wrong?). Precept 10, which reads, "If everyone has not obtained the Tao, do not wish to obtain it yourself," is an adaptation of the Mahayanist Bodhisattva vow to work relentlessly for the salvation of all, rather than merely oneself. The *Dingzhi tongwei jing* is particularly lenient toward the less steadfast, as it provides an escape clause that reads, "If you are encumbered by worldly burdens and cannot completely devote your mind, select from the ten [ordinances] nine, eight, seven, six or even [as few as] five of them which you are capable of [obeying]. The blessings [to be gotten from obeying just] five precepts [are so great that] they are hard to describe" (8a).

Along with these lenient precepts and the harsh Precepts for Monitoring the Body, the Lingbao texts endorse several sets of precepts that prescribe modes of discipline that stand somewhere in between the two extremes. For the sake of brevity, these will not be examined here.[26] However, it should be mentioned that among these precepts we find various items that call for actual hardship and sacrifice and seem to be directed at full-time practitioners. Some of the precepts forcefully enjoin Taoists to foster a pure state of mind through perfect control of the body's "six senses" (the capacities of sight, hearing, smell, taste, touch, and cognition, originally a Buddhist term).

We shall now examine the 300 Great Precepts for Monitoring the Body (of which there are actually 302). The precepts are divided into three sections; the Jade Purity Wisdom Precepts (*Yuqing zhihui jie*) of the Lower Origin (the Way of Superior Immortals, 182 entries), the Middle Origin (the Way of the Peerless Orthodox Perfected Beings, 36 entries), and the Upper Origin (the Limitless Way of the Most High, 84 entries). Because the precepts are far too numerous to quote in full, we shall now summarize those that are of greatest interest and examine their main points.

The Lower Origin Precepts as a whole prescribe an austere lifestyle for full-time adepts. Adepts, we are told, are forbidden from taking the lives of living creatures (which probably also means that they must not eat meat). They must not consume alcohol. They must not eat the five pungent vegetables (garlic, onions, leeks, shallots, and ginger). They must not raise livestock. They must not pluck flowers "for no reason." They must not "teach people to abort children and harm embryos." They must not hoard wealth, nor should they surround themselves with extravagant commodities. They must not own an abundance of clothing and personal articles. They must not receive lavish burials when they die. They must not wish to be famous and wealthy. They must disengage themselves from military matters and must not "meet with emperors, kings and lords for no reason." They must not associate with wicked, worldly people. They must not engage in flattery. They must not "partake in the worldly matter of marriage." They must not walk with women nor speak in private with them. They must not sit next to them nor touch garments with them. They must not "directly instruct women." They must treat people impartially, without showing special favor to family and relatives and without being unfriendly to "those of different surnames." They must not love their disciples overindulgently. They must not get angry at their disciples nor at the people of the world. They must not value themselves. They must not be boastful. They must not neglect and deride the beggars, the aged, or the ill.

The Lower Origin Precepts also include an injunction against fortune-telling and an apparent injunction against geomancy ("One who studies the Tao must not map out hills and plan homes for people."). Also, adepts are enjoined to carry out the required retreats and precepts "while the retreats and precepts are being observed in the various heavens." They must observe the mandatory "Six Retreats of the Year." (As we shall see, certain days were designated as mandatory communal retreat days, and it was believed that the heavenly throngs observed communal retreats on these days as well.)

Three points of emphasis that are particularly striking in the Lower Origin Precepts are the sanctity of life, the corruptive influences of power, and the perils of sexual attraction. Adepts are told to help preserve the life not only of fellow humans, but also of animals, plants, and unborn fetuses. While Buddhistic theories of *karma* certainly provided much of the justification for such precepts, it should also be added that a far-reaching reverence for life is thoroughly consistent with the spirit of the Taoist religion. The Taoist religion sets forth the perpetuation of physical life as a fundamental goal and worships the creative and life-sustaining force of the cosmos (the Tao, or the god[s] that personify it) as its highest Deity.

The injunctions against involvement in political and military affairs are particularly understandable in light of the fact that the earliest adherents of the Lingbao movement probably belonged to the aristocracy. Many were probably in a position quite vulnerable to the vices of ambition, arrogance, and corruption. The precepts also reflect an acute awareness of the fact that power within the religious hierarchy, when abused, could lead to charlatanry. Apparently for this reason, adepts are forbidden from engaging in prognostication and geomancy, practices through which the faith and trust of lay people can be exploited.

As we have seen, the extreme apprehension toward contact with the opposite sex has its precedent in the teachings of the Shangqing movement. The Lower Origin precepts include what appears to be a very early example of a proscription against marriage ("One who studies the Tao must not partake in worldly matters of marriage.") Yet, curiously, we also find an item that reads, "One who studies the Tao must not have separate doorways from his father and mother." This would seem to mean that in spite of the proscription of marriage, monasticism was not approved—at least for those still at the stage of observing the Lower Origin Precepts. Perhaps the idea was that eremitic or cenobitic lifestyles should be pursued only after one's parents had passed on, since filial duty required celibate adepts to care for their parents while they were still alive.

The degree of asceticism intensifies in the Middle Origin Precepts. The importance of humility is given added stress. Adepts are told not to expect politeness and respect from others. They are not to harbor any anger or desire for revenge when mistreated. When they suffer misfortune or illness, they are to simply blame themselves and contemplate how they might reform their immoral conduct. They are to observe austerities that surpass the capabilities of normal people. They must "withstand what others are unable to withstand." They must detach themselves from "what others are unable to detach themselves from." They must "wear what others are unwilling to wear." They must "eat what others are unwilling to eat." They must "study what others are unable to study." They must "tolerate what others are unable to tolerate."

The Middle Origin Precepts also warn adepts not to look women directly in the eyes. This injunction was perhaps dictated by the belief that the demons (Corpses) in the bodies of men and women could emerge from the eyes and interact with each other, regardless of the intentions of the people themselves (see p. 76). Another item in the Middle Origin Precepts that seems to pertain to celibacy is the one that states, "One who studies the Tao must pacify his Mysterious Spring. He must not allow his Source of Life to move deludedly." This probably means to say that he must retain his *jing* (generative force, semen).

The Middle Origin Precepts also stress the purity of body and mind. They proclaim that the *hun* and *po* souls will leave the body if it is unclean. If the adept "has thoughts," "the Heavenly Perfected Beings up on high will distance themselves [from him] and the demon-officials will not submit themselves [to his commands]." If he has an empty mind, "he will find himself face to face with Perfected Beings." If he "has a body" (is concerned about the sustenance of the body), "the various desires will not leave him, and his earnest meditation will elicit no [divine] responses."

The Middle Origin Precepts also contain an entry that reads, "[As for] one who studies the Tao, if he has a family, the Three Poisons (Three Worms?)[27] will not perish and the Three Perfected Beings will not reside [in him]." This, at first sight, appears to be commanding adepts to "leave the family" to pursue eremitism or cenobitism. It seems to contradict the entry in the Lower Origin Precepts that tells adepts not to "have separate doorways" from their parents. A possible interpretation is that the adepts to whom the Middle Origin Precepts were addressed were considered better prepared to pursue eremitism or monasticism (if monasticism had been incorporated into Taoism by this time). However, it also is possible that the phrase "having a family" is used abstractly to describe an inner feeling of attachment to one's family.

The precepts of the Upper Origin outline a regimen of self-discipline and mindfulness that leads to great rewards. The rewards include the transmission of the most advanced methods and scriptures and the gaining of wondrous mystical experiences.

Adepts are told to practice vegetarianism, live in the mountains and forests, and meditate in solitude and silence. They must eat only once a day at noon and do away with all rich delicacies. They must resign themselves to poverty. They must revere the scriptures and precepts and recite them constantly. They must accumulate merits by saving people. They must put others first and never talk about themselves. Their minds must be empty and serene, free of extraneous thoughts.

The Upper Origin Precepts also warn against associating with popular cults that worship "demons and spirits." Adepts are told to distance themselves from demons and spirits, "neither venerating nor scorning them." They must not associate with the "wicked and confused people" who worship these demons and spirits.

Adepts are told to think humble, compassionate, and pious thoughts. They must wish for the well-being of all. They must wish for all people to be freed from their tribulations and their bondage to immorality. They must wish for their parents and their "seven generations of ancestors" to attain deliverance into the "halls of heaven." They must wish for their teachers to quickly achieve heavenly ascension. They must empathize with the sufferings and humiliations of others, feeling their wounds and pains as if they were their own. They must wish to free themselves from the causes that keep them trapped in *samsara*. They must wish for their "tree of life to wither"(?), so their spirits will merge with the Great Non-being.

The Upper Origin Precepts also endorse specific meditation techniques and scriptures. Adepts are told to "constantly visualize the Perfected Man Zidan[28] in the Three Palaces." They are to "contemplate the Female-One" (perform the visualizations of the *Ciyi jing*)[29] and recite the Dadong scripture (the *Dadong zhenjing*). (Here the impact of Shangqing doctrines is clear.) By carrying out such advanced practices, adepts are to aspire to gain wondrous results. They are to "eat the spontaneous delicacies of the kitchens of the heavens without any thoughts of hunger and thirst." They are to command Immortal Boys and Jade Girls. They are to travel to marvelous transcendent realms such as "the Eastern Flowers of the Green Forest," "the Southern Flowers of the Great Elixir," "the Western Flowers of Anyang,"[30] and "the Northern Flowers of Biluo." They are to travel to the northeast, northwest, southeast, and southwest to proclaim the "encouragements of goodness and the admonishments of evil" and deliver people from damnation through the "Eight Gates." They are to wander to the "Jade Purity Palace of the Seven Treasures" and pay their respects to the Heavenly Worthies of the Three Origins. They are to wander to the palaces of the sun and moon, where they will visit the kings and sup the golden nectar of the flowers. They are to listen to the music of celestial singing girls, without entertaining any worldly thoughts. However, the adept must make sure to maintain secrecy in his knowledge of the most sublime matters. He must not carelessly reveal the secret names of Heavenly Perfected Beings.

The aforementioned theme of the "Eight Gates" is featured prominently in the *Taishang xuanyi zhenren shuo santu wuku quanjie jing* (HY455/TT202). There "the Tao" (portrayed as a conscious and willing deity) describes how it set out to alleviate the plight of living beings, after having witnessed their suffering for eons and eons. "The Tao" set up the Eight Gates and instructed the ignorant masses on matters of cause and retribution. "The Tao" then traveled to the hells of the eight directions (N, S, E, W, NE, NW, SE, SW) and witnessed hideous sights of men and women being tortured for their transgressions (the tortures are described in vivid and brutal detail). At each hell, "the Tao" told the Flying Celestial Beings (*feitianren*) to admonish the transgressors toward righteousness so that they could be reborn as humans in the ordinary world. There they could pursue a righteous religious life that could enable them to some day ascend to the immortal realm through the Eight Gates.

According to the Precepts for Monitoring the Body, the advanced adept has the power to emulate this feat of "the Tao." More concretely, this probably means that he possesses the ritual power to deliver damned souls. The deliverance of damned souls was one of the central objectives of the Lingbao *zhai* (retreat) rituals, as we shall see.

By fully observing the Precepts for Monitoring the Body, the adept was to embody all of the virtues of the ideal saint. He would practice a degree of asceticism above and beyond ordinary human capacities. This asceticism was to be thoroughly altruistic, in that the welfare and salvation of others were to be put first. His efforts would strictly follow a set curriculum of methods and scriptures. He was to staunchly oppose demonic cults. Mystical experiences and divine powers were to be a great part of his reward, and these theoretically endowed him with great power in the ritual arena.

Retreats (*zhai*)

In its most basic definition, *zhai* refers to purificatory prohibitions observed for rituals and festivals of all kinds. This usage of the word *zhai* predates the origins of the Taoist religion, as such purificatory prohibitions had long been customary in Chinese official and popular religion. In Taoism, the word *zhai* retained this basic meaning, but also came to denote the rituals and festivals themselves. Because ritual prohibitions typically included dietary restrictions, it also came about that when Buddhism began to spread through China, the word *zhai* was used to translate the Sanskrit word *upasatha*, which denotes the monastic Buddhist practice of fasting after the noon hour. The usage of the word was further expanded to describe the vegetarian food eaten by monks, which laypeople also partook of on special occasions. These Buddhistic usages of *zhai* also are employed in the Lingbao scriptures.

Because the Lingbao scriptures employ all of the aforementioned usages of the word *zhai*, it is often difficult to determine which usage is operative. Also, according to the context, *zhai*, or "retreat," can refer to an elaborate liturgical group ritual carried out periodically over a designated number of days. In some cases, it refers to a solo training regimen that is sustained for a very lengthy period, or even for an entire lifetime. Yet in the minds of the texts' authors, there does not seem to have been a clear-cut distinction between temporary communal retreats and lengthy personal retreats. The latter were extensions and intensifications of the former. In other words, an advanced adept who carried out his own "perpetual retreat" (*chang-zhai*) would observe the same rules that applied to communal retreats. However, he would observe the rules over a much longer period. He would chant the scriptures and liturgies used in the communal retreats, albeit in solitude. His solo rituals bore much of the same meaning and purpose as the communal rituals. In both types of rituals, adepts sought to emulate the gods and attain communion with them. The aim in doing so was to bring salvation and blessings to all sentient beings.

Passages explaining when to carry out retreats are found in the *Zhaijie weiyi jue* (*Lessons on Retreats, Precepts and Mighty Rituals*) and *Taiji yinzhu baojue* (*Precious Lessons with Secret Annotations of the Great Ultimate*). The two texts give different explanations, simply because they mean different things by the term retreat (*zhai*).

The *Zhaijie weiyi jue*, in a passage allegedly uttered by the Perfected Man of the Great Ultimate, states, "The first, third, fifth, seventh, ninth, and eleventh months are the Six Retreats of the Year. The 1st, 8th, 14th, 15th, 18th, 23rd, 24th, 28th, 29th and 30th days are the Ten Retreats of the Month." The retreats mentioned here seem to be communal rituals, and the passage is followed by a short liturgy. In the *Chishu chenwen* (3/1a–8a) we are told that the aforementioned "Ten Retreats of the Month" are days when supreme deities in the heavens of the ten directions gather to carry out retreats, pay their respect to the Lingbao Five Writs, and examine the merits and demerits of the "humans and demons on the earth." It is crucial that humans carry out retreats on these days so that their transgressions will be forgiven and their merits acknowledged. Apparently, the "Six Retreats of the Year" refers to the months during which the designated retreat days (i.e., "Ten Retreats of the Month") had to be observed. The idea, then, was to carry out retreats on ten days out of each of the odd-numbered months, meaning that a total of sixty days per year were mandatory retreat days. However, the same passage also appears to acknowledge that it is worthy and desirable to engage in retreats more often, and thus endorses "perpetual retreats and lengthy contemplation" as a means for "transcending into vacuity." It further proclaims that the "August Elders, Heavenly Worthies and Great Saints" engage in this tirelessly, and therefore "Taoist adepts and immortals" must do so. (*Zhaijie weiyi jue* 1a).

The passage in the *Taiji yinzhu baojue* (also ascribed to the Perfected Man of the Great Ultimate) uses the term *retreat* to refer more generally to the observance of purificatory prohibitions. It asserts that a retreat is a fundamental religious practice that needs to be carried out in conjunction with practically any religious activity. It thus states, "The recitation of scriptures requires a retreat. The editing of scriptures requires a retreat. The writing (copying) of scriptures requires a retreat. The writing of talismans requires a retreat. The preparation of medicines requires a retreat. The concoction of the golden elixir requires a retreat. Concentrated meditation requires a retreat. Visiting and inquiring of a teacher requires a retreat. Bowing and worshipping requires a retreat. Receiving scriptures requires a retreat. Healing diseases and alleviating calamities requires a retreat" (*Taiji yinzhu baojue* 15b).

As may be recalled (pp. 96–97), the *Zhenyi quanjie falun miaojing* tells of how Ge Xuan engaged in a year-long silent retreat on Mt. Tiantai, devoting himself to confession and contemplation. The reward for his austerities was an encounter with the Three Perfected Men of the Obscure Origin and the transmission of holy scriptures. Theoretically, any adept could encounter divine beings by diligently carrying out a retreat. The *Taiji yinzhu baojue* states

> The Perfected Man of the Great Ultimate said, "When a person carries out a pure retreat amidst lengthy stillness, engages in concentrated meditation while basking in the dark mystery, recites scriptures and confesses transgressions, and burns incense in worship, he will eventually see Flying Celestial Beings. Immortal Boys and Jade Girls will descend to his room. Perhaps he will hear [voices] in the room exalting [his] goodness for him.

Perhaps rays of light will illuminate his body. Perhaps he will hear the
sounds of gold and jade [chimes] in the eight tones. These are all signs
that he is about to attain the Tao. Be diligent! Be diligent! The Most High
will not forsake you." (17b)

Here the adept is told to be diligent in his retreat of meditation, scripture
recitation, confession, and worship. By doing so, he is guaranteed to some day
receive confirmation of his progress in the form of a mystical encounter accompanied by extraordinary sights and sounds. The *Zhaijie weiyi jue* describes the
methods employed to bring about mystical encounters in further detail.

The Perfected Man of the Great Ultimate said, "When engaging in a
retreat, everybody should concentrate their minds on the Mysterious
Perfection and always have no external thoughts. Your thoughts must be
upon the scriptures and your teacher. First visualize the Three Ones in
their palaces, residing there peacefully, clearly visible, accompanied by
the three *hun* souls and seven *po* souls. The Great One protects the
Niwan as in the Method of the Whirlwind and the Imperial One.[31]
Afterwards, [the Great One] will participate in the retreat together with
you and listen to the scriptures [that you recite]. [If] you receive [secret
lessons] from the mouth [of the Great One] and contemplate [the lessons]
in your heart, thereby the Three Corpses will run away and the evil *qi*
will be purged. Inside and outside, you will receive the truth. If you do
like this, you will be close to immortality. Complement this (your
visualizations) with [methods of] expelling and taking in, leading and
guiding, and harmonizing fluids. If you practice the above marvelous
ways, the Heavenly Perfected Beings will most certainly descend into
your midst. Upper gentlemen obtain the Tao inside the [meditation]
chamber. Even if you live in a cave, if an external thought even as slight
as a single hair has not been eliminated, you will have but wasted your
strength in futile labor. The study of the Tao is nothing more than the
elimination of mentation. If mentation is eliminated, Immortals will
come down to monitor and test you. Make sure that you are fully aware
of this." (21a)

Specifically recommended here are techniques of visualizing the Three Ones,
the *hun* and *po* souls, and the Great One. Also noteworthy is the reference to the
Shangqing method of the Whirlwind. We can see that Lingbao proponents were
familiar with Shangqing texts and methods and held them in high esteem.
Visualization techniques were supposed to enable the adept to concentrate his mind
in a way that could make communion with divine beings possible. At the same
time, the Three Corpses and wicked *qi* were to be purged from his body, and the
visualizations were to be supplemented with methods of air/saliva swallowing,

breath control, and the guiding of *qi*. As has been discussed in previous chapters, all such methods typically purported to suppress hunger and sustain fasts. Fasts were supposed to purge the body of demonic and impure forces. While the previous passage cites mental concentration as being the primary means of evoking the appearance of divine beings, hunger and fatigue probably also played a role in inducing mystical experiences.

Regarding the dietary restrictions involved in retreats, the *Zhaijie weiyi jue* contains the following information:

> A Taoist adept distances and cuts himself off from human traces and lives quietly in renowned mountains. He practices this perpetual retreat and lives alone in a desolate valley. Thereby he no longer selects a Master of the Doctrines [as his preceptor], but simply makes his mind converse with his mouth. When practicing this retreat amidst people, a Taoist adept practices dietetics. The five grains are cut off by him, and he does not eat anything, and that is all. But if he ingests medicines, he should do so at noon. After the noon hour he may drink water, but must not eat anything. At dawn he may drink porridge and at noon he may eat vegetables. When the retreat comes to an end, and the retreat is to be adjourned with a great feast, [the feast] must be clean and pure (bland, vegetarian) in its form. Serve the fruits that are the seasonal delicacies. You must first burn incense and say prayers [before eating]. Wish for the host of the retreat[32] to ascend to immortality and transcend the world. (21b)

The aforementioned passage starts by describing the personal perpetual retreat of an advanced adept, then seems to move on to set forth guidelines for dietary conduct at communal retreats. Oddly, the text seems to contradict itself. First it says to "cut off grains" and ingest only medicines if complete fasting is impossible. However, it then allows for the consumption of porridge and vegetables. Apparently, complete fasting is endorsed only as an ideal. Medicines, porridge, and vegetables are allowed to be consumed due to the limited capabilities of most adepts.

Later in the same text a passage is found that states, "When observing a retreat, if you reach your limit, you may eat dried jujubes and dried venison. Anything raw or fresh is not allowed to be served" (23b). "Limit" here probably refers to one's capacity to withstand hunger. The underlying assumption seems to be that adepts would do their best to eat nothing until the hunger became unbearable.

In a text issuing from later Lingbao proponents, we find a description of nine different dietary regimens for retreats. The text in question is a section from the now lost *Xuanmen dalun*, preserved in *Yunji qiqian* 37/8a–9a. Japanese scholars have speculated that this scripture, also known as the *Xuanmen dayi*, was written during the Daye era (605–617) of the Sui dynasty.[33] Sunayama Minoru maintains that the scripture was written by members of what he calls the Chongxuan faction, a powerful group of Taoists that carried on the scriptural heritage of the Lingbao and

Taixuan factions into the Sui and Tang periods.³⁴ It is possible that the nine dietary regimens described in the *Xuanmen dalun* were practiced by early Lingbao proponents during retreats. The nine dietary regimens are as follows:

1. Coarse eating: A diet of hemp and millet grains. Purpose/Effect—"To terminate cravings and desires."
2. Rough eating: A diet of vegetables. Purpose/Effect—"To abandon fats (pork)."
3. Limited eating: Observing the post-noon fast. Purpose/Effect—"To eliminate confusion and defilement."
4. Imbibing Essences: The taking of talisman water and "Cinnabar (red?) Flowers." Purpose/Effect—"Your body and spirit will embody and complete the 'flower stems'."
5. Imbibing Sprouts: Eating the Cloud Sprouts of the Five Directions. Purpose/Effect—"You will transform into the sprouts."
6. Imbibing Light: Eating the "Three [types of] Rays of the Sun, Moon and Seven Origins (stars of the Ursa Major)." Purpose/Effect—"You will transform into light."
7. Imbibing *Qi*: Eating "the *Qi* of the Six Awakenings" and the "Great Harmony which is the Wondrous *Qi* of the Four Directions." Purpose/Effect—"You will transform into the Six *Qi* and wander about in the ten directions."
8. Imbibing the Primal *Qi*: Eating "the *qi* of the Three Origins [which are all endowed with] the *jing* of Great Harmony which is in the Great Vacuity." Purpose/Effect—"You will transform into primal *qi* and merge with heaven and earth to form a single body."
9. Womb-eating: Eating "the harmony of the primal *jing* which I, on my own, have obtained. It is the origin of the embryo and the womb. It is, in other words, the pure and vacuous *qi* which descends into the four limbs. No longer do I have a relationship with the outside." Purpose/Effect— "Perpetually you will be in your infancy, and will merge and become one with the Tao."

Entries 1 through 3 describe austere, bland diets observed for the purpose of self-discipline. Entries 4 through 9 describe fasting techniques ascribed with transformative qualities of a symbolic nature. Essentially, the adept "becomes what he eats." Entry 4 is the most difficult to understand, but a tentative interpretation would be that the adept eats flowers with talisman water and acquires the potential to "bloom" with the "flower" of immortality. In entries 5 through 8, the adept eats rarefied substances such as "Cloud Sprouts," light rays, and *qi*. In doing so, his own body becomes rarefied. In entry 9, the adept lives entirely off his own "womb-*qi*," much as a fetus is nourished in his/her mother's womb without eating the food nor breathing the air of the external world.

During Lingbao retreats, participants were expected to engage in worship six times during the course of a twenty-four-hour day. A passage in the *Zhaijie weiyi jue* states, "During the retreat, burn incense and repent of your transgressions three times respectively in the day and evening. Simply, with your entire heart, hear and receive the wondrous and profound teachings of the scriptures and doctrines" (9a). The practice of worshipping six times a day was most likely adopted from Buddhism.[35] The exact times for the six worship sessions are not specified in the Lingbao texts. However, they quite likely occurred at early morning (8 A.M.), noon, afternoon (4 P.M.), night (8 P.M.), midnight, and late night (4 A.M.). (Such was generally the practice within Buddhist circles.)[36] The *Zhaijie weiyi jue* contains a short liturgy for a retreat called the Wushang Zhai (the Peerless Retreat). The liturgy includes verses for summoning gods and immortals and for sending out prayerful petitions. The petitions proclaim the wish that the ritual participants, their ancestors, and all sentient beings throughout the universe will "obtain the Tao and ascend as Immortals." The liturgy also calls for the recitation of confessional verses, followed by scripture recitation. On p. 10a, the text extolls the benefits of observing the retreat over a lengthy period, and provides an annotation describing the routine to be observed.

If you practice the Tao for 1,000 days, with your mind completely devoted to the mysteries, you will certainly be able to beckon down Perfected Men, see Saints and obtain the Tao.

(Comment) Engage in worship six times during the day and night. During three of these [worship] times be at the lecture. During [the other] three [worship] times visualize your bodily deities.

Worshipping six times a day for 1,000 days certainly would have been a pious feat beyond the abilities of ordinary believers. A lengthy retreat of this kind was most likely a practice exclusive to advanced, full-time adepts, since communal retreats usually lasted somewhere between three to twelve days. Thus, the *Zhaijie weiyi jue* later on makes allowances for believers who possessed something less than the greatest piety and endurance. Both the duration of the retreat and the number of daily worship sessions could be modified.

Baopuzi said, "[I, Ge] Hong think that during great retreats that last a great number of days, those nobles or those Taoist adepts who are of naturally frail and weak physique are unable to bear the stress of six times of day and night worship. I would like them to burn incense and worship during the three times [of worship] in the daytime. They may be absent from the nighttime [worship]. They can simply have the doctrines lectured to them instead. Those who are able to burn incense [and worship] six times a day can master the doctrines on their own. I fear that [some] people have not yet obtained the *qi* of the Tao, and [hence] their strength is extremely weak. I only want them to engage in the retreat for one day and one night, during which they should practice the Tao six times. Those who study [the Tao] should employ proper judgment." (23a–b)

The attribution of the previous statements to the alchemist Ge Hong is probably spurious. Whatever the case, the passage acknowledges that worshipping six times daily over any extended period was excessive and dangerous for those who lacked endurance due to physical frailty or lack of prior training. One can surmise that participation in the three nighttime sessions imposed substantial restrictions upon the normal sleep schedules of ordinary people. It is hence understandable that the nighttime sessions were made optional. Further on in the *Zhaijie weiyi jue*, "Ge Hong" proclaims

> As for those who are not mountain dwelling adepts (*shanxue*), [but are practitioners who] reside at home to practice the scriptures, they are certainly not capable of engaging in the perpetual retreat of sustained contemplation. Essentially, they must participate in retreats and practice the Tao (worship) even if it is only for short periods of ten days, nine days, seven days, three days, or even one day. (23b)

A clear distinction is thus made between the "mountain dwelling" full-time adept who can withstand the rigors of a perpetual retreat and the "at home" practitioner who should only participate in retreats to the extent that he or she is capable.

The *Mingzhen ke* contains two ritual liturgies. These rituals probably required the observance of the aforementioned dietary practices and worship schedule. They also required participants to inflict pain and humiliation upon themselves for the expiation of the transgressions of all sentient beings. The first liturgy is entitled "the Upper Item of the Jade Boxes of the Nine Darknesses for Pulling Out and Rescuing the Dead Souls from Punishment" (17a–24b). It is to be carried out during the aforementioned "Six Retreats of the Year and Ten retreats of the Month," and also on the eight seasonal transitions (*bajie*, i.e. the equinoxes and solstices and the first day of each season) and the *jiazi* and *gengshen* days of the sexegenary cycle. In the courtyard of the house that serves as the ritual arena, a lantern post nine *chi* (about 2.17 m.) high is erected, upon which nine lanterns are placed. These symbolize the radiance of the sun, moon, and seven stars of the Ursa Major, which illuminate the Nine Darknesses (hells), while the Primordial Heavenly Worthy expounds the Perfect Doctrines and guides the damned souls toward redemption. In the ensuing ritual, a petition is recited toward the supreme deities of the ten directions (N, S, E, W, NE, NW, SE, SW, above, and below), requesting that all living beings be spared from the Ten Sufferings and Eight Difficulties (*shiku banan*)[37] and that all the souls of the dead be liberated from infernal punishments and reincarnated into a good existence. After each reading of the petition (the petition is read ten times, once for each direction), participants kowtow and "hit themselves" (slap their cheeks)[38] repeatedly.

The prescribed numbers of kowtows and slaps for each direction are: east—81, south—27, west—63, north—45, northeast—9, southeast—9, southwest—9, northwest—9, above—288, below—120. In other words, the participant kowtows and slaps himself a total of 660 times! This was obviously very exhausting and painful. However, such suffering was supposed to enhance the effectiveness of the petitions.

It is so that by prostrating yourself in worship, kowtowing and hitting yourself, you administer words of humble confession. Thereby with your earnest heart and devoted mind, your sincerity is thorough and your suffering is sufficient; naturally [your petitions] will move [divine beings] pervasively.

If your body becomes tired and worn, and can no longer withstand being dragged about, you may worship the Heavenly Perfected Beings in your heart, and need not go to the trouble of prostrating yourself. If you pretend [to be reverent] externally but are lazy in your heart, you will only belabor your body in worship. [As for] gentlemen of faith, their hearts and mouths are consistent. Holding incense, their poignant wishes already [before you know it], permeate the various heavens. The transgressions of the realm of life and death (*samsara*) are all dissipated. This merit is extremely great. It is to be praised throughout the Three Realms.[39] Its blessings and virtues are lofty beyond description. (24b)

The basic aim is to "move" the gods to heed the petitions through one's inner sincerity, which is reflected in external acts of "suffering." However, allowances are made for those unable to follow the demands of the liturgy literally. The text also warns of the futility of suffering that is displayed merely for show, without a genuine feeling of repentance.

The second liturgy in the *Mingzhen ke* is "the Method of the Curriculum of Bright Perfection for the Bureaus of Perpetual Night, the Jade Boxes in the Nine Darknesses" (25b–37a). This is to be performed during national crises such as droughts, epidemics, and wars. Numerous lanterns—as many as 900, depending on the occasion and the severity of the crisis—are set up, symbolizing the divine light that illuminates all existence, including the hells of Perpetual Darkness. Also employed in the ritual are the sacred Five Perfect Writs of the Lingbao, written in red ink and placed on five different tables in the courtyard. Placed beside the Writs are small images of dragons, each made from one *liang* (13.92 grams) of gold. In the ritual's grand finale, the Five Writs are burned. The most interesting feature of the ritual is described as follows:

The great ritual master [stands] in the center [of the ritual arena] with his hair let down and topknot untied. In accordance with the lessons he smears [himself] with soot. Six times [per day] he petitions and repents, carrying out these activities in the courtyard. If men and women of purity and faith [wish to] pray and request on behalf of the nation, they should express their sentiments outside the gates by disheveling their hair and smearing soot on themselves. In the spring, [the ritual should go on for] nine days and nine nights. In the summer, [it should go on for] three days and three nights. In the fall, [it should go on for] seven days and seven nights. In the winter [it should go on for] five days and five nights. During the four *ji* months (third, sixth, ninth, twelfth) [it should go on for] twelve days and twelve nights. (26a–b)

The text continues with petitions to the deities of the ten directions. Again, the petitions—which vary only slightly in their wording—are to be followed by kowtows and slaps (east—81, south—27, west—63, north—45, northeast—9, southeast—9, southwest—9, northwest—9, above—88, below—108; total—448). The petitions include the words, ". . . We now therefore hold a retreat. We open our hearts and expose our bodies. We continuously implore [you] while disciplining ourselves, in order to rid our nation of its misfortunes. . . ."

As was the case with the first liturgy, exhaustion and pain purport to enhance the effectiveness of the petitions. The phrase "expose our bodies" likely means that the participants would strip off their clothing and smear their bodies with soot. Fortunately, we have sources at our disposal that describe the "smearing of soot" (*tutan*) much more vividly.[40] By the latter part of the Six Dynasties period, the "smearing of soot" had itself become a full-fledged retreat called the Tutan Zhai (Retreat of Smearing Soot). The *Wushang biyao* 50 contains a long section (20 1/2 pages) entitled "Section on the Retreat of Smearing Soot," a Tutan Zhai liturgy that incorporates petitions and verses from various scriptures. The liturgy begins with a petition containing the following words:

[We] your subjects . . . [who are like] worms and ants are stinky, filthy, insignificant and lowly as one could be. Due to some kind of a mistake we have had the fortunate destiny of being born into the age of the great evangelism. . . . (50/1a)

Holding us reverently by the hand, for So-and So we follow the instructions of the Celestial Master: [face] smeared with soot, according to the regulations of pardon, presenting ourselves in the sacred place, we are attached, we are linked together, our hair is disheveled, we have smeared our foreheads with mud, we keep our heads averted and our hair in our mouth at the foot of the balustrade, conforming to the [ritual of] pure fasting of the Great Pardon of the Lower Original of the Sacred Jewel, we burn incense and we strike the earth with our forehead; we ask for mercy.

In this day, such-and-such a day of such-and-such a month, on the sacred altar of such-and-such a sub prefecture of such-and-such a commandery, such-and-such a family, carrying out the fast for pure pardon, has lit the lamps and produced the brightness illuminating the heavens.

For three days and three nights, for six hours (*sic*, times)[41] each (of these days and nights), it has carried out repentance to obtain pardon, so that the hundred thousand ancestors, relatives and brothers, already dead or who will later die, including the person of So-and-So (who is performing the ceremony), shall be without evil throughout the *kalpas*. . . . (50/1b)[42]

What is described here is an exercise in self-degradation. Participants compare themselves to worms and ants. They express their remorse by stripping and binding themselves. They further degrade themselves by smearing mud on their faces and striking ridiculous postures. This goes on for three days, probably with severe restrictions on nourishment and rest.

Another interesting passage is found in the *Erjiao lun*, a Buddhist polemical (anti-Taoist) work written by a certain Dao-an in 570 C.E. It states

The Retreat of Smearing Soot was originated by Zhang Lu (the third Heavenly Master). [Participants] roll in the mud like donkeys. Their faces are smeared with yellow mud, and they are grabbed by their heads and hung from their hairpins. [They are then] kneaded until they are ripe (beaten and bruised?). When it came to the beginning of the Yixi reign era (405–418), there was a certain Wang Gongchao who deleted the hitting and slapping [from the procedure]. Lu Xiujing of the Wu region still carried out only the [smearing of] mud on the foreheads and binding of hands behind the back. To resort to these things to deliver oneself from disasters, how extremely foolish. (Taisho Canon 52:140, bottom)

Portrayed here is a frenzied scene where all sense of solemnity and dignity has broken down. Most interesting is the statement maintaining that the ritual was much more abusive and violent prior to the early fifth century, after which the most revolting activities (the beatings) were discontinued. Still, the polemicist tells us, the ritual otherwise retained its elements of self-degradation and wrought much chaotic frenzy. We must keep in mind that the credibility of the *Erjiao lun* is suspect, due to its polemical bias. Nonetheless, Henri Maspero has drawn upon its evidence to surmise that the rituals of the early religious Taoists (Great Peace School, Five Pecks of Rice School)[43] specifically aimed to create a state of frenzy. Furthermore, in his opinion, the delirium caused by deprivation of food and sleep served to heighten the frenzy. Maspero also speculated that the excitement created at rituals was one of the prime factors that enabled the early religious Taoists to win converts at a phenomenal rate.[44]

A Soteriological Puzzle

The Lingbao movement was heavily influenced by Buddhism. But did the Lingbao movement embrace Buddhist doctrines to the point where extinction from *samsara* replaced bodily longevity and immortality as the main goal? This question is of great importance to our study, since the main motive for Taoist asceticism was—or had been—to strengthen and transform the body. An altered view of the body's role in the process of salvation could have had a drastic impact on the form and purpose of asceticism. The *Gongde qingzhong jing* (*The Scripture on the Lightness and Heaviness of Merit*) contains a rather lengthy passage that seems to hold the key to answering our question. The passage, translated in full, reads as follows:

> [The Primordial Heavenly Worthy said], "You die, and you are born again. It becomes dark, and then light is restored. Heaven and earth rotate like the wheels of a cart. The births and deaths of people [follow one after another] like the shadow follows the body, and thus they are difficult to put an end to. Each *qi* follows the other and each seed produces causes. Good, bad, misfortune and blessing all have roots of destiny [by which they are caused]. They are caused not by heaven, earth nor [other] people; they in truth come from your own mind. The mind is, in other words, the spirit. Your bodily form is not proper to you. The reason for why you came to be born was because you came from the self-so-ness of vacuous non-being, and through certain causes entered a womb, underwent transformations and were born. The father and mother who produced you in the womb are not the father and mother of your original birth. Your true father and mother are not here [in the ordinary world]. The love of your [true] father and mother (i.e., the Tao) is great, and their lofty worth is unsurpassed. [As for] the father and mother who gave birth to you in your present existence, you were entrusted to them due to [past] causes and received the favor of their rearing and nurturing. Therefore you [should] repay them with propriety by calling them "father" and "mother."
>
> Therefore, the body that you receive is not your body. You only reside there and make it your house. By means of it you make your home in which you house yourself. You entrust yourself to it and make it your [bodily] form. I shall now teach you about being and non-being.
>
> Therefore, those who acquire the Tao no longer have a [bodily] form. When you do not have a body, what afflictions could you have? The reason for why you have afflictions is only because you have a body. When you have a body, 100 afflictions are produced. If you have no body, you will thereby enter into self-so-ness, and in your carrying out of actions you will merge with the Tao, and thereby your body and spirit will be one. If your body and mind merge into one, this will be your body of Perfection. You will return to your [true] father and mother who first gave birth to you, and thus attain the Tao. You will no longer suffer, and you will never die. Even if you undergo extinction and deliverance

(*miedu*), your spirit will go and your body will not be destroyed. For your entire life you will return to your origin to never leave it again. If the body violates and commits the 100 evil transgressions, it will come to an end and die. This is what is called death. You die and become destroyed, and then return to parents who install you in a womb. If your causes for punishment are not exhausted, you cannot return to your true father and mother. Your spirit will serve the sentence of muddy labor (in hell) and your body will turn to ashes and dust. The dust and ashes fly up and turn into light (*shuang*).[45] The *hun* soul is released [from hell] and merges with the light. Thus the *hun* soul and the light transform and merge into one, and then achieve rebirth and return to existence as a human being. The body and spirit follow each other and never leave each other. In this way, good and evil [actions] in the body each have their appropriate consequence. (33b–34b)

The aforementioned passage first addresses the issue of how to end the cycle of rebirth and suffering. It then states that all causes for one's existence lie nowhere else but in the mind (*xin*), or the spirit (*shen*). It goes on to discuss how by obtaining the Tao, one can avoid hell and rebirth to return to one's true "father and mother."

The body is described as being a mere temporary dwelling for the spirit. Unlike the spirit, it is said to not belong to oneself. The text states that having this body is the cause for all suffering. One who has obtained the Tao no longer "has a body." This apparently does not literally mean to have no body of flesh, since later on in the passage it states that the adept who "has no body" merges his body with his spirit.

The concept of "not having a body" is almost undoubtedly taken from the thirteenth chapter of the *Laozi*. There it reads, "The reason I have great trouble is that I have a body. When I no longer have a body, what trouble have I?"[46] In explaining this passage, the Heshanggong commentary[47]—the Laozi commentary preferred by the Lingbao movement—[48]states

> When you have a body you worry about labor, and are concerned about starving and freezing. Your emotions are affected by humiliations, thereby causing misfortunes.
>
> If you make yourself not have a body, you will embody the Tao spontaneously, lightly ascending upon the clouds, exiting and entering the midst of non-being. Spiritually corresponding with the Tao, what worries could you have? (*Daode zhenjing zhu* [HY682/TT363], 1/10b)

In the passage just cited, "not having a body" does not literally mean to have no physical body. This can be deduced from how the passage describes the state of "not having a body" as a prerequisite for embodying the Tao. "Not having a body" refers to a state of mind that is oblivious to concerns and worries pertaining to the sustenance and survival of the body. In such a state of mind, a person no longer needs to please the senses and gratify the ego.[49] This abstract usage of the phrase "having a body" also is found within the 300 Precepts for Monitoring the Body (see p. 110).

The importance of rising above the concerns and desires of the flesh is also eloquently stated in the *Dingzhi tongwei jing* (*The Scripture on Stabilizing the Will and Penetrating the Subtleties*).

> The essential lesson [you ought to learn] is that you must understand that [all] within the Three Realms and Three Eras (past, present, future) is empty. [You must] understand that the Three Eras are empty [and that] even though you have your body, all is going to return to emptiness. If you are clear on the principle of returning to emptiness, you will thereby be able to forget about your body. [As for] those who are able to forget about their bodies, no longer will they love their bodies. When they no longer love their bodies, they will be able to have nothing that they love. Only the Tao will be [the object of] their love. [As for] those who are able to love the Tao; the Tao will love them too. Those who obtain the love of the Tao will for the first time return to Perfection. (4b)

Taught here is the fundamental Buddhist principle of emptiness (*sunyata*), which is meant to serve as an insight that allows the adept to "forget his body" and attain Perfection. By understanding that neither his body nor any other this-worldly entity possess any permanent and self-sufficient reality, the adept can concentrate solely on seeking the Tao.

Although this ideal of disregarding the body and all other this-worldly objects is certainly conducive to asceticism, it also seems to define Perfection solely in terms of insight and spirituality. If the body is "empty" and is no more than a "temporary dwelling," it would seem that there is no possibility for the flesh to be made immortal. Was the quintessentially Taoist motive for asceticism—namely, the strengthening and transformation of the body—undermined? The key to answering this question seems to lie in how one is to understand the phrase "the body and the spirit will be one" and the term *body of Perfection*, found in the passage from the *Gongde qingzhong jing* (pp. 122–123). A passage from the *Benyuan dajie jing* sheds considerable light on this matter.

> The Perfected Man of the Great Ultimate said, "The Tao is non-being. It expands and wraps around infinitely. If you wish to seek it nearby, within your very own body it also exists. By means of being, enter into non-being. Continuously contemplate [the Tao] in order to obtain what is marvelous. The myriad things in their abundance are all but like mirages. They will all return to emptiness. The same is so with the human body.

When the body dies, the spirit leaves. It is comparable to a house. When the house is destroyed, a person cannot stand there. If the body is damaged, the spirit will not reside there. You [therefore] must control your thoughts to stabilize your will. [You must] make your body still in order to make your spirit peaceful. Treasure your *qi* to preserve your *jing*. Forgetting both your thoughts and concerns, darkly contemplate and look within, and your body and spirit will merge into one. If the body and spirit merge into one, they will soon become the body of Perfection." (2a)

The body is again described here as being a temporary dwelling. However, the passage then describes how, through meditation, one can keep the body and spirit together and stay alive. It also clearly states the importance of avoiding bodily damage. Keeping the body and spirit together involves not only intense meditation and mental discipline but also the stabilization of the body and the retention of *qi* and *jing*. This eventually creates the "body of Perfection." Although the afore-mentioned passage also is very vague about what the "body of Perfection" is, its attainment is apparently tantamount to discovering the Tao that dwells in the body. The text also assures that by employing one's temporal body (being), one obtains and enters the eternal Tao (non-being) latent within it. It thus appears that the body and its maintenance still held an integral place in the new soteriology.

Yet further questions naturally arise regarding the nature of this "body of Perfection." Was it supposed to be a rarefied, transformed body? Is it best under-stood as a metaphor for the innate, ineffable Tao (or Non-being) that the adept somehow comes to terms with? Was it considered an entity that had to be liberated from the flesh at some point, or was the entire flesh supposed to be transformed into an eternal entity? Interpretations may have varied among Lingbao adherents themselves. While they were eager to adopt the doctrines of Buddhism, they also felt the need to leave open the possibility for bodily immortality. It is thus note-worthy that the *Gongde qingzhong jing*, while calling the body a "temporary dwelling," also contains the following passage that affirms the possibility of bodily ascension:

Inside the human body there are the 36,000 gods of the Three Palaces and Six Bowels. When the human body does evil, the bodily deities report it to the Three Officials. When the human body does good, they recommend the person for selection as an immortal. [As for] life, death, punishment and blessing, none of these are not first and foremost caused by the bodily deities. Shadows and echoes respond appropriately in their natural manner. People are born endowed with *qi*. The *qi* gathers and forms the gods. If a person is able to nurture his *qi*, the gods will thus exist [in him] for a long time. If you contemplate internally and guard what is Perfect, what is Perfect will not depart from the body. If there is [an adept] who obtains the Life-Extending Talisman of the Great Mystery, the 36,000 gods will gather their *qi* and manifest their forms, raising up his body as he ascends to the heavens in broad daylight. Hastening about in a chariot of clouds, he will ascend and enter into the vacuous emptiness (the sky). If you lose your *jing* and lose your *qi*, your myriad [bodily] gods will escape and fall out [of your body]. Your gods will wander and your *qi* will scatter, and your [bodily] form will perish as an empty corpse. (21a)

Of note here is the usage of the character *shen* (which I have rendered as "gods" rather than "spirit"), which refers not to a single entity equated to the "mind" (*xin*) but rather to thousands of entities best understood as personifications of the forces that animate each and every part of the body. For the preservation and mobilization of these entities, the adept is told to treasure and nurture the basic vital components (*jing, qi*) of the body. (One Lingbao text, the *Ershisi shengtu jing*, outlines in some detail how the bodily deities are to be mobilized through incantations, visualizations, talisman swallowing, and the imbibing of the Five Sprouts, solar essences, and lunar essences).[50] If we assume that Lingbao adherents took the aforementioned passage literally, we can conclude that in spite of Buddhist influence, they still believed in the perpetuation of the flesh. However, we cannot assume this, and it seems more reasonable to think that Lingbao adherents varied in their understanding of immortality. Also, many of those who believed in "ascension in broad daylight" literally may have seen it as a goal too lofty and elusive for them.

Of paramount interest, when considering the impact of Buddhist doctrines on Taoist theories of immortality, is the usage of the word *miedu*, which I have translated as "extinction and deliverance" (see pp. 122–123). *Miedu* is originally a Buddhist term that denotes the ultimate salvation for Buddhists, the liberation from *samsara* brought on by enlightenment. In the Lingbao scriptures, the term also describes a worthy mode of salvation. However, it is only the second best alternative to the highest ideal, "ascension in broad daylight" (the best alternative is the "liberation from the corpse," where bodily death is "feigned"). When one underwent *miedu*, one was thought to initially die. However, the spirit would not go to hell for punishment, and the body would not decompose. Eventually, one day the spirit and body would be reunited, bringing about resurrection. This belief is most clearly attested to in the *Mingzhen ke* (The Curriculum of Bright Perfection) (4a). This scripture describes how different practices and lifestyles bring about their appropriate retributions. The most blessed are said to ascend to the realm of Yuqing (Jade Purity) "in broad daylight," while the immoral are to suffer the torments of hell (these torments are portrayed vividly in the text). Between these two groups lie those who attain "liberation from the corpse" and those who attain "extinction and deliverance" (*miedu*). The latter are described as follows:

> [As for those who upon being] born into the world, refine their Perfection
> by ingesting the divine elixir and protect and vitalize their Divine

Chambers and Five Palaces (viscera) with the Five Rocks, their merit is slight and their virtue is narrow. Their destiny is not yet to ascend to heaven. Their bodies will achieve extinction and deliverance, and their skeletons (or "bodies"?) will be fragrant and full forever throughout hundreds of thousands of *kalpas*. After a while, they will return to form and once again obtain life and return to the midst of humans. Their wisdom will be thoroughly perceptive and they will foresee good and bad fortune. They will command and control demons and spirits. Transmigrating unceasingly they will definitely be able to receive documents and become Perfected Men of the Nine Palaces [of the realm of Taiqing]. (4a)

Most interesting here is the reference to the method of "protecting" the "Five Palaces" with "Five Rocks." This very likely refers to the method of boiling "white rocks," which was promoted by the Shangqing movement as a means for achieving resurrection and "avoiding grains" (see pp. 65–67).

Also useful for enhancing our understanding of the Taoist usage of the word *miedu* is a story from the *Lingbao benxing jing*, preserved in the *Yunji qiqian* 101/11a–12b.[51] The story is a hagiographical account concerning the Perfected Venerable Lord of Cinnabar Numinosity. Prior to his apotheosis, this Perfected Being was a man named Zheng Ren-an, who lived in the mythical World of Chanli. To summarize the story briefly, Zheng Ren-an, who had been training alone in the mountains since the age of twelve, encountered a certain Master Xuanhe. From him he received the "Perfect Writs of the Black Emperor" (*Lingbao chishu wuqi xuantian heidi zhenwen*) and the "Ten Superior Precepts of Wisdom" (*Zhihui shangpin shijie*). Some time later, a huge flood swept the nation. Zheng Ren-an employed the Perfect Writs to rescue the populace. He then presented the Writs to the king. The Writs immediately flew up to the heavens from which they had originally issued. By relinquishing possession of the Writs, Zheng Ren-an had disqualified himself for heavenly ascension. Thus, we are told

His fate was to undergo extinction and deliverance. He feigned [the end of his] destiny and proclaimed his death at the Hill of Beirong. [There] his holy corpse was exposed for 30-odd years, during which the body never decayed. Its lustrous complexion was fresh and clear, no different from when he was alive. (*Yunji qiqian* 101/11b)

We also are told that when a forest fire raged through the hill, the body and the area surrounding it remained unharmed, while a radiance of three colors emanated from the body. When the king, out of curiosity, built a fire to burn the body, the body was resurrected.

Finally, regarding *miedu*, one must mention the *Taishang dongxuan lingbao miedu wulian shengshi miaojing* (*The Marvelous Scripture on Extinction and Deliverance, the Fivefold Refinement for Reviving the Corpse*).[52] This text contains a funerary liturgy designed to bring about *miedu* for those unable to do so through their own training and merit. The liturgical ritual is supposed to have the effect of preserving the interred corpse, while the *hun* soul is delivered from the underworld and sent to the Southern Palace of Fire (see pp. 81–82) for purification and refinement. Ultimately, after a very long time, the body and po soul are to be resurrected and reunited with the *hun* soul. Eventually, some day heavenly ascension is to be achieved.

Returning our attention to the passage quoted from the *Gongde qingzhong jing* on pp. 122–123, we can see that in the Lingbao version of the transmigration theory, the spirit (*shen, hun*) and body (*shen, qi, po*) are in all cases—good or bad—inalienably associated. Even in the worst scenario, where the transgressor's soul is tortured in hell while the body decomposes into dust, the soul and body (transformed to dust and then light) eventually reunite to form the entity that enters a womb for rebirth. In sum, the Lingbao soteriological scheme upholds the significance of the body. The blessed person is characterized by the degree to which the body is kept intact and how the soul evades the torments of hell.

Still, some of the passages we have examined contain statements that stress the body's impermanence and glorify a merging with the Non-being that sounds suspiciously noncorporeal. An inner tension seems to have existed between views emphasizing the perpetuation of the flesh and views deemphasizing it.

CHAPTER SEVEN

Criticisms of Heretical Asceticism in the *Yuqing jing*

During the next few centuries after the appearance of the Lingbao scriptures, newer scriptures appeared that emulated their format and expanded on their central themes and doctrines.[1] These newer scriptures, some of which survive today, are hefty compositions ranging between 30,000 and 100,000 characters in length. Anonymous in their authorship, they contain stories and discourses allegedly uttered in the inconceivably remote past by gods and immortals in transcendent realms. They claim to expound the Great Vehicle, the highest and truest doctrine that brings forth universal salvation.

One such scripture is the *Yuqing jing* (The Scripture of [the Realm of] Jade Purity, HY1301/TT1022–1024).[2] The *Yuqing jing* is an anonymous work that contains no direct references to actual people and events. While this makes it very difficult to date, it appears to have been written some time in the sixth century. This observation is, however, tentative. The most that can be said with certainty is that it was written after the Lingbao scriptures and before 753 C.E. Internal evidence seems to provide a hint that it was written in northern China.[3]

The *Yuqing jing*, as one would expect from its great length,[4] covers a wide variety of themes. Much of the text deals with topics of interest to general believers, such as the observance of moral precepts, almsgiving, devotion to Taoist deities, and participation in communal retreats. It also covers matters of interest to more advanced practitioners, such as fasting, meditation, and rules of conduct for mountain dwelling.[5] However, the most salient feature of the *Yuqing jing* is its denunciations of heretical forms of asceticism.[6]

The basic heresy attacked in the *Yuqing jing* is the view that maintains that one must destroy the body so the spirit can be liberated and saved. In terms of practice, the text claims that this heresy leads to ascetic abuses that injure or kill the body. The attacks against heresy occur within mythical narratives about demons, "barbarians," and "infidels"[7] who corrupt the world with their perverse ways.

An intriguing question is whether or not these villains are allegorical represen-
tations of the adherents of rival religions. As we shall see, the *Yuqing jing* exhibits a
vehemently antagonistic attitude toward foreigners in general and Buddhists in
particular. This is highly undestandable in light of the acerbic, vindictive quality
that the Taoist–Buddhist rivalry had taken on since the fifth century.[8] However,
closer examination of the *Yuqing qing* seems to show that the text's main objective
was not so much to discredit rival religions as it was to denounce the heresy. In the
opinion of the author (or authors), the heresy existed among both Taoists and non-
Taoists.

"The Chapter on the Original Arising" (*benqi pin*), the first of the *Yuqing
jing*'s twenty chapters, contains the text's first description and criticism of
improper ascetic acts. As a whole, the chapter describes how the power and
teachings of the Primordial Heavenly Worthy act as the sole vehicle for universal
salvation throughout successive cosmic cycles. This it does through a mythical
narrative of events in the "world of Qixian" (*qixian* translates into "abandoning the
morally upright"). According to this narrative, the world of Qixian was nearing the
end of the cosmic cycle. It was afflicted with widespread suffering caused by
general human malice and warfare, combined with natural disasters and epidemics.
Eerie and sinister phenomena took place. The earth grew hair and fur. Animals
began talking like human beings. Under these horrific circumstances, people were
resorting to suicide and cannibalism. The Primordial Heavenly Worthy saw this and
took pity on the world of Qixian. He decided to restore its happiness and vitality
and took special measures to postpone its impending devastation indefinitely. He
thus descended upon the world to expound his doctrines. For seven days and seven
nights, his body emitted a radiance that pervaded the entire world. He inscribed the
Perfect Writs of the Five Monarchs and with them "protected" the five directions,
recharging the world with the creative, life-sustaining force of the Tao. Through the
workings of the good gods commanded by the Five Monarchs, crops became
plentiful, the climate became agreeable, demons were subdued, and morality was
restored among the masses.

The narrative goes on to describe the good deeds of a wise and virtuous king
named Dezheng. Out of gratitude to the Primordial Heavenly Worthy, Dezheng
built temples and monasteries and directed all of his subjects to worship the Tao
and confess their transgressions day and night. After a nationwide retreat of seven
days and seven nights, the Primordial Heavenly Worthy manifested his divine
countenance to the populace and bestowed them with ten precepts.[9] Dezheng
himself was transmitted secret methods, after which he abdicated the throne to one
of his sons and concentrated on Taoist self-training.

The text then describes how the throne was passed down from generation to
generation while Dezheng and his son Shanxiu (who had also abdicated) trained

themselves and attained the status of "Great Perfected Being." One day, a deity called the Perfect Lord Without Superior proclaimed to them what their future task was to be and predicted the horrific events that were to eventually occur in the world.

(I)   The Emperor of Heaven has made his calculations according to the cycles and will order you to go down to indoctrinate and deliver the living masses. Attending the Heavenly Worthy, you will go below the four heavens to teach and indoctrinate the various nations and spread forth the *qi* of the Tao. Why is this? It is to postpone the disasters of this *kalpa*'s fire-*qi*. By adhering to and practicing the religion of the Tao, we can subdue the calamities of the *Yang*-Nine (the Great *Kalpa*),[10] and make the fire essence disappear. When it gets to a later *kalpa*, heaven and earth will be destroyed and the merits of the populace will be exhausted so that [our] doctrines cannot save them. When the cycle comes to its limit, it will naturally be like this.

At the beginning of the Water *Kalpa*,[11] our Tao will greatly flourish. For 370,000 years, people will be pure and naive. But later, the Great Tao will gradually cease to be carried out, and the *yin qi* (evil energy) will become vigorous. The people, in seeking blessings, will set up empty burial mounds and build numerous shrines throughout the world. Men and women with wicked hearts will practice the methods of extinction and will not accord with [our] ritual regulations. Yelling loudly, they will seek death. Some will enter pits of fire and some will throw themselves into deep pools. Mutilating and dismembering themselves, their hordes will worship and sing hymns while sobbing and weeping. Some of them will enter into the empty burial mounds and sit silently. Some will embrace corpses or venerate dried bones. Some will make altars out of manure. Some will smear the earth with fragrant mud. Some, because they do not respect their fathers and mothers, will engage in all kinds of bitter training. Some of them will eat impure and hideous things. There will be nothing that they will not resort to, but to the very end they will not acquire the Tao of Proper Perfection. The minds of people will be prejudiced, and there will be no righteousness between fathers and sons. Amidst the wicked religion(s), factions will arise.

Before the Great Water *Kalpa* there will be a Small Water *Kalpa* (flood)[12] that will subside only after ten years. During the four thousand years after this, from amidst the wicked religion there will arise a military revolt. Plotting harm amongst themselves, some of them will proclaim themselves to be kings, only to self-destruct within 10 to 100 days. There will be no propriety among fathers and sons. Using their force they will exploit those who are weak. Blood relatives will commit lewd acts with each other. Even though they will have human bodies, they will not have human hearts. Viciously and vindictively they will compete with each other and have no mutual trust. In this way the time will come when the Wicked Way will gradually arise and the *yin qi* will flourish to the utmost. Before long, drifting and drowning [in the Great Flood], people will transform into fish, and the scaly dragons will eat the people. At this moment, the Law [of the Tao] will elect its chosen people and place them in the homestead of blessings. You must toil and suffer from morning till evening tirelessly [if you want to be one of the elect]. This is called the Great Tao. Spread it among the people. One's destiny is in one's own hands. [Destiny] is controlled and maintained by people [themselves]. If the mind is proper, the Tao will respond to it. If you follow the wicked, misfortunes will come your way. If you are fond of killing, you will only slay yourself. You must carry out great compassion. (1/11b–12b)

Undoubtedly, the author intended the aforementioned story to serve as a warning to his contemporaries. The "world of Qixian" probably refers to this very world. If so, the myth portrays events of the inconceivably remote past, and the ominous predictions describe events that the author had witnessed or anticipated witnessing during his lifetime. While this interpretation may not be entirely correct, the author certainly intended his readers to see parallels between the "world of Qixian" and their own world.

The author appears to have anticipated a cosmic deluge. He believed that Taoism originated in the inconceivably remote past when the Primordial Heavenly Worthy graced the world with his presence and imbued it with his life-giving force. The author bemoaned the plight of his own age and saw it as a corrupt time pervaded by *yin qi* (evil energy). To his chagrin, he saw a decline in the Taoist religion and a simultaneous emergence of wicked religion ("the Wicked Way").

The author employs the most typical polemical ploy for discrediting his adversaries, accusing them of sedition and extreme moral corruption. More important, the adherents of the wicked religion(s) are portrayed as having a morbid fondness for death that is reflected in their objects of worship and extreme bodily mortifications. The latter include the eating of impurities, self-mutilation, and suicide. The text describes such "bitter training" as "methods of extinction," since they are intended to bring about bodily death. The author denounces these practices as being futile. He urges his readers to remain faithful to Taoism and continue to propagate it amid all the evil surrounding them. He further asserts that while being a Taoist also involves much strenuous hardship, it offers the rewards of survival and eternal bliss.

The nineteenth chapter of the *Yuqing jing*, the "Chapter on Perfected Man Mingwei's Assertion of Might over the Wicked" ("Mingwei zhenren weiye pin"), describes how the Perfected Man Mingwei[13] manifests his doctrines and apotropaic methods in the world to combat evil forces. Denunciations of wicked religion are found abundantly in this chapter as well. In one passage, the emergence of wicked religion is attributed to worldly demons.

(II) The Great Perfected Being Mingwei was aware beforehand[14] of the prejudiced and wicked ways of the later *kalpa*. Wickedness would give rise to *yin qi*, and a filthy and evil world would immediately and easily come to exist. When the purity and simplicity was lost, flippancy and deceitfulness would arise at once. The Four Devas of the lower realm would proclaim themselves to be Divine Kings. Devils such as these would take on the name "God of Heaven," and [in the] filthy and evil world they would pervade the lands down below. Under the Four Devas, the spirits (*jing*)[15] of the rocks of the mountains and forests would possess living people. All of them would mimic each other in claiming to be Immortal Kings. Joining together with the monsters of the wicked *qi* of the Six Heavens, they would form mobs and alliances. Their tributaries would disperse and pervade, establishing their prominence over the generations. Traitors of the Tao would make offerings [to them] and pray for blessings. [The demons] would gnaw on the *jing* and *qi* of people and eat the blood and [blood] vessels of people, shortening their life spans as they remained unaware. Entering into people's bodies they would be able to make them hate life and love death. In this way the various demons would enter into your bodies (the bodies of future people) and their descendants would grow up and flourish. [Because] of the rampant and arbitrary nature of their bodily impulses and forces (*jingqi*), they would have [sexual] intercourse with living people. Worm-monsters and demonic women would also have the ability to make people discern the various doctrines on emptiness and be jealous of the Way of Life. Whenever there were men and women who cultivated and studied the Way of Life, these various evil demons would come to harm them all at once, wanting people to die so they could claim their *hun* souls as companions. For this reason they would resent the Way of Life. As for students [of the Tao] of later times, if your body is able to accomplish the Tao, wicked monsters and evil mobs will submit to your commands and will not be at their free abandon. For this reason, people who study the Tao should clearly be aware of this evil disease that is infidel religion. [They must] have prior knowledge of the methods of Mingwei, so that they can slay [the wicked beings that] haunt them and thereby protect their bodies and spirits. (9/3b–4a)

The founding of the wicked religion(s) is attributed here to worldly demons who entertain pretensions of being mighty and divine. They delude humans into accepting their pretenses, and by doing so gain benefits at their expense. These benefits include more than just offerings of foods and material goods; the demons eat the vital forces of their worshippers (this may be an indirect allusion to human sacrifice) and receive their sexual favors. They brainwash them into hating life and loving death. Most noteworthy here is that those possessed by demons become well versed in doctrines of "emptiness," and these doctrines seem to be at least partially responsible for making them fond of death and disdainful toward life. Taoism, in stark contrast, is "the Way of Life." The arrogant demons are envious of "the Way of Life," presumably because it issues from superior forces and deities. They do their utmost to hinder those who pursue the "Way of Life," and try to keep them entrapped in *samsara* as their own "companions."

This theme of pretentious demons trying to ensnare people through false doctrines is also found in the sixteenth chapter, "Chapter on the Assertion of Might over the Devils." There we are told of how wicked immortals from the two realms of form and desire[16] tried to challenge the Primordial Heavenly Worthy to a contest of divine powers. The self-confidence of the wicked immortals was seemingly justified, since they possessed very marvelous powers and had attained life spans of 80,000 Great *Kalpas*. Their challenge was met not personally by the Primordial Heavenly Worthy, but by his disciple Zhaoling, who easily defeated and rendered them unconscious. Upon regaining consciousness, they became aware of their shortcomings. They realized that their bodies were ultimately doomed to "decaying and rotting" and that they would eventually undergo death and rebirth. Perfected Man Zhaoling then told them the true identity of the deity they had been serving in the lower realms. This deity—who assumed names such as "the Immortal King of the Four Heavens" and "the Divine King"—was actually no deity at all; he was merely a lowly spirit from Mt. Kunlun. Zhaoling then told the wicked immortals to immediately return to the lower realms, since they were polluting the sacred realm with their malodorant, corpselike bodies. After they returned to the lower realm, their leader Luobi reported what they had experienced and heard to the spirit of Mt. Kunlun. The spirit immediately fainted in horror. Upon regaining consciousness, he warned Luobi not to tell anything about it to anybody. This was because if word got out, he would lose all of his power over the people of the world. The text goes on to state that to this very day, the spirit of Mt. Kunlun and his wicked immortals continue to deceive, possess, and receive worship from humankind. However, when the Heavenly Worthy of the Golden Palace Gate (a messianic Perfected Being) appears in the world, they will all be exterminated.

In such a way, the *Yuqing jing* depicts an ongoing conflict between transcendent Perfected Beings and earthly demons. While the demons seem to constantly get their way in the mundane world, the ultimate victory is to be won by the forces of good.

The *Yuqing jing* maintains that people who are demonically deluded into hating life and loving death typically practice excessive and self-destructive austerities. A truly gruesome example is given in the following passage from the nineteenth chapter:

(III) In bygone days at the beginning of the Fire Kalpa,[17] a spirit of a mountain in the Rong region (western lands of the "barbarians") disguised himself in human form. His body possessed all the various marks (*xiang*)[18] [of a saint]. He went about in the world teaching and indoctrinating. He acquired a following of 80,000 [people]. He taught them how to worship fire, along with the method of observing water. For twelve years he sucked on the *jing* and *qi* of people. People all lost sight of what was correct, and their wicked views thus took shape. At that time, the various people of like mind resigned themselves to death, each of them entering into [a pile of] dry grass where they folded their hands together and knelt naked with their cap strings undone. A hired hand then set fire to the hay, and the flames immediately burned and injured the 80,000-odd people. Their hair was charred, their skin was wrent and fluid from their blisters splattered out. Their arms and legs became twisted and shrunken as they fell curled up on the ground. In bitter pain they regretted [what they had done], but were unable to utter a sound. At that time, the mountain spirit snapped his fingers and commended them, saying, "All living species will in the end return to annihilation. The body of confusion is the dwelling place of a hundred poisons. You should quickly distance yourself from it and seek early liberation from it. You must annihilate this body and thereby seek the Dharma Body.[19] If you cannot stand the severity of the fire-poison, you should go into the deep pool." As the mountain spirit finished saying this, the 80,000-odd people crawled into the water. They were sent adrift by the wind and waves, and were devoured by the water creatures. The River Spirit seized their *hun* and *po* souls and the Water Bureau put their essence and light (*jingshuang*)[20] to labor. They have been suffering under this banishment for over 7,000 years, endlessly up to this very day. Once you fall victim to the wicked, you cannot escape from [the bad consequences in] life and death. At that time, the spirit of the mountain of Rong, who had enticed and murdered common folk, knew that he was guilty. Fearing the might of Heaven, he hid himself deep within some rocks. [But] in the spring the God of Thunder exposed him by using his thunder, and put him to the task of tending his dragons. [The mountain spirit now] labors painstakingly day and night without any freedom. In this way, the method for controlling powerful spirits can be carried out by employing the Duke of Thunder to behead them and tear them apart. (9/8b–9b)

Noteworthy first of all here is that the wicked religion is ascribed a foreign origin. The place of its origin is described vaguely as "Rong," a word that was used to refer to any "barbarian" territory west of China. Here we have a prime example of the fierce xenophobia that pervades the *Yuqing jing*. Also interesting, for reasons to be discussed later, is the reference to fire worship. However, of greatest interest is the reasoning by which the mountain spirit justifies and exalts the burning of his followers. The essential idea is that the human body is the "body of confusion,"[21] filled with "poisons" that hinder the enlightenment and liberation of the soul. The mountain spirit also reasons that since life is bound to end anyway, it is foolish to cling to it. He encourages his followers to hasten the body's destruction and the soul's liberation through suicide. The passage goes on to describe the hideous consequences suffered by those who took his advice. The reader is thus sternly warned not to heed doctrines resembling those taught by the mountain spirit.

Also interesting is how the exorcistic method, "employing the Duke of Thunder," is prescribed for combating "powerful spirits." The mountain spirit depicted in the tale may be an allegorical allusion to certain types of preachers active during the time the author lived. However, the mountain spirit also seems to personify the invisible demons that were thought to possess people and cause them to embrace false doctrines. "Employing the Duke of Thunder" appears to have been an exorcism for deprogramming heretics.

The most detailed description of demonic heresies is found in yet another passage from the nineteenth chapter. This passage provides substantial clues, which when combined with information from previously cited passages (I, II, and III), can help us determine what religion(s) the author may have had in mind when describing "wicked religion(s)".

(IV) At that time, also, there was a mountain spirit of [Mt.] Tiewei located in the direction of [the element of] metal [which is] the southwest. He transformed himself into a human and went out into the world to teach and indoctrinate. His doctrine pervaded the wild, barbaric regions of the west. Throughout a hundred nations it changed its form into 500-odd varieties. These (the adherents of the heresies) are called infidels. They worshipped various phenomena such as the sky, the earth, the sun, the moon, the stars, wind, water, metal, wood, hearth-fire, city walls and roads. [They carried out] all kinds of bitter training. They changed their attire and physical appearances. They set up statues and made offerings, and wrote their scriptures on tree leaves. They wounded and harmed their bodies and visages. They wore Rong-style clothing. They employed thaumaturgic mantras. They entered the cities to beg. Each one of them would say, "This is [what brings about] the best of effects." In their retreats and festivals they used blood sacrifices as they praised and cried out to the "King of Heaven." Some of them called themselves "Brahman Masters" and devoted themselves to boiling and slaying [sacrificial victims] for the purpose of serving the God(s) of the Heavens, in hope of gaining great blessings. Seeking worldly wealth and benefits, they would each say, "Anybody who gives alms to me will obtain limitless blessings." Infidels such as these took possession of the bodies of people. [Those possessed] would sob, wail and pull out their hair. They would dance about striking themselves, as they resigned themselves to death and sought annihilation. Some would sit silently in dark rooms, and when they clearly saw forms of light they would claim they had seen a great saint. Some could [fore]see all appearances of punishment and blessing (possessed clairvoyant powers). Common folk would hear about this and compete with each other in coming forth and giving them alms. They abandoned their valuable treasures, wives, children, slaves, horses, cities and farms [and gave them to the infidels]. Some would [even] give up their bodies and lives, their minds not hesitating to relinquish their eyes, bone marrow and brains. This was because those infidels taught them to love death. Whenever they saw a dead person they would sing out praises. They would abandon corpses in wild fields and refer to this as "being born in heaven." Gathering in crowds they would worship and rejoice, exclaiming, "Great stalwarts and superior men hate the world and seek deliverance [from it]. Their bodies fill up [the bellies of] the birds and the beasts as their lumps of consciousness[22] live on in heaven. Confusion no longer continues. Is this not joyous?" Such is the way of the bitter training of the various infidels. They would build large bonfires and say, "If good men and good women are able to enter the bonfire and roast their bodies, they are to be called Great Stalwarts of the First Order. They will be able to depart from their confusion and realize the utmost in results. They will obtain the undefiled ground of perpetual enjoyment. They will get to ascend to the unwavering ground of perpetual enjoyment." These various infidels would praisingly say, "Great Stalwarts are brave and strong. The power of their merit is without comparison. They are able to bring about great benefits to the world." Foolish people would see this and eagerly burn their bodies. At the same time, the infidel roaming spirits would fly about in the air, singing hymns and performing all kinds of music to keep them resigned and content [with being burnt to death]. Thus in the hundred Rong territories, over a span of several decades, more than half the population was injured and killed by the methods and coaxings of these infidels. (9/10a–11a)

Mt. Tiewei, described here as the source of the wicked religion, is the outermost of the eight ring-shaped mountains said to encircle Mt. Sumeru, the cosmic mountain of Hindu and Buddhist legend. According to the Hindu and Buddhist traditions, Mt. Sumeru is the center of the universe and the abode of lofty deities.[23] Here it is described as a mountain in the southwest. Again, the wicked religion is ascribed a foreign origin, and its false doctrines are blamed for wiping out half of the Western "barbarian" population. The passage is most likely meant to warn that the same consequences will be suffered in China if heresy is allowed to prevail.

So what religion (or religions) did the author hold responsible for propagating heresy in China? From where does he get his harrowing images? In light of the fact that Taoism and Buddhism were engaged in a bitter rivalry during the late Six Dynasties and Tang periods, the "wicked religion" would seem most likely to be an allegorical allusion to Buddhism. This speculation can be substantially backed up by information from passages I through IV.

The "empty burial mounds" mentioned in passage I most likely allude to Buddhist stupas. The "dried bones" probably represent the relics, or *sarira*, of saints that are worshipped by Buddhists. The well-known Buddhist veneration of such things was apparently misconstrued by the author (perhaps knowingly) as a fondness for death. The ways of the "wicked religion(s)" are described as "methods of extinction." By describing them in such terms, the *Yuqing jing* seems to be accusing Buddhists of inciting people toward religious suicide by setting forth extinction and liberation as the ultimate goal.

The Four Devas described as pretentious demons in passage II most likely refer to the Four Deva Kings.[24] These four deities bear a prominent place in Buddhist legend and iconography as the faithful and righteous protectors of Buddhism. Describing them as wicked demons seems to be yet another way of deriding Buddhism. In passage II, people possessed by worm monsters and demonic women are described as being good at discussing doctrines of "emptiness." This appears to be a reference to Mahayana Buddhist doctrines that emphasize the "empty" (*sunyata*)[25] quality of all objects and concepts. The passage also may be suggesting that the preoccupation with emptiness has caused Buddhists to disdain human life. The statements uttered by the mountain spirit in passage III, which justify the destruction of the body as a means for cutting off confusion and attaining liberation, seem to most clearly reflect how the author(s) blamed Buddhist doctrines for encouraging self-mutilation and suicide.

Similar statements are attributed to the "infidels" in passage IV. These "infidels" are described as mendicants and practitioners of seated meditation. Begging and meditation were standard activities for Buddhist monks, as the author was presumably well aware. It also has been well documented by modern scholarship how certain prominent Buddhist monks during the Six Dynasties period, especially in the north, achieved great popularity and political patronage due to their alleged clairvoyant powers, efficacious mantras, and other thaumaturgic abilities. These characteristics are ascribed to the "infidels" in passage IV. Although the Tantric Zhenyan school of Buddhism (noted for its mantras) did not flourish in China until the eighth century, Buddhist scriptures containing mantras were translated into Chinese already in the early third century, and numerous others were translated during the fourth and fifth centuries. The author of the *Yuqing jing* was probably aware of Buddhist mantras and thaumaturgy.[26]

However, many of the practices attributed to the "infidels" bear virtually no similarity to Buddhist practices. The worship of profane demons and spirits described in passages II, III, and IV, the blood sacrifice mentioned in passage IV, and the human sacrifice hinted at in passage II, are more reminiscent of the practices of some indigenous Chinese folk cults.[27]

Another foreign religion whose practices may have been known by the author is Zoroastrianism. As has been pointed out by Chen Yuan in his article, "Huoxianjiao ru Zhongguo kao" ("A Study on the Entry of Zoroastrianism into China"),[28] dynastic histories (the *Weishu, Beishi,* and *Suishu*) contain evidence indicating that Zoroastrianism was known to the Chinese by the early sixth century. Certain members within the courts of the Northern Wei, Northern Ji, and Northern Zhou dynasties appear to have practiced Zoroastrian rituals. Admittedly, Zoroastrianism was probably practiced primarily by foreign residents and had very few converts among the Chinese. Still, it is not altogether improbable that the author of the *Yuqing jing* knew of Zoroastrianism and saw it as a rival in the competition for imperial favor. His familiarity with Zoroastrianism is most glaringly hinted at by the mention of fire worship in passages III and IV. In Zoroastrianism, the supreme god Ahura Mazda and his assisting divinities (*amesha spentas* or *yazatas*) are worshipped daily. Their presence in the world is believed to be manifested in various tangible objects, toward which worship is directed. Foremost among these objects is fire. Zoroastrian temples feature a large fire that is kept burning at all times. The sky, earth, sun, moon, and stars also are among their objects of worship. All of these are mentioned in passage IV as being worshipped by the "infidels." Zoroastrian worship also involves blood sacrifice, which is mentioned in passage IV. The terms used in the dynastic histories to refer to the gods worshipped in Persia are *huoshen* (God of Fire) and *tianshen* (God of the Heavens).[29] Chen Yuan speculates that the latter term was used because the Chinese recognized the worship of the sun, moon, and stars as the foremost trait of Persian religion. It is highly noteworthy that the "infidels" in passage IV worship "the God(s) of the Heavens," and passage II tells of how the demons of the world took on the title of "God of Heaven" (*tianshen*). But perhaps most revealing is passage IV's mention of burial by exposure. This practice, also mentioned in the dynastic histories, is customary among Zoroastrians. Because they consider corpses ritually impure and include fire and earth among their sacred objects, Zoroastrians refuse to desecrate fire and earth by cremating or burying corpses. They believe that the souls of the righteous leave the body at death to reside in Heaven, where they await the end of the age. In the end, they are reunited with their bones (left bare of the old flesh devoured by birds and animals) and resurrected in a body of new, pure flesh. From then on they live eternally in Ahura Mazda's new kingdom on earth. In passage IV, the "infidels" express a similar belief, stating that the soul lives on in Heaven while the corpse satiates the birds and beasts.[30] In sum, some of the practices attributed to "infidels" in the *Yuqing jing* may be allusions to Zoroastrian practices, and Zoroastrians may have been among the foes the author sought to discredit.

One thing is certain; the "infidels" depicted in the *Yuqing jing* are not modeled exclusively on the adherents of any single religion. They are best understood as composite creations of the author's imagination. To create his villains, the author seems to have blended the images of various religious opponents and embellished them with gruesome details derived from his own morbid fantasy.

Admittedly, something resembling self-mutilation and self-cremation seems to have been carried out by some Chinese Buddhists. Kenneth K.S. Chen has brought to attention some shocking descriptions of happenings that occurred during festivals in honor of a famous relic (a finger bone of the Buddha) enshrined at the Famen Temple near the Tang dynasty capital Chang'an.[31] During these festivals, the relic was brought to the imperial palace and kept there for three days to be worshipped by members of the court. It was then put on public display, whereupon ferocious religious frenzy would ensue. A description of one such festival that occurred in 819 is found in a memorial presented in protest by the Confucian scholar Han Yu. In it, Han Yu alleges that multitudes of people burned their heads and roasted their fingers in a show of piety. A firsthand description of another such festival in 873 (which has been translated and quoted in full by Chen) is found in Su E's *Duyang zapian.*

> At that time, a soldier cut off his left arm in front of the Buddha's relic, and while holding it with his hand, he reverenced the relic each time he took a step, his blood sprinkling the ground all the while. As for those who walked on their elbows and knees, biting off their fingers or cutting off their hair, their numbers could not be counted. There was also a monk who covered his head with artemisia, a practice known as disciplining the head. When the pile of artemisia was ignited, the pain caused the monk to shake his head and to cry out, but young men in the marketplace held him tight so that he could not move. When the pain became unbearable, he cried out and fell prostrate on the ground. With his head scorched and his deportment disorderly, he was the object of laughter of all the spectators.[32]

The author of the *Yuqing jing* may have witnessed or heard of events similar to this. However, many of his most powerful images of ascetic abuses may actually be drawn from passages in Buddhist texts that describe the austerities of non-Buddhist Indian ascetics. One scripture that the author of the *Yuqing jing* may have derived his images from is the *Guoqu xianzai yinyuan jing,* a well-known narrative of the Buddha's life, translated into Chinese around 450 C.E. Included in the narrative is an episode where the young prince Siddhartha Gautama (the Buddha), shortly after leaving his home in pursuit of enlightenment, visited a forest inhabited by anchorites (*xianren*). There he witnessed their austerities.

[The prince] observed the activities of those various anchorites. Some of them made their garments out of grass. Some of them made their clothing out of the bark and leaves of trees. Some of them ate only weeds, trees, flowers and fruits, eating just once per day, once every two days, or once every three days. In such ways they practiced the methods of self-starvation. Some of them worshipped water and fire. Some of them venerated the sun and moon. Some of them stood on one leg. Some of them lay down in the dust and dirt. Some of them lay down on thorns. Some of them lay down next to water and fire. The prince, upon witnessing bitter training such as this, asked the anchorite Baqie, "Your present practicing of these deeds of hardship is truly extraordinary. What results do you seek to attain from this?" The anchorite answered, "We practice this bitter training because we want to live in heaven." The prince again asked, "Even though the various heavens are enjoyable, [existence there] comes to an end when your merits expire. Transmigrating in the six paths of existence, in the end it will be but a bundle of suffering. Why do you put to practice what is but the cause for suffering, only to receive the retribution of suffering?"[33]

The resemblance between the ways of the anchorites here and the "infidels" in the *Yuqing jing* (passage IV in particular) is quite striking. Described here are extreme austerities accompanied by the worship of water, fire, sun, and moon. The motive cited for the austerities is the attainment of life in heaven, as is the case in passage IV. The Buddha rejects their methods because they do not bring about emancipation from suffering.

Another possible source for the *Yuqing jing*'s imagery is the *Nirvanasutra* (*Daban niepan jing*), a Mahayana sutra first translated into Chinese in 421 by Dharmakshema. This sutra is best known for its doctrine of the innate Buddha nature possessed by all sentient beings. The passage of greatest relevance to our study, however, is the following:

Understand [the following]. [There are those who practice] the methods of self-starvation. [Some] throw [themselves] into pools or enter into fire. [Some] fall off high cliffs. [Some] constantly stand on one leg. [Some] roast their bodies with five sources of heat. [Some] constantly lie down amidst soot, dirt, thorns, woven rafters (?), tree leaves, bad weeds or cow dung. [Some] wear coarse hemp garments, or wear manure-stained woven woolen garments abandoned amid burial mounds. [Some wear] *qinboluo* (?) robes, deer skin belts and garments of straw. [Some] eat vegetables or eat weeds. [Some eat] lotus roots and fruits defiled with grease, grime and cow dung. [Some], when they go about begging, only go to one house. If the master of the house says he has no food, they take leave of him and do not pay attention even if he calls for them to come back.

[Some] do not eat salted meats or the five varieties of beef dishes. [Some] always eat boiled porridge made from chaff. [Some] uphold precepts [against eating] beef while others observe ordinances against eating dogs, chickens or pheasants. [Some] smear their bodies with soot and grow their hair long. [Some,] when they carry out their worship with sacrifices of sheep, first say a mantra before killing. In the fourth month they worship fire and imbibe wind for seven days. They offer hundreds, thousands, and hundreds of millions of flowers to the various heavens. Their various wishes are to thereby supposed to be realized. As for these various methods, there are none that can become causes for the ultimate liberation.[34]

The preceding passage describes austerities that harm and kill the body. It also describes begging, the eating of impurities, fire worship, and blood sacrifice. An important side note here is that the *Yuanyang jing* (*The Scripture of the Primal Yang*), another Taoist scripture of the late Six Dynasties or early Tang, plagiarizes this same passage almost word for word.[35] This indicates beyond a doubt that Taoists were well acquainted with the *Nirvanasutra* and were willing to borrow its material for their own use.

However, it should be noted that the *Yuqing jing*, unlike the *Nirvanasutra* or the *Guoqu xianzai yinyuan jing*, does not mention dietary restrictions and fasts among the misguided austerities of heretical ascetics. This is probably because the author, being a Taoist, had great faith in fasting as a training method, provided it was carried out correctly.

It seems likely that the images of the "infidels" in the *Yuqing jing* are partly modeled upon the non-Buddhist Indian ascetics depicted in Buddhist sutras. Nonethess, this does not account for all of the traits attributed to the "infidels." They possess various other traits that would seem to identify them as Buddhists. Even though the references to things such as fire worship and blood sacrifice could have been borrowed from the Buddhist sutras, the references to burial by exposure and the "God(s) of Heaven" still seem to hint at an awareness of Zoroastrianism. It is undeniable that the author must have been at least partially driven by polemical aims.

But if his primary goal was to discredit rival religions, why did he dilute his depictions of "infidels" with images of austerities carried out by non-Buddhist Indian ascetics whom Buddhists themselves discredited? Would his polemics not have been much more effective if he had limited himself to describing and discrediting beliefs and practices that were quintessentially Buddhist? Did he really mean to say that Buddhists were demon worshippers who were fond of self-mutilation and suicide?

The author's primary purpose was probably not polemical. As xenophobic and anti-Buddhist as he may have been, he did not necessarily desire his readers to identify the "infidels" with anybody in particular. His fundamental purpose for depicting the "infidels" was to denounce heresy in general. The gruesome depictions were intended to provide a stark contrast with the blessed attributes of those who adhere to the orthodox way. His descriptions and denunciations of heresy serve to enhance his positive exhortations.

The essential heresy attacked in the *Yuqing jing* is the disdain for the body and human life, along with the ascetic abuses that can result from it. More precisely, it is the belief that salvation is a liberation of the soul from the body, which can be expedited by bodily annihilation. This heresy may or may not have been expounded by rival religions. What probably troubled the author most was that some *Taoists* had embraced the heresy. This, in his mind, threatened the very integrity of the Taoist religion. The following passage from the *Yuqing jing* clearly expresses this apprehension:

> Gentlemen of later times who study [the Tao], if you want to eliminate the divergent ways you should practice the methods of the Orthodox One and equip yourself with great and mighty gods and thereby subdue them. With the marvelous *qi* of the Great Tao and the perfect might of the Gods of Life, [you should] eliminate them. The infidels of ordinary bodies will naturally be converted. The infidel spirits will naturally cease to exist. Students who study [the Tao] in later times, if you want to eliminate these evils, you should adeptly use the Way of the Fire Bells,[36] and thereby the evils will perish. As for these various infidels, even though they seek the best results, they will never be able to attain them. The way of annihilating life is not the [way of] attaining Perfection. It is to be called "the wicked and false way of the walking corpses (*xingshi*)."[37] *Even within the Religion of the Great Way, there are people like this* (emphasis added). The hearts of people change and waver and their bodies do what is incorrect. Wicked gods employ them. These people are also to be called infidels. People such as these cannot distinguish between true and false. With purity and turbidity not distinguished, they naturally bring forth wicked specters. Once their minds have thus become prejudiced and spiteful, the Great Tao will not be carried out [by them]. If tempting spirits have gotten into their hearts, how can they hear the Way of Life? (9/11a–b)

Most noteworthy here is the italicized sentence that clearly states that the heresy has infiltrated Taoism. How could this have come about? The text blames it on "infidel" spirits that possess people. What were these "spirits"? What actually caused Taoists to embrace heresy?

Some Taoist doctrines (both indigenous and foreign influenced), if misinterpreted, could have led to disdain and abuse of the body. As we have seen in previous chapters, some Taoist texts convey a strong loathing toward the human body in its ordinary, untrained condition. It was seen to be full of filthy *yin qi* that made it heavy, weak, and corruptible. It was thought to be infested with internal demons (the Three Worms in particular) that tempted people to succumb to corruptive desires and emotions. As long as it was in such a condition, the body was considered a hindrance to the adept's progress. Along with this loathing for the untrained body, there existed a longing to escape the mundane world and to participate in a transcendent realm. This longing and loathing may have occasionally led to bodily abuse, or even religious suicide.

By the time the *Yuqing jing* was written, the innate potential for Taoist doctrines to engender heresy and ascetic abuses had become even greater, due to the massive incorporation of Buddhist elements. Most noteworthy is the new soteriology of the Lingbao movement, in which the highest levels of immortality are equated to the liberation from *samsara*. As we have seen, some passages in the Lingbao scriptures describe the body as being a mere temporary dwelling for the spirit, or emphasize the "empty" quality of the body. The adept is told to "forget" his body and stop "loving" it. Mythical deities and personages are extolled for their willingness to sacrifice their lives, whether for the welfare of others or the attainment of personal religious goals. The inherent tension between the ideals of longevity and transcendence had been heightened as never before, and the importance of the body within the soteriological scheme seems to have been waning.

Heresy of the kind attributed to the *Yuqing jing*'s "infidels" could well have been embraced by some Taoists, solely as a result of how they interpreted their own doctrines. It is therefore interesting that in the *Yuqing jing*'s fourth chapter (Prefatory Chapter to the Precepts of Compassion), the origin of heresy is attributed to the misinterpretation of the "less profound truths of the Taoism" (the form of Taoism taught to the "barbarians," i.e., Buddhism). The exposition of this theory comes from the mouth of a Heavenly Worthy.[38] His exposition is directed at a throng of youths from the Snowy Mountains (this probably refers to the Himalayas), self-proclaimed immortals who had studied under a certain "ancient master." It reads

> Good men, as for your saying that you encountered an ancient master and obtained conversion and salvation, [this] ancient master was my disciple. I made him evangelize in the frontier regions, expounding the [doctrines] of the Three Vehicles, [in order to] make the masses achieve extinction and deliverance *(miedu)* so that they could cultivate their fruits for later times. [This was] because those lands were hard to convert. The people had no harmonious *qi*. [Because they were the] kin of animals, they were intellectually and mentally deficient. They drank blood and ate fur and were violent and unrestrained. [The ancient master] thus performed miracles and preached extensively, using metaphors in order to open up enlightenment for people of inferior capacities. Doctrines such as these [that the ancient master expounded] do not fathom the ultimate principles, but merely reveal forms and traces expediently. After

the master left [the world], he pulled back his traces and returned to the origin. The forms and traces [that he had revealed] gradually dissipated. Even though some of them have barely survived, they are full of mistakes. Some people proclaim themselves to be immortals or claim to be the god Brahma.[39] Some of them sit silently in empty rooms. Some of them burn their bodies and kill themselves. Some of them fall off tall cliffs. Some of them make offerings to fire and water. Some of them make statues of heavenly beings. [They have] various kinds of god-images with three faces and a thousand arms. They slaughter [sacrificial victims] and carry out their ritual worship. The crowds of worshippers, in carrying out their worship, yell out and seek extinction. Some of them clearly see images of light. Ways such as these are called fallacies. Even though they have scriptures and texts, they do not have the true doctrines. Wickedness and orthodoxy are intermingled so that they cannot acquire the Tao. (1/30a–b)

Set forth here is a unique version of the infamous *huahu* (conversion of the "barbarians") legend.[40] This legend claimed that Buddhism was a derivative version of Taoism best suited for the intellectually and morally inferior "barbarians." Some versions of the legend claim that Laozi founded Buddhism when he traveled to the west. Others claim that the Buddha was Laozi's disciple. The legend's foremost purpose was to undermine the dignity of Buddhism. It also purported to be a viable defense against those who criticized Taoism for imitating Buddhism. If one accepted the legend, one had to conclude that Taoism did not borrow anything from Buddhism, since Buddhism itself was Taoism in a lower form. The "Three Vehicles" is a clear reference to Buddhism, since it is a Buddhist term that denotes three types of enlightenment for people of three different levels of capability.[41] The "ancient master" apparently refers to Laozi (whom the author may also have deemed to be one and the same person as the Buddha).[42] The doctrines "the ancient master" taught in the frontier regions were of a rudimentary nature, mere "forms and traces" of the ultimate truths of Taoism, which could enable the ignorant "barbarians" to achieve "extinction and deliverance," or *miedu*. Unclear here is the meaning of *miedu*. As was discussed in chapter 6, *miedu*, when used in Buddhist texts, refers to the decisive enlightenment and liberation. In the Lingbao scriptures, it refers to a mode of salvation that ranks below heavenly ascension and liberation from the corpse. Its main benefits were that the spirit evaded damnation and the corpse did not decay, resulting ultimately in resurrection. The Lingbao movement's definition of *miedu* is probably intended here, since the author seems to perceive *miedu* as a good, yet less than ideal mode of salvation. The doctrines of the "Three Vehicles" are not denounced as heresy; they are merely described as lower Taoist truths that confer no more than *miedu*. The heresies glorifying death are thus seen as misinterpretations of these "lower truths of Taoism," which arose in foreign lands after the "ancient master" (Laozi) had left. The author was seemingly aware that some Taoist doctrines (albeit the "forms and traces") held the potential for engendering bodily abuse and other abominations if misinterpreted. However, unsurprisingly, he blames foreigners for twisting Taoism into heresy.

The youths from the Snowy Mountains represent Buddhists who have managed to roughly adhere to the "forms and traces" taught by the "ancient master." In this sense they are much better than the "infidels" denounced throughout the *Yuqing jing*. The narrative goes on to describe how they were easily swayed to convert to Taoism in its "highest form." But how about those who have sunken deeply into blasphemy and heresy? Does the *Yuqing jing* acknowledge any hope for them?

The answer is "yes," albeit only after a very painstaking process. This is well illustrated in the eighth chapter, the "Chapter on Penetrating the Dark and Obscure." There (3/19a–27a) we are told that the Heavenly Worthy, while residing in his Cloud Palace in the Heaven of Jade Purity, was visited by a horde of demons who claimed to be "the gods of the clouds and mists, the divine kings of the Four Heavens and the gods of the Eighty Heavens of the Four Directions of [Mt.] Kunlun." All of these demons possessed the "32 marks, 80 good signs and 18 divine powers." The earth shook when they walked, their bodies produced water and fire, and they emitted light rays from between their eyebrows. Naked and barefooted, they came and paid their respects from afar toward the "cloudy gates", kneeling and pressing their hands together in a "barbarian" manner. However, the Heavenly Worthy instantly knew they were "infidels" (from this point on, the text refers to them merely as the "various wicked ones" or the "various devils"). He refused to entertain their inquiries personally, and instead assigned a "minor Immortal" to the task. The minor Immortal appeared before them, manifesting his "marks"[43] and divine powers. He emitted light rays from all of his hairs and pores, and the sky and ground shook violently. As they witnessed this, the demons trembled and perspired profusely in horror, while their own bodily radiances completely disappeared. The Immortal then rebuked them for all of their past wrongdoings. They had vainly pretended to be gods and holy men. They ate meat, committed lascivious acts, and taught people improper methods of meditation that brought forth "luminous apparitions" of a delusionary nature. After pointing out these wrongdoings, the Immortal rebuked them for their heretical doctrines that extolled death and extinction as the "method of ultimate enjoyment," and caused people to "kill themselves and mutilate their bodies in order to transform their ordinary bodies into diamond bodies"[44] (3/20b).

The Immortal then told the demons that their transgressions disqualified them from "seeing the Tao." This meant that they did not deserve a direct audience with the Heavenly Worthy. The demons immediately felt intense remorse. They wailed and sobbed and hopped about hitting themselves until blood flowed all over their bodies. They pulled out their hair on their scalps and sideburns. They prostrated themselves, trembling before the feet of the Immortal (3/22a).

Their propensity for excessive bodily mortification thus showed itself even in how they expressed remorse. The Immortal reprimanded them, stating that repentance only requires a change of heart, and that the body must not be harmed in the process. However, at this point, the demons' sincere remorse managed to win the sympathy of the Heavenly Worthy in the Cloud Palace. The Heavenly Worthy indicated this to the Immortal from afar by emitting a purple light from his eyes.

The demons then tried to curry the Heavenly Worthy's favor with lavish gifts. However, the Immortal told them that their treasures would only defile the Cloud Palace, and that the Heavenly Worthy "values people's heart-treasures." To this the demons replied, "Bodies of flesh from the Realm of Desires contain no treasures in the heart." The Immortal then suggested, "If your bodies contain no treasures, why not give your hearts?" The demons took his words literally. One of them, who called himself the "Brahman King," borrowed a sword from the Immortal, cut open his own belly, and took out his five viscera to show his heart to the Immortal. The rest of the demons immediately started to do the same thing. The Immortal restrained them, explaining that by "give your hearts," he merely meant that they should abandon their false views and concentrate on seeking the Great Tao. He then laid his hands on their self-inflicted wounds and healed them. Thereupon the demons all expressed the wish to be taught the Way of Perpetual Life and No Death. However, the Immortal rejected their request, citing two basic reasons. First of all, they lacked the proper physical constitution. In their advanced age, their "marrow and brains" were "empty and depleted," and their bodily fluids had become "dirty and stagnant." Second, they had accumulated a great many transgressions by "deceiving and confusing" the people of the world. For these reasons, he told them, it would be exceedingly difficult for them to gain the ultimate salvation (3/24a–b).

The Immortal then told them that if they were to have any hope at all, they had to first gain the approval of the Heavenly Worthy of Great Compassion. Taking to heart what they had been told, the demons did as follows:

The entire throng, outside the cloudy gates, worshipped the Heavenly Worthy from afar, burning incense and proclaiming their wishes for seven days and seven nights. They kowtowed and prostrated themselves to seek a response. These various infidels, at high noon, suddenly smelled a divine fragrance that permeated their noses and entered their hearts. In their hearts they rejoiced, and their confusion was eliminated. Inside, they felt neither hunger nor thirst. Their sight and hearing became twice as clear as it was when they first came forth. These various infidels snapped their fingers and looked at each other, and remarked at how their bodily complexions had taken on a moist luster. At that time, the Immortal in his heart understood that the Heavenly Worthy had taken pity on the various Infidels. These various infidels, in their hearts also sensed [that the Heavenly Worthy had taken pity on them]. With joy in their bosoms they were left speechless, and they simply bowed and gave thanks, visualizing the Perfect Monarch of Great Compassion. Again for seven days and seven nights they bowed and knelt by the cloudy gates. (3/24b–25a)

The Immortal then declared to the demons that they had "obtained the Power of the Tao" (*de daoli*). They had finally managed to take the proper approach toward correcting their faults. In seeking the Heavenly Worthy's mercy, they had prostrated themselves and worshipped nonstop for many days and nights, in the hope of evoking a positive sign. It should be noted here that they had engaged in a very mentally and physically demanding deed. However, they did not harm their bodies in any way. To the contrary, they became healthier. Their senses became sharper and they became impervious to hunger and thirst. The days and nights of religious rapture and oblivion toward bodily concerns enhanced their physical well-being. This was because they directed their faith and reverence toward the sole deity (the Tao, or the Heavenly Worthy who personifies it) capable of generating the life-bestowing Power of the Tao.

In thus obtaining the Power of the Tao, the Immortals had made a great step in the right direction. However, it was nonetheless only the first step. Although their lives had been extended indefinitely and their most evil transgressions had been forgiven, the *qi* of their bodies and minds still required much more purification. The demons were thus told to return to the Realm of Desires (the mundane world) and to engage in a retreat for three *kalpas*. During this retreat they were to practice Taoist dietetics, "eating the harmonious [*qi*] and ingesting pills." Only after doing so could they meet the Heavenly Worthy in person and learn the methods that would confer the highest immortality (3/26b–27a).

The aforementioned narrative presents a striking contrast between the religion of the "infidels" and the religion of the Tao. "Infidels" do not understand the importance of purifying and strengthening the body, and therefore readily resort to bodily abuse. Taoism demands austere discipline, but the austerities actually enhance physical health.

This contrast is presented even more clearly in the seventeenth chapter ("The Chapter on the Tao Converting the Four Barbarian Peoples"). This long chapter describes events that allegedly took place in a mythical nation governed by a righteous and pious sage–king name Chongguang. Chongguang, we are told, was actually an avatar of Baoguang, a Superior Perfected Being of the Heaven of Jade Purity. Baoguang had taken on his human form through a miraculous conception in the womb of the nation's queen. One day, after he had taken the throne, an army of bloodthirsty "barbarians" attempted to invade his nation. Because they had heard that the nation possessed no troops or weapons, they anticipated an easy conquest. However, before they even reached its borders, they were afflicted with contagious diseases that wiped out three-tenths of their troops. They initially retreated, but then tried to reorganize their assault. The epidemic immediately afflicted their own homelands. It killed eight-tenths of their population and still showed no signs of subsiding. Many of the "barbarians" contemplated human sacrifice as a means of imploring the gods of heaven to end the epidemic. However, one of the wiser among them suggested that it would be better to go apologize to the sage–king, who was obviously in good divine graces. Thus, 125 "barbarian" generals, leading an entourage of 84,000 strong, went to the virtuous nation bearing lavish gifts. There, after presenting their gifts, they demonstrated their remorse before King Chongguang by cutting off their noses, pulling out their hair, and beating themselves until they were covered with bruises. Chongguang, however, refused their gifts and told them that he personally harbored no grudge or pity toward them. This was because their agonies were caused only by their own misdeeds. Desperate and unable to understand what they were being told, the "barbarians" contemplated suicide as a means of appeasing the king and ending the epidemic. Chongguang then told them that the way to seek blessings was not through material offerings and self-torture. Rather, the only viable means was to "serve the Tao with an empty heart." In regard to their contemplating suicide, Chongguang reprimanded them, saying,

> Why, in seeking blessings do you contrarily[45] annihilate your body? The annihilation of the body is not to be called a "blessing." Why do you barbarians want to annihilate your bodies? The body is the basis of blessings. Why should you annihilate it? To annihilate the body is to be called "annihilating blessings." Also, the body is the basis of the Tao. To annihilate the body is to be called, "annihilating the Tao." It is not the annihilation of transgressions. Those who annihilate their transgressions do not annihilate their transgressions by relying on their blessings (by sacrificing their blessed bodies). Those who seek blessings do not bring about their blessings by committing transgressions. (7/7a–b)

Thus he told them that it was essential for them to keep their bodies intact. The barbarians, however, still did not understand. They asked to hear more about the religion of the Tao. Chongguang obliged them with a lengthy discourse that included the statement

> The Most High Ultimate Tao begins with the perpetuation of life as its basic tenet. Immediately within this body one makes the Dharma Body. (7/8b)

This statement makes it clear that the perpetuation of life is a fundamental concern in Taoism. This is because the ultimate goal, described here as the attainment of the "Dharma Body," must be realized within the living flesh. However, the discourse also included statements of a more obscure nature.

[The Taoist religion] regards the body's being able to follow the spirit as non-being. It regards non-doing as self-so-ness. It regards formlessness as perpetual life. (7/8b–9a)

Here, formlessness is equated with eternal life. Taken literally, a statement such as this would seem to imply that the blessed being no longer possesses a body of flesh. This seemingly contradicts the ideal of bodily immortality and the notion of "obtaining the Dharma Body within this Body." The statement, "it regards the body being able to follow the spirit as non-being," may hold the clue to resolving the seeming contradiction. It perhaps means that the body, somehow transformed to a formless state, accompanies the spirit into a state of non-being, and this non-being is eternal life. The understanding of the author seems to be that such a transformation is tantamount to the perpetuation of the body.

After this explanation by the sage–king, the text tells us (unsurprisingly) that the "barbarians" still could not understand. The narrative continues by describing how King Chongguang summoned forth a certain Grand Master of the Cold Forest (an avatar of the Most High Lord of the Tao) and all of the family-leaving Taoist monks (*chujia daoshi*) of the nation. The Grand Master and his monkish entourage performed a ritual of purification and repentance for seven days and seven nights on behalf of the frontier nations. The epidemic immediately ended, and all of the nations sent envoys to express their gratitude. All of the citizens of the blessed nation also came forth to pay their respects to the Grand Master. A grand festival was then staged, sponsored by the sage–king. While the monks sang hymns and circumambulated, the Grand Master took his seat upon a high platform and revealed his true countenance as the Most High Lord of the Tao. King Chongguang, obeying the instructions of the Most High Lord of the Tao, burned incense, "bowed from afar to the Heavenly Worthy of Great Compassion in the Cloud Palace," and proclaimed ten wishes.[46] This immediately evoked a wide variety of miraculous phenomena that included the resurrection of dead bodies and the blossoming of dead trees and plants.[47] The Heavenly Worthy of Great Compassion himself, together with his sacred throngs, appeared in the sky above the eastern walls of the nation. Due to their remote distance, they appeared to the eyes of their beholders as a murky purple radiance surrounded by a bright mist. The Grand Master then produced a duplicate of his Perfect Form (*zhenxing*), which ascended and entered the clouds to join the Heavenly Worthy. The text then states

Within the great assembly, [all] humans and non-humans became silent and motionless. With their hearts never tiring, they joyfully gazed up and enjoyed the Perfect [Forms] by observing their countenances. They devoted their hearts and concentrated their thoughts without even sensing they had bodies. For nine days and nine nights they remained serene without hungering nor thirsting. Their bodies and minds were motionless. (7/13b)

Described here once again is a state of rapture experienced by those who devote their attention solely to the Tao's theophany. The rapture renders them impervious to bodily needs, presumably because they have become imbued with the Power of the Tao. Unfortunately, our text tells us, the "barbarians" still had not overcome their chronic ignorance. Upon witnessing the scene before them, they became terrified and overwhelmed with feelings of guilt. They proceeded to pull out their hair, slice off their noses, and strike their bodies. They also harbored the desire to give their bodies to the Tao as sacrifices by gouging out their eyes, chopping off their heads, and burning their bodies. King Chongguang promptly reprimanded them for defiling his nation with their vulgar ways, and reminded them that the Tao could not be sought through bodily annihilation. He then lectured them on the importance of "completing" the body.

> If you want to hear the Tao, you must complete your sense of hearing. Do not listen to the Tao by listening with your ears. If you want to see the Tao, you must complete your sense of sight. Do not look at the Tao with eyes that are defective and damaged. If you want to practice the Tao, you must complete your life. Do not practice the Tao by annihilating life. If you want to practice the Tao, you must first complete your body. Do not practice the Tao with a deficient body that violates. If you want to embrace the Tao, you must eliminate the ten evils.[48] You must not practice the Tao after entertaining thoughts of committing the five deadly transgressions.[49] You now must understand that those whose lives are not completed are not worthy of hearing the Tao. Those whose bodies are not completed are not worthy of studying the Tao. (7/14a–b)

Here, "completing" something means to realize its full potential. In terms of the human body, it means to live out one's life span and train the body to its best possible condition. Thus Chongguang is telling the "barbarians" that in order to worship and practice the Tao, they must take care of their bodies and not allow their lives to end prematurely. At the same time, they must work to improve the quality of the body and its functions so an understanding and direct experience of the Tao are possible. The clear implication here is that the "barbarians" possess "incomplete" bodies that need to be "completed." To seek the Tao by further damaging such bodies is a misguided approach.

The king then told the "barbarians" that even though they were not yet worthy of seeking the Tao, the merit they had just gained by seeing the Heavenly Worthy from a distance would enable them to be reborn 10,000 *kalpas* later as citizens of the blessed kingdom. He added, however, that from that day on they had to "complete their bodies." If they ever engaged in bodily mutilation again, they would lose all hope.

The guilt and impurity of the foreigners was thus so profound that they had to train for an inconceivably long period to achieve rebirth in the blessed kingdom.

Only after this rebirth was true salvation possible. The implication of the story—assuming that the blessed nation is an allegory for China—is that foreigners, by sheer fault of their ethnicity, are unable to attain Perfection without first being reborn as Chinese. However, while the author of the *Yuqing jing* is again clearly xenophobic, his real adversary is the heretical doctrine that seems to have infiltrated the beliefs of Taoists themselves. The author advocates the life-affirming soteriology that he considers Taoist orthodoxy and appeals to the xenophobia of fellow Chinese and Taoists by labeling all supporters of the heretical viewpoint "barbarians" and "infidels."

The *Yuqing jing* sets forth—albeit vaguely—a soteriological scheme in which an eternal, transcendent existence is attained without compromising the objectives of bodily health and longevity. Coherence to this soteriological scheme is meant to be the standard by which the validity of a belief or practice can be determined. We do not know who the author (or authors) of the *Yuqing jing* was, and it is uncertain how influential and prevalent his views were among his Taoist contemporaries. Nonetheless, the *Yuqing jing* is a text of profound importance, in that it addresses a doctrinal issue that was, and always will be, of critical importance, namely, the role of the flesh in the quest for the highest immortality. The *Yuqing jing* adamantly argues that the human body is extremely valuable, and this view prevails to this day as a definitive trait of the Taoist religion.

CHAPTER EIGHT

Conclusion

During roughly the first six centuries of the common era, many Taoists practiced asceticism in the hope of gaining everlasting life. As new beliefs and practices were developed (or adopted from Buddhism), ascetics were provided with further motivation and justification for their austerities. While the Taoist religion certainly accommodated less austere modes of religiosity, asceticism was demanded of advanced adepts who sought immortality in its highest forms. Inevitably, some of the new beliefs—particularly those inspired by Buddhist influence—created contradictions and tensions with older beliefs and practices. However, an effort was made to retain the old beliefs and practices in ways that were coherent to the new beliefs.

The principal ascetic practices included fasting, celibacy, sleep avoidance, wilderness seclusion, and self-imposed poverty. However, over the course of the period examined, the soteriological and cosmological beliefs justifying these practices changed considerably. Some of these changes intensified the inherent tension between two primary objectives: longevity and transcendence. This was because they provided a theoretical basis for thinking that transcendence could be achieved without seeking longevity. The emergence of such thinking created a greater possibility for ascetic abuses (the harming and killing of the body) to be carried out and condoned.

Up until roughly the mid-fourth century, Taoist ascetics mostly functioned within small schools and master-disciple lineages that did not share any clearly defined cosmology, soteriology, or ethical code. Buddhist influence was still sparse, and physiological theories, rather than ethical concerns, provided most of the rationale for self-denial. Celibacy, for example, was practiced primarily because the loss of sexual fluids was thought to deplete one's vital forces, not because sex was deemed inherently immoral. Monasticism akin to the Buddhist model had yet to be developed. However, many adepts consciously secluded themselves from society and shunned basic worldly needs and comforts.

Most striking is the intensity and resourcefulness with which adepts fasted. Because Taoist texts frequently employ terms such as *the avoidance of grains* (*bigu*) or *cutting off grains* (*duangu*) to denote the practice of fasting, modern scholars have commonly been led to believe that the primary objective of Taoist dietetics was merely to abstain from eating the "five grains" (rice, glutinous millet, panicled millet, wheat, and soybeans). However, the actual objective was to radically reduce one's intake of all foods. To do this, adepts ingested an amazing variety of hunger-suppressing substances and potions and devised numerous techniques such as visualization, incantation, air swallowing, saliva swallowing, breath holding, and talisman swallowing.

During the latter part of the fourth century and onward, the Shangqing and Lingbao movements came to assert pervasive influence, providing larger, commonly shared doctrinal and institutional frameworks into which ascetic practices were incorporated. By the fifth or sixth century, at the latest, male and female monasticism based on the Buddhist model came to be practiced by Taoists, as is well attested to by evidence in the *Daoxue zhuan*.

The Shangqing movement (that began in the late fourth century) incorporated asceticism into its comprehensive training regimen that culminated in the transmission, study, and practice of the *Dadong zhenjing* and other "revealed" scriptures. While ascetic training methods of the kind pursued in earlier years were no longer in themselves deemed capable of conferring the highest salvation, they were nonetheless deemed essential for qualifying and conditioning adepts to receive the holiest scriptures and practice their methods.

While its borrowing of Buddhist doctrines and practices was not as extensive as that of the Lingbao movement, the Shangqing movement did draw upon the teachings of the Buddhist *Sishi-er zhang jing* to enjoin its followers to train rigorously, reduce their desires, and renounce sex and marriage. The Shangqing movement also promoted celibacy vigorously on indigenous principles. According to the Shangqing texts, sexual activity depleted the body's vital forces and could even cause instant death in certain cases (when engaged in by practitioners of specific training methods). Sexual desires rendered adepts susceptible to the malice of demons and incapable of communication with divine beings. Chastity in thought and action could enable adepts to enter sublime, platonic companionships with immortal beings of the opposite sex. Ascetic discipline in general was promoted as being conducive to gaining the sympathy and assistance of gods and immortals. Under their benevolent gaze, adepts hoped to withstand the numerous trials imposed by demons during their quest for perfection.

Beliefs anticipating the imminent destruction of the corrupt world formed a central component of the Shangqing worldview, and the mood that pervades the Shangqing texts is decidedly pessimistic and antiworldly. This antiworldly sentiment is perhaps best exemplified by how the Shangqing movement promoted certain methods tantamount to religious suicide and lauded the immortals of yore who feigned gruesome deaths before proceeding to eternal life.

The Lingbao movement of the fifth century also made asceticism an integral part of its religious system. Lingbao Taoism was strongly influenced by Mahayana Buddhism. Probably largely for this reason, its asceticism bore a strongly altruistic tinge. The ideal saint of the Lingbao tradition, much like the Bodhisattva of Mahayana Buddhism, was one who made great efforts and sacrifices for the benefit of all living beings, not just for his or her own salvation. A fundamental claim of the movement was that personal training methods—however rigorous—could not confer the highest immortality if one did not exhibit great altruistic virtue over many incarnations.

The Lingbao movement's teachings on morality and discipline are set forth in sets of precepts (*jie*) addressed to believers at various levels, and hence vary in their degree of austerity and self-sacrifice. The more advanced sets of precepts appear to be addressed to adepts who make religious training their exclusive vocation and demand a high degree of asceticism. These advanced precepts may have served as codes of discipline within early monastic settings.

The Lingbao movement emphasized the conscientious observance of communal "retreat" (*zhai*) rituals. These typically lasted three or more days and entailed strict dietary prohibitions and strenuous liturgical procedures. To express remorse for their transgressions, participants would kowtow and slap their cheeks hundreds of times. In some cases, they would humiliate themselves by stripping their garments, disheveling their hair, and smearing soot over their faces and bodies. The ultimate object was to implore the lofty Taoist deities to grant happiness and salvation to all sentient beings. The austere daily regimen of advanced adepts was considered a "perpetual retreat" (*changzhai*), an extension of the communal "retreat" ritual wherein the devotional and purificatory observances were maintained permanently at a personal level.

The Lingbao scriptures provide discourses on soteriology that present us with a complicated puzzle. Some passages in the Lingbao scriptures describe the body as being a temporary dwelling for the spirit, or emphasize the "empty" quality of the body. The adept is told to "forget" his body and to stop "loving" it. The spirit (*shen*), equated to the mind, is described as something more proper to the adept. Its state of perfection or lack thereof is claimed to be the primary factor that determines whether one will gain a desirable rebirth or—preferably—become liberated from *samsara*. This would seem to imply a belief in a singular soul that can survive death and perpetuate one's personality in a blessed afterlife state. However, in some passages, heavenly ascension in the full physical body still is set forth as being the highest form of salvation. In such passages (of which prime examples are found in the *Gongde qingzhong jing* and the *Ershisi shengtu jing*), the *shen* (the spiritual component of one's being) is described as thousands of gods that personify the *qi* that pervades the body and animates it. Immortal ascension is claimed to come about when these internal gods combine their forces to propel the adept's body upward.

The ambiguities and seeming discrepancies in Lingbao soteriology were a product of the latent tension that had always existed between the two primary objectives of Taoist adepts: longevity and transcendence. Taoist adepts yearned to live eternally in a realm beyond this imperfect world. To believe in the immortality and ascension of the human flesh is undoubtedly difficult, since everybody witnesses the grim reality of death, while nobody ever seems to witness the marvel of heavenly ascension. Empirical evidence seems to constantly undermine any faith in physical immortality. A belief in the immortality of an invisible, nonphysical entity is less readily refutable on empirical grounds. If one accepts Buddhistic theories on *karma* and reincarnation and infers that there exists an immortal soul that can transcend the world (contradictory as this may be to the Buddha's authentic teachings), one has created a doctrine that requires a lesser leap of faith. An ascetic who adopts such a soteriology could then conceivably maintain that spiritual perfection is the sole priority and that the body can and should be neglected and mortified to the point of destruction.

Such is the doctrine denounced throughout the *Yuqing jing* in its gruesome depictions of heretical asceticism. While the author seems to blame the propagation of the heresy mostly on foreigners and "infidels," he also maintains that the heresy has infiltrated the Taoist religion itself. The soteriology of the *Yuqing jing* itself is somewhat ambiguous, since it describes the highest immortality as a liberation from *samsara* and a merging with a formless non-being. The idea seems to be that the adept somehow transforms his physical body into such a state. Nonetheless, the *Yuqing jing* is unequivocal in its assertion that the body ("the basis of the Tao") must be treasured. The *Yuqing jing* encourages adepts to train rigorously, but forcefully asserts that they absolutely must not inflict irreversible harm on their bodies, much less bring about premature death.

The latent tension between longevity and transcendence, along with an uneasy sense of doubt toward the possibility of physical immortality, certainly must have existed throughout the period covered in this study. Ascetic abuses probably occured intermittently, especially when adepts were overcome by their desire to leave the world, or by their disgust toward their imperfect bodies. Suicidal methods may have largely occurred as a result of such sentiments, even though such methods theoretically constituted a mere "feigning" of death. However, when reading the *Yuqing jing*, one gets the impression that ascetic abuses may have become more common by the sixth century, and that the latent tension between longevity and transcendence had been aggravated by the adoption of Buddhistic doctrines.

We shall end this study with a brief look at the present state of the Taoist religion and some speculative comments on the course that Taoist asceticism took after ca. 600 C.E.

Today Taoism lives on as an organized religion, and asceticism continues to be an important aspect of it. Two major forms of Taoism have survived: the priestly and the monastic. The former has been carried on primarily by the Heavenly Masters School, while the latter has been carried on primarily by the Complete Perfection (Quanzhen) School.

The priests of the Heavenly Masters School, which is now also known as the Orthodox Unity (Zhengyi) School, are all men. They are allowed to marry, and in many cases, the priestly vocation is passed on from father to son. The primary activity of priests is the performance of rituals of various kinds. These include both private and communal rituals, along with healings and exorcisms. In the People's Republic, the Heavenly Masters School survives primarily in the south and has its headquarters at Mt. Longhu in Jiangxi Province. However, many priests live outside mainland China, especially in Taiwan.

The Complete Perfection School was founded by Wang Chongyang (1112–1170). In its early years, it had its strongholds in present-day Shaanxi and Shandong provinces. Today it has its headquarters at Beijing's White Cloud Monastery (Baiyun Guan), and has numerous monasteries scattered throughout the People's Republic. Its clergy include both monks and nuns, who lead disciplined, celibate lives. Their primary pursuit is self-cultivation, which involves the adherence to monastic rules and the practice of internal alchemical meditation.[1]

Generally speaking, priestly Taoism emphasizes ritual, while monastic Taoism emphasizes self-cultivation. However, this distinction is not absolute. Many priests practice internal alchemical meditation. Some monks and nuns are trained to administer rituals. Nonetheless, it would be accurate to say that the ascetic strain in the Taoist religion has been perpetuated primarily in the monasteries.

During the Cultural Revolution, a concerted effort was made by the government to eliminate Taoism from the People's Republic for good, which would have meant the virtual extinction of monastic Taoism. Fortunately, the government has adopted a more tolerant policy toward organized religion since the early 1980s, and Taoism is gradually restoring itself. At the same time, the nation's doors have been opened to foreign visitors, making it possible for non-Chinese scholars to encounter monastic Taoism. In my own visits to China, I have been impressed by how Taoist monks and nuns are upholding strict standards of discipline. On one of my trips I met an adept named Lingdanzi ("the Master of the Miraculous Elixir") at the foot of Mt. Wudang in western Hubei Province, who claimed to go on fasts of up to 100 days. From monks at the Southern Peak Mt. Heng (Hunan Province) I heard a rumor about a nun on Mt. Wudang who had not eaten for three years. While I am skeptical about such claims, I was able to verify that celibacy, vegetarianism, and the renunciation of luxuries were generally mandatory for monks and nuns. Unfortunately, it must also be added that much of the grandeur of the monasteries, along with their wealth of personalities, has been lost as a result of the Cultural Revolution.[2]

Undoubtedly, many things have occured in the history of Taoist asceticism since 600 C.E., the approximate point in time at which our study ends. Evidence in the *Yuqing jing* seems to indicate that Taoism and its asceticism had come to a critical crossroad. New, largely Buddhist-influenced trends in doctrine were bringing to question the value of the human body. The teachings of the *Yuqing jing* represent a fervent attempt to reassert the value of the human body and keep ascetic practices within boundaries that were consistent with this outlook. Unfortunately, we do not know the extent to which the message of the *Yuqing jing* was heard and embraced by Taoists at the time.

We do know that Taoists were to continue to draw upon Buddhist teachings. Texts of the late Six Dynasties and the Tang betray the influence of various forms of Mahayana thought. Taoist internal alchemists of the Song and Yuan were strongly influenced by Chan (Zen) Buddhism in particular. The highest forms of immortality continued to be equated to the complete liberation from *samsara*. At the same time, physical longevity was still a cherished goal (it still is), and macrobiotic techniques continued to be carried out and developed. The underlying tension between the dual objectives of transcendence and longevity was probably never fully resolved, and controversies of the kind addressed in the *Yuqing jing* probably reemerged from time to time.

However, this tension may have been partially resolved in some of the speculations of the internal alchemists of the Song (960–1279) and Yuan (1279–1367) dynasties.[3] While not all internal alchemical texts appear to be in full agreement about exactly what immortality is, many make the claim that the adept creates a divine, immortal entity within his body. This entity proceeds to a godly and an eternal existence once the body of flesh has perished. However, physical health and longevity are nonetheless deemed essential, since the body of flesh is to act as the apparatus for concocting this immortal entity. This view provided adepts with the hope of transcending the evils and agonies of worldly existence, while at the same time posing a deterrent against bodily abuse. Of course, one can never assume that a particular religious doctrine will bring the consequences one might imagine, and in actual practice adepts may well have fallen into excesses—or laxity—from time to time.

The development of internal alchemy—which reached its apex during the Song and Yuan—was probably the most significant event in the evolution of Taoist self-cultivation. One result seems to have been that ancient texts (such as the Shangqing and Lingbao) largely went out of fashion as guides for self-cultivation.[4] This was at least in part because internal alchemists emulated Chan Buddhists in their tendency to value personal experience and direct oral teaching from master to disciple, rather than the study of old texts. Internal alchemists developed their own intricate theories about cosmology and physiology and attempted to pursue their daily discipline and meditation techniques in a way that fully integrated the mind with the body, and in turn synchronized these with the cyclical workings of nature.

To the extent that they accomplished this—or so thought—they claimed superiority for their approach over the ways of past Taoists. While they acknowledged some of the standard macrobiotic techniques of the past to be of value, and often included them within their overall regimen, they considered none sufficient on their own for conferring eternal life.

While a significant portion of internal alchemists were monastics and ascetics, it is hard to say exactly how large this portion was. Certainly not all internal alchemists were ascetics, and it should be noted that some pursued sexual yoga as an integral part of their regimen. We do know that Complete Perfection School founder Wang Chongyang and his inner circle of disciples were extreme ascetics who begged for their living, braved the harsh elements of nature, and avoided food and sleep for lengthy periods. (Of course, their tremendous ascetic feats may be grossly exaggerated in the hagiographical accounts that record them.) It also appears that the Complete Perfection School revitalized Taoist monasticism and played a central role in defining the shape that it would carry to the present day.[5]

Undoubtedly, before and after the founding of the Complete Perfection School, there were many other significant movements and developments that deserve mention. It must be admitted that much needs to be learned before we can properly trace the evolution of Taoist asceticism between ca. 600 C.E. and the present. This task hopefully will be carried out in a future full-length study.

Appendix

*Summary Information on the Lingbao Scriptures
Cited in Chapter Six*

Benyuan dajie jing (The Scripture of the Great Precepts of the Original Vow; HY344/TT177)—Full title, *Taishang dongxuan lingbao zhihui benyuan dajie shangpin jing* (18 pp). This text contains instructions that were allegedly conferred upon Ge Xuan by the Perfected Man of the Great Ultimate on Mt. Tiantai. The text covers various topics pertaining to training. It exhorts the reader to "stabilize the mind and treasure the *qi*." It forcefully recommends the study and recitation of the *Laozi*. It describes progressively intense levels of training that are to be pursued in their proper order. It gives a list of fifty-nine "original vows of wisdom," pious and compassionate wishes that the adept must harbor when witnessing various things. It also describes horrendous punishments that are to be suffered by those who become dishonest and immoral after entering the religious life full time. The text states unequivocally that it is better to remain a layperson than to become a corrupt clergy member.

Benxing yinyuan jing (The Scripture on the Causation from Past Deeds; HY1106/TT758)—Full title, *Taishang dongxuan lingbao benxing yinyuan jing* (7 1/2 pp). On Mt. Laocheng, Ge Xuan responds to questions from a group of thirty-three earthly Immortals and Taoist adepts. He describes the long process spanning countless rebirths through which he gained his lofty status of Left Immortal Duke of the Great Ultimate.

Chishu yujue (Jade Lessons on the Red Script; HY352/TT178)—Full title, *Taishang dongxuan lingbao chishu yujue miaojing*. Two *juan* (62 1/2 pp). The opening portion of the first *juan* describes how the Most High Lord of the Tao revealed the scripture to a certain Wang Long and conferred upon him the Lingbao Ten Precepts and the Twelve Precepts to be Obeyed; these precepts are enumerated in the text.

161

The text then presents two short liturgies of repentance. These are followed by the all-important Lingbao Perfect Writs, which are presented in ordinary, legible script. The Writs are accompanied by detailed instructions on how to utilize them to gain various benefits. These benefits include: 1) attaining immortality, 2) correcting inauspicious alignments of the stars, 3) surviving the anticipated cosmic flood, and 4) protection from demons. The second *juan* begins by describing how the five *qi* or "sprouts" are dispatched every morning from the highest heavens to recharge the world with vitality and nourish the adepts who are capable of eating them. The text then narrates the story of a pious girl named Aqiu Zeng (see p. 101). This story is followed by descriptions of various methods. These include the method for eating the "sprouts," a technique for visualizing and summoning the Five Monarchs of the Five Peaks, and a ritual method for invoking deities with the Perfect Writs. The text concludes with a liturgy for the transmission of the Perfect Writs.

Chishu zhenwen (The Perfect Writs in RedScript; HY22/TT26)—Full title, *Yuanshi wulao chishu yupian zhenwen tianshu jing*. Three *juan* (75 pp). The first *juan* begins by describing the primordial origins of the Perfects Writs. It further describes how the Primordial Heavenly Worthy made them legible, after which their marvelous power brought about the miracles of creation. The Writs themselves are shown, written in seal script and accompanied by talismans. Next in the text are descriptions of the Five Monarchs, also accompanied by talismans. These are followed by general descriptions of the various purposes for which the Writs can be utilized. The second *juan* displays various talismans, most of which purport to enable one to survive the cataclysm at the end of the cosmic era. The third *juan* lists the days for carrying out retreat rituals. It also provides lists of the wondrous attributes of the Perfect Writs and the blessings to be obtained by those who employ them.

Dingzhi tongwei jing (The Scripture on Stabilizing the Will and Penetrating the Subtleties; HY325/TT167)—Full title, *Taishang dongxuan lingbao zhihui dingzhi tongwei jing* (24 1/2 pp). Teachings bestowed upon the Perfected Men Zuoxuan and Youxuan by the Heavenly Worthy of the Lingbao. The text contains a discussion about how the spirit, originally pure, becomes corrupted as it takes on a bodily form and receives stimuli through the six senses. The "emptiness" of all worldly phenomena is set forth as an insight that can enable one to sever all attachments and return to the original state of Perfection. It also sets forth a rudimentary set of ten precepts to be propagated among the living masses. Two lengthy parables are included as well. One of these extols the merits of generous stewardship toward the Taoist clergy; the other promotes the observance of the rudimentary ten precepts.

Ershisi shengtu jing (The Scripture of the Twenty-four Life-Bestowing Diagrams)— Full title, *Dongxuan lingbao ershisi shengtu jing* (HY1396/TT1051) (48 pp). This text contains twenty-four verses that once accompanied twenty-four diagrams. The contents of the verses endorse special fasting techniques (methods for imbibing the Five Sprouts, solar essences, and lunar essences) and outline a process by which the internal gods that animate the body are concentrated into one great divine entity that can propel the adept's body to the heavens.

Gongde qingzhong jing (The Scripture on the Lightness and Heaviness of Meritorious Virtue; HY456/TT202)—Full title, *Taishang dongxuan lingbao sanyuan pin jie gongde qingzhong jing* (37 1/2 pp). Instructions bestowed upon the Most High Lord of the Tao by the Primordial Heavenly Worthy. The text includes detailed descriptions of the divine bureaucracy of the Three Origins of Heaven, Earth, and Water, which monitor human conduct and administer punishments and rewards as necessary. It also describes how the deities inhabiting the human body report the deeds of humans to the divine bureaucracy. Of greatest interest is the discourse on how *karma* and rebirth are determined primarily by one's state of mind. The text claims that this causal principle is of earlier origin and greater influence than hereditary factors. Nonetheless, it also acknowledges that hereditary merit and guilt assert some impact on the fate of people. The text also lists 180 sins that incur punishment from the divine bureaucracy.

Mingzhen ke (The Curriculum of Bright Perfection; HY1400/TT1052)—Full title, *Dongxuan lingbao changye zhifu jiuyou yugui mingzhen ke* (39 pp). This text contains discourses allegedly expounded by the Primordial Worthy to the Youth of Superior Wisdom. It describes twelve ways of living and training that bring forth auspicious consequences. It also describes fourteen kinds of bad behavior that incur hideous punishment and provides two liturgies for rituals of repentance that purport to benefit all beings, living and dead.

Shangpin jie jing (The Scripture of the Upper Section Precepts; HY454/TT202)—Full title, *Taishang dongxuan lingbao shangpin jie jing* (HY454/TT202) (8 pp). Instructions bestowed upon the Most High Lord of the Tao by the Primordial Heavenly Worthy. This text stresses the importance of performing rituals and sending up petitions on the first day of each month; the purpose is to gain divine recognition for one's virtue. The text also contains exhortations that encourage good behavior and warn of the consequences wrought by bad behavior. It also provides a variety of lists: 1) the poignant, compassionate wishes proclaimed by the Heavenly Girls of Resolved Mind and Immortals who Withstand Humiliations, 2) the Precepts for the Six Senses, 3) the twelve "diseases" (types of evil behavior), and 4) twelve "medicines" (moral virtues serving to eliminate the "diseases"). For some reason, Ofuchi Ninji does not match this scripture with any of the entries in Lu Xiujing's catalog. However, its title resembles catalog entries 8 and 9. Large portions of it (1a–b, 3a–4a, 5a–b) match passages in the *Zhihui shangpin dajie* and *Taishang dongxuan lingbao zhihui shangpin dajie* (Pelliot 2461), texts that Ofuchi believes to correspond to entry 9. (See Ofuchi [1974], pp. 48–49)

Shangqing dongzhen zhihui guanshen dajie wen (Text of the Great Precepts for Monitoring the Body; HY1353/TT1039) (24 pp). A list of 302 precepts that are to be observed by the most advanced and serious practitioners. This is not one of the catalogued Lingbao scriptures, but its precepts were apparently known and esteemed by Lingbao proponents.

Taiji yinzhu baojue (The [Perfected Man of] the Great Ultimate's Precious Lessons with Secret Commentary; HY425/TT194)—Full title, *Shangqing taiji yinzhu yujing baojue* (19 1/2 pp). This text contains discourses on various matters, presented as utterances of the Perfected Man of the Great Ultimate. The predominant theme is how to receive, venerate, and utilize sacred texts such as the *Laozi*, the *Dadong zhenjing*, the Lingbao scriptures, the *Sanhuang wen*, and the Shangqing scriptures and talismans. The Heshanggong commentary is endorsed as the best commentary to the *Laozi*. The text also includes instructions pertaining to meditation and the observance of retreats.

Taiji zuoxiangong qingwen jing shang (The Scripture on the Inquiries of the Left Immortal Duke of the Great Ultimate, Upper Volume; Dunhuang manuscripts, Stein 1351, 5 1/2 pp). Teachings bestowed upon Ge Xuan by "the Peerless Master of the Doctrines, the Lofty and Superior Laozi of the Most High Great Ultimate." Major themes include: 1) the importance of accumulating merit through good deeds, 2) the merit gained through the Lingbao and Santian (Three Heavens) retreat rituals, 3) the benefits gained by properly reciting the *Laozi* and the *Dongxuan lingbao yuqingshan buxu jing*, and 4) the importance of striving "bravely and fiercely" in various aspects of the religious life.

Taishang zhutian lingshu duming jing (The Most High Miraculous Book of the Various Heavens, the Scripture on the Deliverance of Lives; HY23/TT26, 19 pp). Teachings uttered by the Primordial Heavenly Worthy to the Most High Lord of the Tao. This text describes at length how the Lingbao scriptures were manifested in the five lands of the blessed. It also describes how the Primordial Heavenly Worthy has assumed different titles and appeared in the world during various cosmic eras to instruct living beings. The final part of the text presents four sets of verses to be recited toward the heavens of the east, south, west, and north. These purport to confer longevity to practitioners and deliver their ancestors to the Southern Palace for posthumous purification and deliverance.

Xuanyi quanjie falun miaojing (The [Perfected Man of] the Mysterious One's Marvelous Scripture of the Exhortations and Admonishments of the Wheel of the Doctrine; HY348/TT177)—Full title, *Taishang xuanyi zhenren shuo quanjie falun miaojing* (6 1/2 pp). This is one of the four scriptures that correspond to entry 14 of Lu Xiujing's catalog (the other three scriptures are the *Zhenyi quanjie falun miaojing* [see text that follows], the *Taishang xuanyi zhenren shuo santu wuku quanjie jing* [HY455/TT202], and the *Taishang xuanyi zhenren shuo miaotong zhuanshen ruding miaojing* [HY347/TT177]). These four scriptures once formed a single text. (See Ofuchi [1974] p. 50) Presented as sayings uttered by "the Tao," the *Xuanyi quanjie falun miaojing* describes how one's fate is inalienably linked to the quality of one's religious training and moral conduct. Particular emphasis is put upon describing the causes (good deeds in past lives) that confer one with privileged social status. It appears that the author had an aristocratic audience in mind and sought to encourage moral rectitude in them by addressing their worldly concerns.

Zhaijie weiyi jue (Lessons on Retreats, Precepts, and Mighty Rituals; HY532/ TT295)—Full title, *Taishang zhenren fu lingbao zhaijie weiyi zhujing yaojue* (23 1/2 pp). Presented as utterances of the Perfected Man of the Great Ultimate, with commentary attributed to Ge Xuan. This text contains various instructions pertaining to the observance of retreats. It specifies the mandatory retreat days and describes the conduct that is required during retreats. Another prominent theme is the sacredness of the *Laozi*, the *Dadong zhenjing*, and the Lingbao scriptures; these are described as indestructible scriptures that have existed from the beginning of time. A short liturgy also is provided, which bears the title, the Peerless Retreat (*wushang zhai*).

Zhenyi quanjie falun miaojing (The Perfect One Marvelous Scripture of the Exhortations and Admonishments of the Wheel of the Doctrine; HY346/TT177)— Full title, *Taishang dongxuan lingbao zhenyi quanjie falun miaojing* (5 1/2 pp). As has been mentioned in the summary of the *Xuanyi quanjie falun miaojing*, this is one of the four scriptures thought to correspond to entry 14 of Lu Xiujing's catalog. It appears to have been the prologue to the single text that the four scriptures once formed. It describes the scripture's celestial origins and the events that led up to its conferral upon Ge Xuan on Mt. Tiantai.

Zhihui shangpin dajie (The Great Upper Section Precepts of Wisdom; HY177/ TT77)—Full title, *Taishang dongzhen zhihui shangpin dajie* (16 pp). Teachings bestowed upon the Most High Lord of the Tao by the Primordial Heavenly Worthy. The text lists various precepts: the Ten Precepts of Wisdom, the Twelve Precepts to be Obeyed, the Precepts for the Six Senses, the Great Upper Section Wisdom Precepts for Delivering the Living, the Great Precepts of the Ten Good Deeds of Encouragement and Assistance (ten types of meritorious, pious conduct), and the Wisdom Upper Section Precepts on the Retribution for Meritorious Virtue (descriptions of the blessed consequences of generous stewardship and almsgiving).

Zuigen dajie jing (The Scripture on the Roots of Sins and the Great Precepts; HY457/TT202)—Full title, *Taishang dongxuan lingbao zhihui zuigen shangping dajie jing*. Two *juan* (28 pp). The first *juan* consists of instructions allegedly given to the Most High Lord of the Tao by the Primordial Heavenly Worthy. After describing how the Primordial Heavenly Worthy appeared in the world during various cosmic eras to indoctrinate the living masses, the text provides lists of precepts. The second *juan* consists of conversations between the Most High Lord of the Tao and the Flying Heavenly Perfected Beings of the various directions. In these conversations, the Perfected Beings describe how men and women have come to suffer the torments of the various hells and specify the ritual methods and offerings required for their release.

Notes

1. Introduction

1. The *wuxing* or five agents theory was first developed during the Warring States Period (403-222 B.C.E.) by Zou Yan and his school of cosmological thinkers. Various English translations have been proposed and used for the concept of *wuxing*, such as five agents, five elements, five phases, or five forces. The five agents are "elements" in the sense that they are five modes of *qi* (see note 25 later) that constitute things. However, the term *elements* seems too passive, since the five agents also are active, abstract forces that interact in logically ordained ways and dictate the flow and flux of the cosmos. The Chinese envisioned the cosmos as a logical system in which the five agents had their correlates in various things at various levels. The agents had the following among their correlates: Wood—east, Jupiter, liver; Fire—south, Mars, heart; Earth—center, Saturn, spleen; Metal—west, Venus, lungs; Water—north, Mercury, kidneys.

2. Walter O. Kaelber, "Asceticism," in *The Encyclopedia of Religion*, edited by Mircea Eliade (New York: Macmillan, 1987), 1: 441.

3. The *Laozi* and *Zhuangzi*, in keeping with the custom of the Warring States period (403–222 B.C.E.), bear the names of their putative authors as their titles. Laozi ("the Old Master") was traditionally thought to have been a royal archivist named Li Er, an older contemporary of Confucius (551–479 B.C.E.). Most modern scholars doubt whether Li Er was an actual historical figure. The *Laozi* book first appeared in something close to its present form during the late fourth or early third century B.C.E. Opinion is divided regarding whether it is of a singular or composite authorship. The "Inner Chapters" (chs. 1–7) of the *Zhuangzi* ("Master Zhuang") are generally accepted as the writings of Zhuang Zhou (fl. ca. late fourth century to early third century B.C.E.). The rest of the book's thirty-three chapters appear to have been written by various authors of heterogeneous schools, only some of whom subscribed to Zhuang Zhou's line of thinking.

4. *Tao Te Ching*, translated by D.C. Lau (London: Penguin, 1963), p. 68.

167

5. Ibid., p. 75.

6. Ibid., p. 107.

7. In expounding the concept of "evening things out," the *Zhuangzi* endeavors to do more than just discredit common conceptualizations and distinctions. It questions the validity of reasoning itself. According to A.C. Graham, the *Zhuangzi* enjoins that "we should abandon reason for the immediate experience of an undifferentiated world." See *Chuang-tzu: The Seven Inner Chapters and other writings from the book* Chuang-tzu, translated by A.C. Graham (London: George Allen and Unwin, 1981), pp. 9–14.

8. Graham, p. 58.

9. Graham, p. 46.

10. These rulers included King Wei (r. 355–320 B.C.E.) and King Xuan (r. 319–301 B.C.E.) of the Qi kingdom, King Zhao (r. 311–279 B.C.E.) of the Yan kingdom, the First Emperor (Shihuangdi, r. 221–210 B.C.E.) of the Qin dynasty, and Emperor Wu (Wudi, r. 140–87 B.C.E.) of the Han dynasty.

11. Good discussions on the immortality beliefs and methods of the court magicians are found in Ofuchi Ninji, *Shoki no dookyo* (Tokyo: Sobunsha, 1991), pp. 438–68 and Qing Xitai, ed., *Zhongguo daojiao shi* (Chengdu: Sichuan Renmin Chubanshe, 1988), pp. 49–56.

12. This portion also could be rendered as ". . . seeking [to encounter a] Divine Immortal. . . ."

13. *Sibu congkan chubian*, 18:10. The translation is my own, but I have consulted that of Yu Yingshi borrowed by Joseph Needham in *Science and Civilization in China*, vol. 5: 2 (Cambridge: Cambridge University Press, 1974), p. 111.

14. See Anna Seidel and Michel Strickmann, eds. "Taoism" in *Encyclopedia Brittanica* (1994 ed.), vol. 28, p. 388. Also see Anna Seidel, *La divinisation de Lao tseu dans le taoisme des Han* (Paris: Ecole Francaise d'Extreme-Orient, 1969), pp. 17–25.

15. See Sakade Yoshinobu, "Changshang shu" (original title, "Choosei jutsu") in Fukui Kojun et al., *Daojiao*, vol. 1 (*Dookyoo 1: Dookyoo to wa nani ka*), translated by Zhu Yueli (Shanghai: Shanghai Guji Chubanshe, 1990 [Original Japanese edition published in 1983]), p. 203.

16. *Lun heng* (Shanghai: Renmin Chubanshe, 1974), p. 113. I have consulted the translation of Alfred Forke. See Alfred Forke, *Lun-heng: Philosophical Essays of Wang Chung* (Leipzig: Otto Harrassowitz, 1907), p. 346.

17. The deification of Laozi during the Han is discussed masterfully in Anna Seidel, *La divinisation de Lao tseu dans le taoisme des Han.*

18. The earliest historical sources refer to this organization as the Five Pecks of Rice School (*wudoumi dao*). This was because the organization collected five pecks of rice as revenue from each of its adherents. Whether the organization's adherents themselves referred to it by this name is unclear. It has always been known as the Heavenly Masters School due to the fact that the leader is given the

title of Heavenly Master. Today, it is also known as the Orthodox Unity School (*zhengyi pai*) and has its headquarters at Mt. Longhu in Jiangxi Province.

19. The most thorough and informative study of these two movements is found in Ofuchi Ninji, *Shoki no dookyoo* (Tokyo: Sobunsha, 1991), pp. 5–406.

20. A very large number of religious and secular manuscripts were recovered from the Mogao Buddhist Grottos at Dunhuang (western Gansu Province) in 1908 by the party of M.A. Stein and Paul Pelliot. Included among these were many Taoist texts that would have been otherwise unavailable to modern scholars.

21. See Anna Seidel, *La divinisation de Lao tseu dans le taoisme des Han*, pp. 58–75.

22. See Kenneth Scott Latourette, *A History of Christianity* (New York: Harper & Brothers, 1953), pp. 122–23; E. Glenn Hinson, *The Early Church* (Nashville: Abingdon Press, 1996), p. 166.

23. See M.G. Bhagat, *Ancient Indian Asceticism* (New Delhi: Munshiram Manoharlal, 1976), p. 199.

24. See Kurt Rudolph, *Gnosis: The Nature and History of Gnosticism* (San Francisco: Harper and Row, 1984), pp. 326–42.

25. *Qi* in its most common usage refers to steam, air, or gas of some form. (The character's radical 气 derives from a pictograph depicting rising steam.) It also can refer to an invisible force or energy. In its broadest sense, it refers to the basic material that makes up all in the universe. The idea is that before the creation of the world there existed only an undifferentiated, chaotic mass of *qi* that eventually condensed and differentiated itself into various forms and consistencies. Thus essentially all that exists is *qi* in its varying degrees of turbidity (*yin*) and rarefaction (*yang*).

26. See Henri Maspero, *Taoism and Chinese Religion*, translated by Frank Kiermann (Amherst: University of Massachusetts Press, 1981), pp. 266–67.

27. As we shall see in chapter 4, the commentary to the *Zhonghuang jing* in some portions seems to convey a belief in the immortality of a subtle internal entity. However, this interpretation is uncertain. Even if it is correct, the commentary probably dates no earlier than ca. 700 and may expound a soteriology inconsistent with that held by the author of the main text (that may date as early as the fourth century).

28. Two informative studies about these beliefs include Isabelle Robinet, "Metamorphosis and Deliverance from the Corpse in Taoism," *History of Religions* 19.1 (1979), pp. 37–70 and Anna Seidel, "*Post-mortem* Immortality—or: the Taoist Resurrection of the Body." In S. Shaked, D. Shuman, and G.G. Stoumsa, eds. *Gilgul: Essays on Transformation, Revolution and Permanence in the History of Religions*, (Leiden: E.J. Brill, 1987), pp. 223–37.

29. Sozomen, *Ecclesiastical History* (ca. 443–448), translated by Kathleen O'Brien Wicker in *Ascetic Behavior in Greco-Roman Antiquity: A Sourcebook*, edited by Vincent Wimbush (Minneapolis: Fortress Press, 1990), p. 338.

30. This sentence is quoted from Psalms 26: 2.

31. Jacob of Serug (ca. 449–521), *Homily on Simeon the Stylite*, translated by Susan Ashbrook Harvey in Wimbush, p. 21.

32. See Jacques Gernet, *A History of Chinese Civilization*, translated by J.R. Foster (Cambridge: Cambridge University Press, 1982 [original French edition, 1972]), pp. 149–57, 174–94.

33. There is considerable controversy over the authorship of this text. Fukui Koojun argues that it probably dates no earlier than the Tang dynasty. Suzuki Yoshijiro cites internal evidence to argue that it indeed must have been written in the Latter Han. See Stephen Eskildsen, "Severe Asceticism in Early Daoist Religion," Doctoral Dissertation (University of British Columbia, 1994), pp. 196–97, ft. nt. 4; Fukui Kojun, "A Study of *Chou-i Ts'an-t'ung-ch'i*," *Acta Asiatica*, no. 27 (1974), pp. 19–32; Suzuki Yoshijiro, *Shuu-eki sandookei* (Tokyo: Meitoku Shuppansha, 1977), pp. 5–12.

34. See Kenneth Chen, *Buddhism in China: A Historical Survey* (Princeton: Princeton University Press, 1964), pp. 138–42. Also see Nakajima Ryuzo, *Rikuchoo shisooshi no kenkyuu* (Kyoto: Heirakuji Shoten, 1985), pp. 547–52.

35. The leader of the Great Peace Sect who orchestrated the Yellow Turban revolt.

36. See p. 29.

37. A Taoist priest-turned-government official who is thought to have masterminded Northern Song Emperor Zhenzong's (r. 998–1016 C.E.) ploys to solidify his authority on religious grounds. Zhenzong claimed that he had seen divine beings in visions, after which "heavenly books" appeared declaring divine blessing for his regime. In response to these "signs," Zhenzong performed the *feng* and *shan* sacrifices at Mt. Tai. Temples were built and lavish Taoist rituals were performed nationwide to commemorate these events. See Ren Jiyu, ed., *Zhongguo daojiao shi* (Shanghai: Renmin Chubanshe, 1990), pp. 464–72.

38. A Taoist priest who won the favor of Northern Song Emperor Huizong (r. 1101–1127 C.E.) through flattery, declaring him a worldly incarnation of a supreme heavenly deity called the Great Imperial Lord of Long Life (*changsheng da dijun*). See Ren Jiyu, ed., *Zhongguo daojiao shi*, p. 474.

39. An alchemist who concocted the toxic pill that poisoned Tang Emperor Xianzong (r. 805–820 C.E.). See Ren Jiyu, ed., *Zhongguo daojiao shi*, p. 427.

2. The Lives of Taoist Ascetics (1)—Depictions in the *Liexian zhuan* and *Shenxian zhuan*

1. See Eskildsen (1994), pp. 44–46; Max Kaltenmark, *Le Lie-sien tchouan* (Beijing: University of Paris, 1953), pp. 1–5; Sawada Mizuho, "Ressenden, Shinsenden kaisetsu" in *Chuugoku koten bungaku taikei 8: Hoobokushi, Ressenden, Shinsenden, Sengaikyoo* (Tokyo: Heibonsha, 1969), pp. 559–70; Fukui Kojun,

"Ressenden koo" in *Tooyoo shisooshi kenkyuu,* (Tokyo: Shoseki-Bunbutsu Ryutsukai), pp. 113–44.

2. See Eskildsen (1994), pp. 46–48; Kominami Ichiro, "Jin-yaku kara zonshi e" in Yoshikawa Tadao ed. *Chuugoku Kodookyooshi Kenkyuu* (Kyoto: Dohosha, 1992), pp. 4–19; Sawada Mizuho, "Ressenden, Shinsenden Kaisetsu" in *Chuugoku Koten Bungaku Taikei 8: Hoobokushi, Ressenden, Shinsenden, Sengaikyoo,* pp. 564–69; Fukui Kojun, "Shinsenden koo" in *Tooyoo shisoo no kenkyuu* (Tokyo: Risosha, 1955), pp. 30–66.

3. In its original usage, the character *jing* denotes refined white rice. However, it has a wide variety of other uses. It commonly denotes the pure, subtle essence of a thing. When used in a physiological context, it refers abstractly to the body's vitality and its generative forces or, more concretely, to seminal fluid. In some contexts, as we will see, it refers to the nutrients in foods. Also, in some contexts it refers to the spiritual component of a human or an animal, or to nature spirits that dwell in trees, rocks, and so on.

4. Page references for the *Liexian zhuan* are from the Taoist Canon edition (HY294/TT138).

5. Most extant editions of *Liexian zhuan,* including that in the Taoist Canon, refer to her as Nü Wan, which seems to be an error, since she is referred to as Nü Ji in the *Yongcheng jixian lu* (6/9b), *Taiping yulan* (828/4b), *Taiping guangji* (59/6b), and *Zhenxian tongjian houji* (2/13b).

6. References to Pengzu are found in various ancient books such as the *Shiji, Zhuangzi, Xunzi,* and *Huainanzi.* According to legend, his family name was Jian and his personal name was Keng. He was the grandson of the legendary Emperor Zhuanxu. He served as a high official during the reign of Emperor Yao and continued to serve in government up until the end of the Shang dynasty. He allegedly lived for over 700 years.

7. This refers to certain forms of fungi thought to possess great efficacy for bestowing long life.

8. Page references for the *Shenxian zhuan* are from the *Guang hanwei congshu* version text in the *Daozang jinghua lu,* comp. Ding Fubao (fl. 1922) (Hangzhou: Zhejiang Guji Chuban She, 1989).

9. In 220 C.E., the Han dynasty officially came to an end as the throne was usurped by the Cao clan. The Cao clan then established the Wei Kingdom in northern China.

10. See *Sandong zhunang* 2/4a.

11. Quoted along with Jiao Xian's story are the *Liexian zhuan*'s story of Youbozi and the *Shenxian zhuan*'s story of Kong Yuanfang (the text of *Sandong zhunang* is missing the character *fang* 方 from his name). Youbozi "always wore a single-layered garment in the winter and wore a jacket and trousers during the peak of summer." Kong Yuanfang "always ate the tukahoe (*fuling, Pachymo cocos*) plant and pine seeds. He wore bad clothes and ate coarse food"(2/3b).

12. See *Sanguo zhi* (Zhonghua Shuju edition), pp. 363–64. See also Aat Vervoorn, *Men of the Cliffs and Caves: The Development of the Chinese Eremitic Tradition to the End of the Han Dynasty* (Hong Kong: Chinese University Press, 1990), pp. 11–12.

13. See Eskildsen, "The Beliefs and Practices of Early Ch'üan-chen Taoism," M.A. Thesis (University of British Columbia, 1989), pp. 40–42.

14. This mountain is located in Xingpingxian, Shaanxi Province.

15. This is only a tentative translation of the word *shizhongru*. *Zhongrushi* is the most common word used to refer to stalactite. This passage seems to be claiming that Qiong Shu invented the word.

16. Located in Dengfengxian, Henan Province. This mountain and nearby Mt. Shaoshi are referred to collectively as the Central Peak Mt. Song (Zhongyue Song-shan) and revered as one of the sacred Five Peaks of China. Located at the foot of Mt. Taishi is a large active Taoist monastery called the Zhongyuemiao (The Shrine of the Central Peak).

17. This was a region located in what is today the southwestern portion of Shanxi Province and northern portion of Henan Province.

18. Another name for the Western Peak Mt. Hua.

19. An entry on Gu Chun is found in *Liexian zhuan* 2/6b–7a.

20. The location of this mountain is unclear. Longmei may have been an alternate name for Mt. Qingcheng.

21. This is another name for the Central Peak Mt. Song.

22. A few examples are the "grave of Laozi" at Mt. Zhongnan, "Ge Hong's alchemical furnace" at Mt. Luofu, "Zhang Daoling's hatchet" at Mt. Qingcheng, and "Hao Guangning's Cave" on the summit of Mt. Hua.

23. There seems to have once been a Taoist nunnery located here, but now there is only a rest station.

24. The "Qishenpian" chapter in the eighteenth *juan* of the *Daoshu* (HY1011/ TT641–648), a twelfth-century internal alchemical anthology compiled by Zeng Zao.

25. See Jean Levi, "L'abstinence des cereales chez les Taoistes," *Etudes Chinoises* 1 (1983): 3–47 and Kristofer Schipper, *The Taoist Body* (Berkeley: University of California Press, 1993), pp. 167–70.

26. *Congshu jicheng chupian* (1939), 1342: 40. Although the *Bowuzhi* is attributed to Zhang Hua (232–300 C.E.), the original text has been lost. The present version is a collection of writings gathered from various sources, only one of which was Zhang's actual work.

27. The character "gu", 穀 or perhaps "li" 粒 for "grains" is not found in the extant editions of the *Liexian zhuan*, but there seems to be a lacuna here, with *gu* (or *li*) being the missing character. Some more recent editions of the *Liexian zhuan* (Wang Zhaoyuan's revised edition in the *Daozang jinghua lu* and the corrected edition of Qian Xizuo in the *Zhihai*) make this same speculation and insert the character *gu* 穀 into the text.

28. The *Sandong zhunang* has a passage that reads, "The sun is the fruit from which the mist issues. The mist is the essence of the sun" (*"Fushipin"* 3/3b–4a. Quoted from a scripture entitled *Jiuhua jing*).

29. At various times, especially during the late Six Dynasties and Tang periods, Taoists promoted the controversial *huahu* (conversion of the barbarians) legend. This legend maintained that Laozi and Yin Xi went to India and founded Buddhism. Liu Xiang himself probably lived too early to have been familiar with this legend. The text has almost certainly been embellished here, although it is difficult to say when or by whom.

30. Located in Zhuxixian, Hubei Province.

31. Location unsure. This could either refer to the Mt. Huo in Shanxi Province or the one in Anhui Province.

32. A region (once an independent state during the Warring States period) located in present-day western Shandong Province. It was the home of Confucius. Kong Anguo's surname suggests that he may have been a descendant of Confucius. During the reign of Han Emperor Wu (140–87 B.C.E.), there was scholar (and descendent of Confucius) named Kong Anguo who wrote a commentary to the *Shujing* (Book of History). It is unclear whether the Kong Anguo in the *Shenxian zhuan* is supposed to be the same person.

33. Located in Qianshanxian, Anhui Province.

34. Located in Shanxi Province.

35. See Needham, *Science and Civilization in China* 5:5 (1983), pp. 144–45.

36. Such is the attitude of the *Shenxian zhuan*'s narrative. However, in the *Weilüe*, Jiao Xian is not clearly described as a Taoist adept, and the impression one gets is that he may have avoided women out of a feeling of loyalty and mourning for his deceased wife.

37. A district in present-day Hebei Province.

38. Located in Fengjiexian, Sichuan Province.

39. The Wu kingdom was a kingdom that extended over southeastern China during the Three Kingdoms period that followed the Han dynasty.

40. A good and concise discussion about sexual yoga is found in Joseph Needham, *Science and Civilization in China* 2 (1956), pp. 146–52. A good recent book on the subject is Douglas Wile, *Art of the Bedchamber: The Chinese Sexual Yoga Classics including Women's Solo Meditation Texts* (Albany: State University of New York Press, 1992).

41. Zhang Daoling, who was active during the mid to late second century, is revered today as the first Heavenly Master. His sect reached its height as a religious and political body under his grandson Zhang Lu (the third Heavenly Master). (See Ofuchi Ninji, *Shoki no dookyoo* [Tokyo: Sobunsha, 1991], pp. 5–406.) The extant accounts of Zhang Daoling vary greatly. As mentioned in chapter 1, the Five Pecks of Rice Sect emphasized ritual healing and rudimentary ethics and may not have been involved in propagating immortality techniques. No other

source depicts Zhang Daoling as an alchemist, and his depiction as such in the *Shenxian zhuan* seems to be a reflection of the author's own alchemical leanings.

42. This, we are told, he did by means of a method of "liberation from the corpse" (*shijie*). He feigned illness to become bedridden, after which he magically transformed a bamboo cane into a likeness of his corpse. Leaving this fake corpse behind in his bed, he went to join his master.

43. The text is unclear about exactly how he ended up with his master. Perhaps the idea is that after carrying out the procedure of "liberation from the corpse," he was magically transported to the dwelling of his master.

44. Ning was a village located in present-day Huojiaxian, Henan Province.

45. One of the ancient Nine Regions. It spanned over the present-day Hebei and Shanxi provinces, as well as the portion of Henan Province north of the Yellow River.

46. This seems to be a textual corruption, since Xizhou is the name of a dynasty (Western Zhou) and not a place name. Max Kaltenmark points out that the text here should read "Quzhou" (located in southern Hebei Province), since this is how it is rendered in the commentary to the *Wenxuan* (6/33a), the *Chuxue ji* (26/13a), and the *Taiping yulan* (697/5b). See *Le Lie-sien Tchouan*, (Beijing: University of Paris, 1953), 74 nt. a.

47. This probably refers to a middle-aged woman or an elderly woman, since "Liangmu" would translate into something like "the mother from the state of Liang" or "the mother of the beams."

48. The meaning of "three brightnesses" is unclear, but it perhaps refers to certain celestial realms, or to the sun, moon, and pole star.

49. This probably is also a textual corruption. It should probably read "Quyi," which refers again to Quzhou.

50. This is the name of a Warring States period kingdom that existed in present-day eastern Shanxi Province and northern Henan Province.

51. The *Daozang* edition of *Liexian zhuan* has a note here that says that a certain version of the text reads *tang* 碭 instead of *zhuo* 涿 . Tangjun spanned over parts of the present-day Henan, Shandong, Jiangsu, and Anhui provinces.

52. Located between Xi'an and Huaxian in Shaanxi Province.

53. This is a river located west of Zhuoxian, Shaanxi Province.

54. We also are told that he was welcomed as a guest at the home of King Kang of the Song Kingdom because he could play the drum and lute. He is said to have practiced the methods of Juanzi and Pengzu.

55. The revolts took place during the waning years of the Eastern Jin dynasty (317–419). The fighting occurred in areas south of the Yangzi River and along the southern seacoast.

56. See *Jin shu*, pp. 2631–2634 (all page references from the official histories are from the Zhonghua Shuju editions). See also p. 44 of Akizuki Kan-ei, "Daojiao

shi" ("Dookyooshi") in Fukui et al. *Daojiao* vol. (*Dookyoo 1: Dookyoo to wa nani ka*), translated by Zhu Yueli, pp. 35–36. A lengthy, in-depth discussion of Sun En's revolts is found in Miyakawa Hisayuki, *Chuugoku shuukyooshi kenkyuu*, Vol. I (Kyoto: Dohosha, 1983), pp. 193–270.

3. The Lives of Taoist Ascetics (2)—Depictions in the *Daoxue zhuan*

1. Bibliographical citations of the *Daoxue zhuan* are found in several texts; the *Sui shu jingjizhi* (by Changsun Wuji d. 659), *Jiu tang shu* (by Liu Xu 887–946), *Xin tang shu* (by Ouyang Xiu 1007–1072 and Song Qi 998–1067), *Tongzhi lüe* (by Zheng Qiao 1104–1162), *Daozang quejing mulu* (comp. 1275), and *Maoshan zhi*. The *Jiu tang shu*, *Xin tang shu*, and *Tongzhi lüe* give the name of Ma Shu as the author, while the others do not name an author. Both the *Jiu tang shu* and *Xin tang shu* refer to the work as the "*Xuedao zhuan*." See Chen Guofu, *Daozang yuanliu kao*, vol. 2 (1963), pp. 454–55.

2. These texts include the following: *Daode zhenjing guangsheng yi* (HY725/TT440–448), *Xianyuan pianzhu* (HY596/TT329–330), the *Sandong qunxian lu* (HY1238/TT992–995), *Chuxue ji*, the *Taiping yulan* and the *Shilei fu*, and Li Shan's (d. 689) commentary to the *Wenxuan*. The eminent modern Chinese scholar Chen Guofu has patched together all of the available text fragments to create a restored version of the *Daoxue zhuan*.

3. See Yao Sulian (557–637), *Chen shu* (Beijing: Zhonghua Shuju, 1972), pp. 264–65; Li Yanshou (fl. seventh century), *Nan shi* (Beijing: Zhonghua Shuju, 1975), pp. 1907–8.

4. All of the bibliographies that cite it, with the exception of the *Xin tang shu*, describe it as a work of twenty *juan*. The *Sandong zhunang*, which generally mentions the *juan* of the *Daoxue zhuan* it quotes from, makes numerous quotes from the twentieth *juan*.

5. Of course, some of these figures (if they actually lived) did not see themselves as Taoists, but nonetheless came to be revered within the Taoist tradition.

6. Preserved in the first *juan* of the *Xianyuan bianzhu*. See Chen Guofu, *Daozang yuanliu kao*, p. 489.

7. Preserved in the eighth *juan* of the *Daode zhenjing guangsheng yi*. See Chen Guofu, *Daozang yuanliu kao*, p. 489.

8. Preserved in Li Shan's *Wen xuan* commentary and the *Taiping yulan*. See Chen Guofu, *Daozang yuanliu kao*, p. 456.

9. The text of the 663rd *juan* of the *Taiping yulan*—which preserves the passages on Jie Xiang, Jiao Xian, and She Zheng—appears to be corrupt. It gives the names of these three personages, respectively, as Jie Xiang 介像 , Jiao Guang 焦光 , and Bu Zheng 步正 . The content of the fragments indicates that they describe the same personages described in the *Shenxian zhuan*.

10. The text tells us that he hailed from Langzhong, which was located in the northern part of present-day Sichuan Province, near its borders with Gansu and Shaanxi provinces. It also says he moved to Fucheng in "the fourteenth year of the Taiyuan reign era of the Liu-Song Dynasty". Fucheng was located in present-day Jingnandao, Hubei Province. Oddly, there was no Taiyuan reign era during the Liu-Song dynasty (420–479 C.E.). During the Eastern Jin dynasty there was a Taiyuan reign era that lasted from 376 to 396.

11. This may refer to one of the generals who played an instrumental role in founding the Northern Wei dynasty.

12. This allegedly took place in the fourteenth year of the Yuanjia reign era (424–553 c.e.).

13. The Southern Peak (*nanyue*), one of China's renowned Five Peaks, located near Hengyang in Hunan Province.

14. It is unclear whether they had moved to Mt. Heng or had been living there all along. We are told that Liu Ningzhi was "a man of Zhijiang, Nanjun" (located in present-day Jingnan Dao, Hubei Province), but sometimes a statement like this only means that his family roots were in the named area.

15. Near present-day Shaoxing, Zhejiang Province.

16. He hailed from the vicinity of present-day Suzhou, Jiangsu Province.

17. From present-day Yanling County, Henan Province.

18. From present-day Anqiu County, Shandong Province.

19. Yan Jizhi hailed from Jurong near present-day Nanjing.

20. He hailed from what is present-day Xinye County, Henan Province.

21. The text actually reads, "Chaozong," which apparently is an error, since other passages in the *Sandong zhunang* refer to him as "Zongchao." He hailed from what is present-day Jiao County, Shandong Province.

22. Ozaki Masaharu, "Dooshi, Zaike kara Shukke e" in *Rekishi ni okeru Minshuu to Bunka* (Fetschrifte for Sakai Tadao, Tokyo: Kokusho Kankokai, 1982), pp. 205–20.

23. Ozaki, p. 207.

24. The text fragments tell us that Zhang Min went on a fast in the first year of the Dajian (*sic*; Taijian) era of the Chen dynasty (569). Xu Mingye was active as a monk during the Taiqing era of the Liang dynasty (547–549). Xu Shizi was made abbot of the Zhongxu Daguan monastery by Chen Emperor Wu (r. 557–580). Li Lingchen healed the illness of the crown prince during the reign of Liang Emperor Yuan (there was no such emperor, but this likely refers to Emperor Wu [r. 502–556]). Cheng Tongsun was made abbot of the Jingsheng Guan monastery in the sixteenth year of the Tianguan era (517). Zhang Yu established the Zhaozhen Guan monastery on Mt. Yu (near Changshou County, Jiangsu Province) during the Tianguan reign era (502–519).

25. See Ozaki, p. 207.

26. *Sandong qunxian lu* 2/17a.

27. There is a Mt. Yunmeng near Baocheng County, Shaanxi Province. However, since Lu Xiujing hailed from Wuxing (the present-day Zhejiang Province), it seems likely that this passage is referring to a different Mt. Yunmeng that was located near Wuxing, where his family presumably still lived.

28. A comprehensive catalog of Taoist scriptures that established the standard of categorizing Taoist scriptures into the "Three Caverns" or Sandong (Dongzhen, Dongxuan, and Dongshen).

29. Shan is the name of a county and a mountain range in the Eastern Zhejiang Province.

30. Near Tiantai County, Zhejiang Province.

31. This episode also is recorded in *Xianyuan pianzhu* 2/4b, *Xuanpin lu* 3/19b–20a, *Sandong qunxian lu* 6/20b–21a, and *Nanshi*, 1873–1874. According to the version in the *Xianyuan pianzhu*, Chu Boyu fled from his wedding when he was sixteen, and pursued his training on Mt. Tiantai.

32. See Michel Strickmann, "The Mao Shan Revelations: Taoism and the Aristocracy," *Toung Pao* 63 (1977), p. 31.

33. Located in the vicinity of present-day Shaoxing, Zhejiang Province.

34. By Yao Sulian (557–537).

35. This is found in the twenty-sixth *juan* of the *Guang hongming ji*, Taisho Canon 52: 294, middle, p. 298 bottom.

36. See Nakajima Ryuzo, *Rikuchoo shisoo no kenkyuu* (Kyoto: Heirakuji Shoten, 1985), pp. 370–78.

37. She was the aunt of Zhou Ziliang, who was a disciple of Tao Hongjing.

38. See Michel Strickmann, "Liang Wu Ti's Suppression of Taoism," *Journal of the American Oriental Society*, no. 98.4 (1978), pp. 467–75.

39. He hailed from Bo County in present-day Hebei Province.

40. This seems to be the name of a specific liturgy for the confession of sins, which purported to benefit all living and deceased beings. In the Taoist Canon today we have a scripture entitled *Taishang shifang yinghao tianzun xian* (HY542/TT296). The text is largely incomplete, as it preserves only the second and tenth *juan* of what was originally a work of ten *juan*. This scripture could well have been the liturgy used by Fang Qianzhi, although this is difficult to ascertain. The scripture, as its title indicates, is a liturgy of worship and repentance directed at the Heavenly Worthies of the Ten Directions (*shifang tianzun*). The liturgy is designed to bring about universal salvation, which was the central concern of the Lingbao movement. Based on this fact, the scripture probably was written no earlier than the late fourth century.

41. Guisun may have still been ill at this time. However, this is difficult to determine since the portion of the story dealing with Guisun's illness and the portion dealing with the events at the "eastern fringes" are found in separate places in the *Sandong zhunang*. It appears that Xuanche and Guisun fled to the "eastern fringes" together, since the text says "*they* went together into the eastern fringes."

As far as it can be determined, the flight may have taken place during Guisun's three years of illness.

42. For full translations of these passages, see Eskildsen (1994), pp. 266–69.

43. Tao Dan and Xu Mai lived during the fourth century. Xiao Zheng probably lived during the sixth century, when nunhood had been established in Taoism.

44. Wang Jia lived around the late fourth or early fifth century.

45. A county located near present-day Jing County, Anhui Province.

46. This refers to the approximate height of the human body.

4. Taoist Methods of Fasting

1. See Henri Maspero, *Taoism and Chinese Religion*, translated by Frank Kiermann (Amherst: University of Massachusetts Press, 1981), pp. 333–39. Jean Levi, "L'abstinence des cereales chez les Taoistes," *Etudes Chinoises* 1 (1983): 3–47; and Kristofer Schipper, *The Taoist Body*, pp. 167–70.

2. *Lun-heng*, p. 113; Forke, p. 347.

3. Full title, *Taiqing zhonghuang zhenjing*. Two slightly varying versions of the text are found in the Taoist Canon. One version is contained in the *Yunji qiqian* (HY1026/TT677–702), a voluminous anthology of Taoist writings compiled in 1028 or 1029 C.E. The other is found independently (HY816/TT568).

4. A detailed discussion on the dating of the *Zhonghuang jing* is found in Eskildsen (1994), pp. 93–103.

5. For example, the commentary to the fifth chapter states that the eyes have apertures on them that are connected to the liver, which is connected to the heart, which is in turn connected to the nose. Thus when a person has a sad feeling in his heart, tears well up in the eyes and a "sour sensation" becomes present in the nose. Also, because the nose is connected to the brain, a "fever in the brain" causes the nose to dry up.

6. Translations from the *Zhonghuang jing* are based on the HY816/TT568 version. Here, because the topic of the chapter seems to be the retention of inhaled air, rather than the swallowing of air, I have chosen to translate the character *fu* 服 as "subdue" rather than "imbibe." A hint indicating that it is correct to interpret the character in this way is found in the *Yunji qiqian*'s version of the text that employs the character 伏 (*fu*) here, rather than the character 服 .

7. The *Yunji qiqian*'s version of the text reads, ". . . the yellow color will flourish."

8. What exactly is being referred to here as "womb *qi*" is hard to say. Perhaps it refers to the *qi* that gathers and congeals in the belly. Perhaps it refers to the *qi* that is held in during the practice of womb breathing.

9. This probably means that the adept can transform his old, doomed body into a new immortal body. A popularly held notion in China was that when one dies

and the *hun* souls leave the body to return to the heavens, the mourners of the deceased can try to revive their loved one by coaxing the *hun* soul into returning to the body. There is even a type of incense called "*hun* returning incense," the aroma of which is supposed to be helpful for coaxing back the *hun* soul.

10. The *qi* of the liver cures "feverish diseases," boils, and rashes, as well as emaciation. The heart's *qi* cures "chilly diseases."

11. It is unclear whether the word "corpse" here is a disdainful reference to the ordinary body, or is rather a reference to the demons that inhabit the body.

12. The large ones are several *zhang* (one *zhang* is 241 cm.), the small ones are the size of swallows and sparrows. Some have wildly disheveled hair and others emit lightning from their eyes.

13. The two versions of the *Zhonghuang jing* cite different scriptures as the source of the passage. The version in the *Yunji qiqian* cites the *Taihuang jing*, and the HY816/TT568 version cites the *Taiwei xuanjing*.

14. A detailed and highly informative study of this scripture is Livia Kohn, *Taoist Mystical Philosophy: The Scripture of the Western Ascension* (Albany: State University of New York Press, 1991). Two annotated versions of the *Xisheng jing* exist today in the Taoist Canon (HY726/TT449–450, HY666/TT346–347).

15. It should be noted that the statements in question here are found in only one of the two extant versions of the *Zhonghuang jing*. They are not found in the version in the *Yunji qiqian*.

16. This compound *jingqi* is difficult to translate, especially since we do not know the actual exercises prescribed in the *Daoji tuna jing* and *Tuna jing*. However, in combining the words *jing* (generative force, seminal essence) and *qi* (material force, energy, breath) it seems to vaguely designate something in the body that keeps it alive.

17. The two characters *qian* 前 ("before") and *zhi* 至 ("reach") fit in poorly here. There may be a textual corruption.

18. Eight limits" refers to infinitely remote regions situated in the north, south, east, west, northeast, northwest, southeast, and southwest.

19. These texts dealt with various topics, including prognostication, cosmology, numerology, and macrobiotics. They began to appear in the early first century and purported to be commentaries and supplements to the Confucian classics—*jing* or "woof" texts—authored by Confucius and other great sages.

20. See Eskildsen (1994), pp. 137–41; Kobayashi Masayoshi, "*Taijoo reihoo gofu jo no seisho katei no bunseki*," *Toho shukyo* 71 (April 1988), pp. 20–43, 72 (October 1988), pp. 20–44; Yamada Toshiaki, "Longevity and the *Lingbao Wufu xu*" in Livia Kohn, ed. *Taoist Meditation and Longevity Techniques* (Ann Arbor: University of Michigan Press, 1989), pp. 99–124.

21. The Jade Girl rides the Beast of the Nine Mountains and the Most High True King rides the *Kun* Dragon.

22. This deity seems to embody three personalities, as he also is called "Perfected Man Zidan" and the "Jade Girl of the Heavenly Storehouse of the *wuji* of the Yellow Court."

23. This apparently refers to a spot on the roof of the mouth from where saliva is secreted. This term also is found in the *Huangting neijing jing*. There it refers to a spot under the tongue (*Yunji qiqian* 11/20b). In the *Huangting waijing jing*, it refers to a place in the middle of the throat (*Yunji qiqian* 12/31b).

24. These variant methods for imbibing the Five *Qi* are examined in Eskildsen (1994), pp. 366–72, 503–14.

25. See Kristofer Schipper, "Le Calendrier de Jade: Note sur le *Laozi zhongjing*." *Nachrichten der deutchen Gesellschaft für Natur- und Volkerkunde Ostasiens* 125 (1979), pp. 75–80 and *The Taoist Body* (Berkeley: University of California Press, 1993), ch. 6; Maeda Shigeki, "Rooshi Chuukyoo Oboegaki" in Sakade Yoshinobu, ed. *Chuugoku kodai yoosei shisoo no soogooteki kenkyuu* (Tokyo: Hirakawa Shuppansha, 1988), pp. 491–97; Eskildsen (1994), p. 95, ft. nt. 3.

26. It would seem logical here for the adept to first visualize the *qi* of the kidneys. An omission may have occurred in the text. The version of the lunar essence method in 1/19a–b includes a visualization of white *qi* that emerges from the kidneys and permeates the body.

27. See Eskildsen (1994), pp. 372–79, 486–503.

28. According to tradition, the *Sanhuang wen* was discovered by Bao Jing in the second year of the Yuankang reign era of the Western Jin dynasty (292 C.E.). He found the text on Mt. Song, engraved on the wall of a cave. Bao Jing later transmitted the scripture to Ge Hong (see *Yunji qiqian* 6/12a). A passage in the *Baopuzi* reads, "I have heard Sir Zheng say, 'Among the important Taoist books, none surpass the *Sanhuang wen* and the *Wuyue zhenxing tu*'" (19/8a). The surviving fragments of the *Sanhuang wen* are mostly found in the *Wushang biyao* (25th *juan*) and the *Dongshen badi miaojing jing* (HY640/TT342). See Robinet, *La revelation du Shangqing dans l'histoire du Taosime*, 1: 12, pp. 26–29. Also Fukui Kojun, *Dookyoo no Kisoteki Kenkyuu* (Tokyo: Shoseki-Bunbutsu Ryutsukai, 1964), pp. 170–78 and Ofuchi Ninji, *Dookyooshi no Kenkyuu* (Okayama: Okayama Daigaku Kyoseikai Shosekibu, 1964), pp. 277–344.

29. The final sentence here could perhaps be translated as "Divine Immortals will naturally be made to come [before you]."

30. It contains a toxin called phytolacctoxin (C24H3008).

31. 2/23b–24b. "The Immortal's Method for Expelling the Three Worms and Subduing the Corpses."

32. This large mountain range spans across parts of Henan, Hebei, and Shanxi provinces.

33. *Xun* is a variant name for the *nanzhu* shrub, and *fan* denotes cooked rice. Thus, *xunfan* simply means "rice cooked with *nanzhu*." A longer name for the potion is *qingjing ganshi xunfan* (blue refined dried stone *xun* rice). The *nanzhu*

grows to a height of one to three meters. Its leaves have a sour and bitter flavor. See *Zhongyao dazidian*, entry no. 3,261.

34. This fragment is preserved in the *Sandong zhunang* 3/6b.

35. This translates into "The Miraculous Method of Superior Immortals for Blue Refined Rice Dried Stone Xunfan of the Perfected Man of the Great Ultimate."

36. One *liang* was equal to 13.92 grams.

37. One *jin* was equal to 222.73 grams.

38. What kind of disease this refers to is unclear.

39. Hollow azurite, perhaps due to its blue color—and the correlates that blue has in the five element scheme—was thought to "enter" the liver and cure eye ailments. It also was thought to cure other conditions such as palsy. Cinnabar, being red, was thought to "enter" the heart. It was commonly used to treat, among other things, mental conditions such as fear, anxiety, and insomnia. See *Zhongyao dazidian*.

40. This probably refers to an esoteric biography that is now lost. The biography apparently included teachings on the merits of eating white rocks. See Robinet, *La revelation du Shangqing dans l'histoire du taoisme*, 1: 56.

41. Oddly, his entry in the *Shenxian zhuan* does not depict him as an ascetic, nor as a practitioner of fasting. While it does say that he boiled and ate white rocks, it also says that he drank liquor and ate dried meats and ordinary food. It also says that he excelled at sexual yoga and the ingestion of liquid gold. He opted for the perpetual enjoyment of worldly things, rather than heavenly ascension. (2/6a)

42. 1. *Yunji qiqian* 74/7b–13a, in a section entitled "Taishang jushengyu zhu wushiying fa" (The Most High Method for Boiling Five Quartz Pieces in Sesame Oil).

   2. *Ciyi jing* 53b–56b, in a section entitled "Dadong ciyi taiji dijun zhensheng wuzang fa."

   3. *Wushang biyao* 87/6a–13a, quoted from a certain *Dongzhen taiji dijun zhensheng wuzang shangjing*.

43. These references appear within quotes from the *Xuanmu bamen jing* (*The Scripture of the Eight Gates of the Mysterious Mother*) and the third and seventh *juan* of the *Dengzhen yinjue*.

44. Michel Strickmann also describes this method in "On the Alchemy of T'ao Hung-ching," pp. 183–84.

45. The *Dengzhen yinjue*, quoted in the *Sandong zhunang* 3/6a.

46. This narrative also is found in *Zhengao* 4/16a–b and *Wushang biyao* 87/11a–12a. It also is described in Strickmann, "On the Alchemy of T'ao Hung-ching," pp. 182–83.

47. The *Tuna jing* states: "[In pursuing] the Tao [you must] regard your [*jing*] as a treasure. If you administer it you will create a person. If a man retains it he will give life to his own body. If he gives life to his own body he will forever transcend the world and take on the rank of an immortal. If he gives life to a person, his

worldly merit will be accomplished, and he may go into seclusion. People of the world regard this as severe. But how much more [severe the consequences are] if one carelessly administers and abandons [his *jing*]. [By] discarding and damaging [their *jing*] and not studying [the Tao], many [people] thereby decline, age, and lose their lives" (*Tuna jing*, quoted in *Sandong zhunang* 4/1b).

5. Asceticism in the Shangqing Texts

1. *Nanshi*, 1896.

2. See p. 3 of Michel Strickmann, "The Mao Shan Revelations: Taoism and the Aristocracy," *T'oung-pao* 63 (1978), pp. 1–63.

3. See Isabelle Robinet, *La revelation du Shangqing dans l'histoire du taoisme* (1984), 1:107–8.

4. See Miyakawa Hisayuki, *Rikuchoo shi kenkyuu: Shuukyoo hen* (Kyoto: Heirakuji Shoten, 1964), p. 139, and Michel Strickmann, "The Mao Shan Revelations: Taoism and the Aristocracy."

5. Luoyang was sacked by the armies of Liu Yao (of Xiongnu ethnicity) and Shile (of the Jie tribe) of the new Han kingdom.

6. See *La revelation du Shangqing dans l'histoire du taoisme* (1984), 1:108.

7. Ibid., p. 109.

8. For more details on the early proliferation of the texts, see Strickmann, "The Mao Shan Revelations: Taoism and the Aristocracy," pp. 16–54. Strickmann has provided a full English translation of the *Zhengao* 19/9b–20/4b, which describes the process in detail. The man responsible for writing much of the apocryphal material was Wang Lingqi (see pp. 19–24, 45–49 of the article).

9. See Strickmann, "The Mao Shan Revelations: Taoism and the Aristocracy," pp. 31–32.

10. This apprecticeship took place during the mandatory three-year mourning period (484–486) for his mother's death.

11. See pp. 139–40 of Michel Strickmann, "On the Alchemy of T'ao Hung-ching" in Anna Seidel and Holmes Welch, eds., *Facets of Taoism* (1979), pp. 123–92.

12. The version in the Taoist Canon today has only three *juan*. The original work apparently had as many as 24 *juan*, as evidenced in the earliest biography of Tao Hongjing, the *Huayang yinju xiansheng benji lu* (*Yunji qiqian* 107/1b–14a), written ca. 499 by Tao Hongjing's nephew, Tao Yi. The "Dadong zhenjing mu," a catalog of Shangqing texts found in the *Dongxuan lingbao sandong fengdao kejie yingshi* (HY1117/TT760–761, written ca. 550) 5/1a–2b, lists it as having 26 *juan*. Almost all of the passages quoted in other works are not found in the Taoist Canon version. See Robinet, *La revelation du Shangqing dans l'histoire du taoisme*, 2: 347.

13. See Strickmann, "On the Alchemy of T'ao Hung-ching," pp. 157–58 and "The Mao Shan Revelations: Taoism and the Aristocracy," p. 39. Strickmann also has speculated, however, that even Tao Hongjing and his sect eventually felt the

impact of the suppression of 517, which was why Tao built facilities for Buddhist worship on Mt. Mao and personally carried out Buddhist rituals. See Strickmann, "Liang Wu Ti's Suppression of Taoism," pp. 471–72.

14. In our examination of Shangqing asceticism, we will rely on texts that convey the original teachings of the revelations, or at least reflect the beliefs of Shangqing proponents during the fourth through sixth centuries. To be on the safe side, I have relied heavily on the *Zhengao* and *Dengzhen yinjue*, since their contents are most readily verifiable as the authentic writings of Yang Xi and the two Xus. I have also cited various scriptures (*jing*), "esoteric biographies" (*neizhuan*), and lessons (*jue*) that modern scholars consider the products of the early Shangqing movement. In my selection of source materials, I am particularly indebted to Isabelle Robinet, whose work I have consulted repeatedly.

15. See Zürcher, "Buddhist Influence on Early Taoism," *T'oung-pao* 65 (1980), pp. 84–146 and Robinet, *La revelation du Shangqing dans l'histoire du taoisme*, 1: 87–106.

16. *Taisho Canon* no. 784 (vol. 17, p. 722). The first to discover the *Zhengao*'s borrowings from the *Sishi'er zhang jing* was Hu Shi (see "Tao Hongjing de *Zhengao* kao" in *Hu Shi lunxue jinzhu diyi ji* [1935], pp. 155–67), who vehemently criticized Tao Hongjing for plagiarism and deception. Yoshioka Yoshitoyo has pointed out that Tao, as a compiler and an annotator of the writings of Yang Xi and the Xus, was not guilty as accused, since the passages in question came from the manuscripts of Yang Xi. Tao's "innocence" also is attested to by the fact that borrowings from the *Sishi'er zhang jing* also are found in the seventh *juan* of the *Wushang biyao*, as quotes from the *Zhenji* and *Daoji*. The *Zhenji* predated the *Zhengao*, as perhaps did the *Daoji*. See Yoshioka Yoshitoyo, *Dookyoo to bukkyoo*, vol. 3 (Tokyo: Nihon Gakujutsu Shinkokai, 1976), pp. 3–38. Yoshioka provides a very useful table that places the text of the *Sishi'er zhang jing* alongside the cognate passages in the *Zhengao* and the *Shangqing zhongzhen jiaojie dexing jing* (HY458/TT203).

17. By the late fifth or early sixth century, this claim had been generally accepted. However, modern scholars are skeptical. Estimates of the *Sishi-erzhang jing*'s date (in its Chinese form) range between the Latter Han and the early fifth century. It has also been questioned whether it is actually a translation of an Indian original. The fact that large portions of it were found among manuscripts belonging to Yang Xi and the Xus would indicate that the *Sishi-erzhang jing*, or a large portion of it, was in circulation by the fourth century.

18. The cognate portion in the *Sishi'er zhang jing* reads, "From illness they reach [the point of] death."

19. The italicized portion of this passage matches the thirty-fifth chapter of the Buddhist *Sishi'er zhang jing*.

20. This portion matches the fortieth chapter of the *Sishi'er zhang jing*. The text of the *Sishi'er zhang jing* concludes simply, "When the evils are eliminated, you acquire the Tao."

21. This passage matches the twentieth chapter of the *Sishi'er zhang jing*.

22. This passage matches the twenty-second chapter of the *Sishi'er zhang jing*.

23. This passage matches the twenty-first chapter of the *Sishi'er zhang jing*. A note by Tao Hongjing states that the portion reading, "[When you are] shackled . . . tiger's bite" is missing from a "different manuscript from a different hand" of this same passage.

24. See *Yunji qiqian* 5/3b–4b.

25. This most likely refers to those who, by virtue of personal and hereditary merit, are predestined to gain access to the Shangqing scriptures and achieve immortality in the realm of Taiji. Taiji, according to Shangqing belief, was a lofty realm of Perfected Beings that ranked below the realms of Yuqing and Shangqing.

26. In his annotation, Tao Hongjing comments that this "lesson" probably is not a product of one of Yang Xi's visions but is nonetheless consistent with the teachings of the revealed scriptures.

27. The meaning of "female palaces" and "male palaces" is unclear, but these terms perhaps denote certain compartments in the bodies of women and men where the Corpses reside.

28. The ninth of the twelve "branches." It correlates to the seventh month, 4 P.M., and the direction of west-southwest.

29. The third of the twelve "branches." It correlates to the first month, the element of Wood, 4 A.M., and the direction of east-northeast.

30. What all this means is unclear, but apparently it is this correlation of the male and female palaces with the branches of *yin* and *shen* that dictates the days when contact with the opposite sex must be most carefully avoided.

31. The first and final days of each lunar month, along with the *gengshen* (fifty-seventh) and *jiayin* (fifty-first) days of the sexegenary cycle.

32. These deities were believed to examine the merits and misdeeds of the living and the dead and thereby determine their just rewards and punishments. According to the early Heavenly Masters Sect, the Three Officials were the Official of Heaven, the Official of Earth, and the Official of Water. Writs of confession were offered to them during healing rituals. However, the *Xiaomo jing* (full title, *Dongzhen taishang zhihui xiaomo jing*, HY1333/TT1032) 1/5a–b, contains a passage that states that the Three Officials—who live in the Eastern Peak Mt. Tai—are 1) the Water Official of the Left who monitors the sins of the living, 2) the Fire Official of the Right who monitors the sins of the dead, and 3) the Woman Official who monitors the sins of women. Strangely, *Zhengao* 13/4a says that the Three Officials reside in the northern mountain of Fengdu, where they are in charge of the Palaces of the Six (Infernal) Heavens. Tao Hongjing, in his annotation, takes note of the *Xiaomo jing*'s alternative theory and also states that the three posts are currently filled by the three Mao brothers.

33. This apparently refers to sexual desire. "Red" and "white" most likely indicate sexual secretions, with "red" denoting the blood of childbirth and menstru-

ation and "white" denoting sperm. Another less likely interpretation could be that "red and white" refer to the rosy lips and fair complexion of a beautiful woman.

34. Passages concerning the celestial betrothal of Yang Xi are found in *Zhengao* 1/11b–18a.

35. This concept is explained in *Zhengao* 2/2a, in a discourse ascribed to Lady Ziwei. In describing the nature of the liaisons, the discourse states, "Even though you are called husband and wife, you do not carry out the traces of husband and wife (have conjugal sexual relations). Here an empty name is merely used to show to sight and hearing. If yellow and red (erotic passion) exist in your chest, Perfected Beings cannot be seen, and contact cannot be made with holy beings."

36. The character *jian* 漸 seems to be a mistranscription of the character *zhan* 斬 .

37. Full title, *Taishang yupei jindang taiji jinshu shangjing* (HY56/TT30). Robinet speculates that this scripture was part of the original Shangqing corpus. The present edition of the text seems to have mostly maintained its original form, judging from how well its contents match the quotations found in the *Wushang biyao* and *Sandong zhunang*. However, the portion describing the Mingtang Xuanzhen method was originally contained in the esoteric biography of Mao Ying and later added to the *Yupei jindang jing*. See Robinet, *La revelation du Shangqing dans l'histoire du taoisme*, 2: 213–18.

38. This method has previously been translated and discussed by Edward Schafer. See Schafer, "The Jade Woman of the Greatest Mystery," *History of Religions* 17: 3/4 (1978), pp. 387–98. A shorter version of the method, which does not include the amorous imagery, is found in *Zhengao* 9/18a. According to Robinet, the longer version represents the original form of the method. (See Robinet, *La revelation du Shangqing dans l'histoire du taoisme*, 2: 396.) Schafer, to the contrary, says that the longer version is a later, expanded version of the shorter one.

39. Here I have borrowed Schafer's translation.

40. This could refer to the ocean. It could also refer to a mythical island of immortals.

41. This refers to Mao Gu, the second eldest of the Mao brothers.

42. The text states, ". . . I eventually lost my life [drowning] in the harbor of a long embankment."

43. Here Tao Hongjing adds a note stating that Xin Xuanzi's case is comparable to that of the daughter of a certain Wang En, who also had drowned. Tao remarks that in such cases, the body cannot be restored to life and one can only "return the substance to the womb-spirit." This seems to mean that the person gains posthumous regeneration in the Southern Palace. The understanding is apparently that something other than the ordinary body is regenerated. However, Tao Hongjing's attitude seems to be that the perpetuation of the body is still the highest ideal. This Xin Xuanzi failed to achieve in spite of his dedication, due to a lack of what Tao Hongjing calls "deeds of the Tao"—which apparently refers to hereditary merit.

44. This theme is particularly prominent in the *Taiping jing*. See Wang Ming, *Taiping jing hejiao*, pp. 22–24 ("Jie chengfu jue") and pp. 57–61 ("Wushi jie chengfu fa").

45. As has been pointed out by Strickmann, *Zhengao* 3/13b–14a gives a good example of how the beliefs in reincarnation and hereditary merit were combined. There it states that Xu Mi was predestined to attain heavenly immortality. It further states that his blessed destiny and his faith in the Tao were caused by the merit that his distant ancestors had accumulated by saving the lives of 408 people during a famine. The text also claims that Xu Mi was the reincarnation of a Han dynasty adept named Xue Lü, who had failed to attain Immortal-hood because of his concupiscence. Xue Lü had requested rebirth into the Xu family in the hope of benefitting from their hereditary merit. See Strickmann, "On the Alchemy of T'ao Hung-ching," p. 188, ft. nt. 192.

46. See Robinet, *La revelation du Shangqing dans l'histoire du taoisme*, 1:132.

47. See Robinet, *La revelation du Shangqing dans l'histoire du taoisme*, 1:172.

48. Tao Hongjing, in his annotations, speculates that this "Lord" is Peijun (Lord Pei). Peijun was a semilegendary adept of the Former Han. His esoteric biography is found in *Yunji qiqian* 105.

49. As Strickmann points out ("On the Alchemy of Tao Hung-ching," p. 180), the Nine Palaces is the fifth highest tier of divine realms, situated directly under the Taiqing, according to Tao Hongjing's "Chart of Ranks and Merit of the Perfected Holy Beings" (*Dongxuan lingbao zhenling weiye tu* HY167/TT73. This chart also is preserved in *Wushang biyao* 83).

50. Tao Hongjing, in his annotation, states that such a status is conferred if one of the scriptures or methods is mastered. If all of the methods are mastered, one becomes a Perfected Man of the Great Ultimate.

51. This refers to the immortal Chisongzi (Master of the Red Pine), who is mentioned in Peijun's esoteric biography as his teacher. Biographies of Chisongzi, the contents of which differ almost completely from each other, are found in both the *Liexian zhuan* (1/1a) and *Shenxian zhuan* (2/6). The Chisongzi of the *Shenxian zhuan* is the one revered in the Shangqing tradition.

52. Qingwugong was a disciple of Pengzu, according to Tao Hongjing's annotation.

53. Located in Huangyan County, Zhejiang Province.

54. Located in Dantu County, Jiangsu Province.

55. A recipe for a golden elixir that was to be ingested while reciting the *Dadong zhenjing*, is found in the *Ciyi jing* 57b–58b. This elixir has cinnabar, mica powder, and honey as its ingredients. The elixir purports to allow the adept to return to the world and resume a normal diet once he has mastered the recitation and practice of the *Dadong zhenjing* (this is stated in *Ciyi jing* 16b). It is unclear

whether the golden elixir mentioned in the story of Huangguanzi is the same potion.

56. The narrative ends with the comment, "This is not something that the Buddha is able to bring about. It is because his inner inch (his heart) was stable" (5/7b–8a). Thus measures are taken here to prevent readers from crediting Huangguanzi's success to the Buddha.

57. There are several possibilities, but this probably refers to the Zhongshan located near present-day Jingyang County, Shaanxi Province.

58. Located near Mian County, Shaanxi Province.

59. The Yixian Palace is the name of a paradise for women located in the subterranean Huayang Grotto Heaven in Mt. Mao. This was where Xu Hui's mother was thought to dwell after her death (*Zhengao* 13/2a–6b). See Robinet, *La revelation du Shangqing dans l'histoire du taoisme*, 1:136.

60. "Esoteric biographies" are elaborate legends of ancient semilegendary adepts who were revered within the tradition. These works contain detailed descriptions of the techniques allegedly employed by the protagonists. The existence of an esoteric biography of Peijun among original Shangqing materials is attested to by a reference in *Zhengao* 2/18a. According to Robinet, the version found today in the *Yunji qiqian* is not the original; it mixes fragments of the original with fragments from other Shangqing texts. See Robinet, *La revelation du Shangqing dans l'histoire du taoisme*, 2: 375–83.

61. Fufeng was located in present-day Hancheng County, Shaanxi Province. The historicity of this story is clearly dubious because Peijun's alleged date of birth is almost two centuries prior to the official introduction of Buddhism to the court of Latter Han Emperor Ming.

62. There are eight different Mt. Jings, each of which could well be the mountain referred to here; two in Henan Province, two in Anhui Province, two in Hubei Province, one in Shandong Province, and one in Shaanxi Province.

63. Full title, *Taishang shuo zhihui xiaomo zhenjing* (HY1333/TT1032). According to Robinet (*La revelation du Shangqing dans l'histoire du taoisme*, 2:183), the first two *juan* of the extant Taoist Canon version can be deemed authentic Shangqing material, based on comparisons with the citations of the *Xiaomo jing* found in the *Zhengao*.

64. The first few pages of the first *juan* tell how Jinque Dijun (The Imperial Lord of the Golden Palace Gates), who had heard this first section preached by Taishang Daojun, transmitted it orally to Lord Blue Boy, who in turn transmitted it to Chisongzi.

65. Located in Jinhua County, Zhejiang Province.

66. These "heavens" are not paradises; rather, they are six infernal realms of punishment located in Mt. Fengdu.

67. The official history of the Former Han dynasty, written by Ban Gu (32–92 C.E.).

68. See Eskildsen (1994), pp. 144, 230–35.

69. These expositions are found the *Dongzhen santian zhengfa jing* (quoted in *Wushang biyao* 6), *Shangqing santian zhengfa jing* (quoted in *Sandong zhunang* 9 and *Yunji qiqian* 2), and *Shangqing housheng daojun lieji* (HY442/TT198). See Kobayashi Masayoshi, "Jooseikyoo to Reihookyoo no Shuumatsu Ron" in *Toohoo Shuukyoo* 75 (May 1990) and Isabelle Robinet, *La révélation du Shangqing dans l'histoire du Taoîsme* (1984), pp. 138–41.

70. See subsequent nt. 77.

71. I do not understand this sentence clearly, but I think it means that traces of what are good and divine are scarcely to be found in the world, as the demonic entities carry out their proper duty to punish evil people by afflicting them with misfortunes.

72. As is noted by Tao Hongjing, Chen Anshi's story appears in the *Shenxian zhuan* 8/33b–34a (see p. 22).

73. The body of flesh where the *po* souls make their abode.

74. This text's full title is *Shangqing gaoshang miemo yudi shenhui yuqing yinshu* (HY1345/TT1038).

75. This text's full title is *Shangqing gaoshang jinyuan yuzhang yuqing yinshu* (HY1347/TT1038).

76. See Robinet, *La revelation du Shangqing dans l'histoire du taoisme*, 2: 237–44.

77. The precise meaning here of "Six Heavens" and "Three Heavens" is difficult to ascertain. However, the theme of the sacred Three Heavens (the heavens of Qingwei, Yuyu, and Dachi) that subdue the demons of the profane Six Heavens (the gods of non-Taoist folk cults) was prominent within the beliefs of the early Heavenly Masters Sect. Eventually, the Three Heavens came to be described as the Three Pure Realms (*sanqing*) of Yuqing, Shangqing, and Taiqing (see Chen Guofu, *Daozang yuanliu kao*, pp. 311–14). Robinet points out, however, that the Heavenly Masters Sect's names for the Three Heavens are nowhere to be found in the Shangqing texts, and the Six Heavens are described in the Shangqing texts as infernal realms located in Mt. Fengdu. See Robinet, *La revelation du Shangqing dans l'histoire du taoisme*, 1: 67.

78. This refers to the first days of the four seasons, the spring and fall equinoxes and the summer and winter solstices.

79. This original Shangqing scripture (which survives today only in fragments preserved in various sources) is listed in the "Dadong zhenjing mu" (see nt. 12) as *Shijing jinguang zangjing luxing jing*. In the *Zhengao* it is referred to as the *Baojian jing*, or simply *Jian jing* (Scripture of the Double-edged Sword). The *Daodian lun* quotes it under the title *Taiji zhenren feixian baojian shang-jing*. See Robinet, *La revelation du Shangqing dans l'histoire du taoisme*, 2: 137–40.

80. This passage also is found in *Daodian lun* 2/11a–12b.

81. After being a Master in the Underground for 1000 years, they "manage demons and spirits for 1,400 years" and finally become "Intermediate-level Immortals of the Nine Palaces of the Great Purity" (*Zhengao* 16/10b, *Daodian lun* 2/11b).

82. For a detailed discussion on these lofty meditations, see Isabelle Robinet, *La Meditation Taoiste* (1979), which is now available in English translation (*Taoist Meditation*, translated by Norman Girardot and Julian Pas (Albany: State University of New York Press, 1993).

83. The full title of the text is *Dongzhen gaoshang yudi dadong ciyi yujian wulao baojing* (HY1302/TT1025) 9b. According to Robinet, the *Ciyi jing* we have today is a collection of materials that originally belonged to various different texts, some of which were written by Yang Xi, and others which were early Shangqing apocrypha. The text did not take on its present form until the seventh century or later. Robinet's speculations are based primarily on the observation that the *Wushang biyao* and *Sandong zhunang* contain various passages that match the contents of the *Ciyi jing*, but are presented as quotes from different scriptures. This would indicate that the *Ciyi jing* itself does not predate the *Sandong zhunang*, even though the bulk of its material does. *Ciyi jing* 1a–19b deals primarily with how to prepare oneself for the recitation and practice of the all-important *Dadong zhenjing*. Robinet points out that this section differs stylistically from the original Shangqing writings, and that p. 11a contains a reference to the Primordial Heavenly Worthy (Yuanshi Tianzun, the supreme deity introduced and venerated in the Lingbao scriptures). This suggests that the section was not written before the fifth century. The passage in question here is nonetheless relevant to our study, since it does convey the religiosity of the proponents of the *Dadong zhenjing*. See Robinet, *La revelation du Shangqing dans l'histoire du taoisme*, 2: 261–76.

84. The underlined portion also is found in a fragment from the *Dengzhen yinjue*, preserved in *Sandong zhunang* 3/13a.

85. On the various usages of the term *dadong*, see Robinet, *La revelation du Shangqing dans l'histoire du taoisme*, 2: 30.

86. See Michel Strickmann, "On the Alchemy of T'ao Hung-ching," pp. 130–36.

87. According to Strickmann, "abandoning the waist band" means to cast aside the restrictive coil of formal social relationships. See "On the Alchemy of T'ao Hung-ching," p. 137, ft. nt. 37.

88. The passage also states that the adept can relieve the chest pain if he knows "the name(s) of the drug(s)." Strickmann understands this as an allusion to the secret names of the medicine's ingredients. In my opinion, it also could refer to celestial medicines of the kind exalted in the *Xiaomo jing* (see p. 86). The text also provides the adept with the option of remaining in the world; he can do so by limiting the amount of water he drinks. In other words, an escape route is provided for those who change their minds because of their fear of death. See "On the Alchemy of T'ao Hung-ching," p. 137.

89. His story is found in the *Liexian zhuan* 2/4b.
90. This likely refers to Chouzi, whose story is found in the *Liexian zhuan* 1/8.
91. This could refer to Mt. Qiao near Zhongbu County, Shaanxi Province.
92. His story is found in *Yunji qiqian* 85/8a–9a.
93. This apparently refers to Ningfengzi. See p. 00.
94. See *Liexian zhuan* 1/7b.
95. The sentence about Bocheng is also quoted in *Taiping yulan* 670/2a.
96. See Eskildsen (1994), pp. 190–92.

6. Asceticism in the Lingbao Scriptures

1. Although numerous texts of diverse periods bear the term *Lingbao* in their titles, "Lingbao scriptures" in this study refers to the texts categorized as such by Lu Xiujing in his famous catalog, the *Sandong jingshu mulu* of 471 C.E. The catalog divides the scriptures into two categories, which modern Japanese scholars have conveniently named the "Primordial's category" (*genshi kei*) and the "Immortal Duke's category" (*senkoo kei*). Scriptures of the Primordial's category are generally presented as teachings uttered by the Primordial Heavenly Worthy. As has been pointed out by Kobayashi Masayoshi, these scriptures were apparently believed to have been revealed and expounded throughout the universe by the Primordial Heavenly Worthy in the first year of the Shanghuang reign era (a mythical era in the inconceivably remote past). Scriptures of the Immortal Duke's category are presented as lessons bestowed upon Ge Xuan by divine beings, or as discourses delivered by Ge Xuan himself. These scriptures were believed to have been revealed to Ge Xuan during the Chiwu reign era (238–251 C.E.) of the Three Kingdoms Wu dynasty. While such are their ascribed origins, the Lingbao scriptures appear to have been written some time between 420 and 471 C.E.

The full text of Lu Xiujing's catalog, in its original form, has not survived. However, most of its contents were preserved in two manuscripts found at Dunhuang (Pelliot manuscripts 2861 and 2256). Ofuchi Ninji has reconstructed the whole catalog by supplementing the information in these manuscripts with information found in a few other texts ("Lingbao zhongmeng mulu" in Pelliot manuscript 2337 *Sangdong fengdao kejie yifan* and "Zhaitan anzhen jingmu" in *Wushang huanglu dazhai licheng yi*, HY508/TT278). He has also made a gallant effort to determine which scriptures extant today in the Taoist Canon and the Dunhuang manuscripts correspond to the titles enumerated in the catalog. (See Ofuchi Ninji, "On *Ku Ling-pao ching*" in *Acta Asiatica* 27 (1974) pp. 34–56.)

2. A widely held theory among modern scholars has been that Ge Chaofu wrote the texts around the year 400. However, this theory has been forcefully refuted by Kobayashi Masayoshi, who argues for a later date and speculates that Ge Chaofu only wrote the set of five sacred verses known as the *Lingbao chishu wupian zhenwen* (Lingbao Five Perfect Writs in Red Script). For detailed discus-

sions on the authorship of the Lingbao scriptures, see Kobayashi Masayoshi, "Ryuu-soo ni okeru Reihookyoo no keisei," *Toyo Bunka* (March 1982), pp. 99–137; and Eskildsen (1994), pp. 386–91.

3. See Bokenkamp, "Sources of the Lingbao Scriptures," pp. 445–46.

4. These are found in the *Chishu zhenwen* (*The Perfect Writs and Red Script*) 1/7b–29a, *Chishu yujue* (*Jade Lessons on the Red Script*) 1/8b–16a, and *Wushang biyao* 24/7b–15a (in a section entitled "Dongxuan chishu jing"). The Writs are written in a special seal script in the *Chishu zhenwen*.

5. Full title, *Taishang dongxuan lingbao benxing yinyuan jing* (HY1107/ TT758).

6. The *Dongxuan lingbao yuqingshan buxujing* states, "The Mysterious Capital of Jade Capital Mountain exists above the Three Pure Realms . . . it is the Heaven of Daluo that is without a superior, the place governed by the Most High Vacuous Emperor of the Limitless" (1a).

7. His story is found in the *Liexian zhuan* 1/14b–15a.

8. Full title, *Dongxuan lingbao zhihui benyuan dajie shangping jing* (HY344/TT177).

9. The point being made here is unclear. It could be saying that good retribution cannot yet be had with only 1,200 merits. On the other hand, it could be saying that the accumulation of 1,200 merits assures one of evading bad retribution (early death, damnation, etc.).

10. Although this title resembles Lingbao catalog entry 13, Ofuchi ("On *Ku Ling-pao ching,*" 51) states that it is not the same scripture. This is because its contents do not resemble the *Taishang dongxuan lingbao zhenwen duren benxing miaojing* (Pelliot 3022), which he believes to correspond to entry 13. My impression is that the *Taishang dongxuan lingbao jieye benxing shangpin miaojing* conveys the religiosity of the Lingbao movement. However, it contains elaborate discourses on themes (such as an enumeration of grades of saints, or *sheng*) not present in the Lingbao scriptures. It appears to be the work of somewhat later Lingbao adherents.

11. On pages 8b–9a, the "places of the ten goodnesses" are enumerated by the Heavenly Worthy of the Primordial One (*yuanyi tianzun*). These are traits to be exhibited by truly righteous people, which include an all-embracing compassion and love, generous almsgiving, and the observance of retreats and precepts. The sixth item in the list is "to be able to die while maintaining your goodness, withstanding disgrace without killing and not stealing." If this is not a clear enough exhortation toward martyrdom, one later finds (on p. 10a) the following words of advice on how to deal with persecution at the hands of the unrighteous: "I revealed the superior section on the ten goodnesses in order to make all gods and people throughout the ten directions avoid the ten places of evil. Being so, if there are those who practice the ten evils, you must not follow them. If you go amidst them, and there are those who say the praises of [sensual] pleasures, you should avoid

them. If there are those who say they want to come and harm you, you should with your whole heart contemplate the remonstrances about *karma* and concentrate upon the Perfect, and thereupon let them kill you. The principle [of cause and effect] will then naturally work so that there can be no harm. Your own body will transform into an Utmost Perfected Being that is without Superior. Those people [who kill you] will naturally suffer the retribution (punishment) for murder."

Thus, a true adept was supposed to be willing to die for the purpose of maintaining his moral integrity. Rather than commit a violent act, he was to allow himself to be harmed or even killed. Such martyrdom is the ultimate expression of faith and the renunciation of evil and greed.

12. As Bokenkamp has illustrated, this notion of five lands is inspired by the Pure Land Buddhist belief in Amitabha's Western Pure Land, a theme adopted and grafted upon that of the heavens of the Five Directions. See "Sources of the Ling-pao Scriptures," pp. 472–73.

13. A similar story belonging to the Lingbao tradition is found in the "Chronicle of the Worthy God of the Southern Extreme," quoted from the *Dongxuan benxing jing* in *Yunji qiqian* 102/12b–13b.

14. "Sources of the Ling-pao Scriptures," p. 474.

15. Taisho Canon no. 557 (vol. 14, p. 909, bottom).

16. Bokenkamp interprets this portion of the narrative differently. According to him, the Demon–Kings told her that her father was about to be reborn as a woman and that she must follow his example by remaining a woman. He has apparently misinterpreted the phrase 汝父當出女身.

The accuracy of my interpretation is attested to by the text of the same story found in the *Yunji qiqian* 102/11b. There, the corresponding portion reads 汝父當娉汝身. Clearly, the passage means to say that her father had made plans for her marriage.

17. The text tells us that during his life as a prince, he acquainted himself with a circle of future religious figures (who were palace attendants at this particular incarnation and time). These included the Buddhists Shi Daowei and Zhu Falan and the Taoists Zheng Siyuan and Zhang Tai. Nothing is known by modern scholarship about Shi Daowei and Zhang Tai. Zheng Siyuan was a disciple of Ge Xuan and the teacher of Ge Hong. Zhu Falan is the name of one of the Indian Buddhist masters in the famous legend of Han Emperor Ming's dream (which led to the introduction of Buddhism into China), who putatively came to Luoyang in 67 C.E. However, Bokenkamp speculates that the Zhu Falan mentioned here is a monk by the same name who trained together with Zhi Qian on Mt. Qionglong. Bokenkamp further speculates that during the third century, the Ge clan may have had connections with an early southern Buddhist tradition for whom Zhi Qian had carried out translation work. See Bokenkamp, "Sources of the Ling-pao Scriptures," pp. 466–67.

18. The legendary cosmic mountain in the west.

19. Another possible translation is, ". . . burdens of forms."

20. One of the Three Pure Realms. It ranked below the realms of Yuqing and Shangqing. Tao Hongjing's *Zhenling weiyi tu* places another realm, Taiji, in between the Shangqing and Taiqing realms.

21. The *Foshuo amituo sanye sanfo salou fotan guodu rendao jing* (Taisho Canon no. 362), a Buddhist scripture translated by Zhiqian of the third century C.E., describes three categories of devotees who gain rebirth in the Pure Land of the Amitabha. The *Xuanyi quanjie falun miaojing*'s three categories of gentlemen may have been formulated partially under the influence of this Buddhist concept.

In the Buddhist formulation, the categories consist of 1) monks who live a pure, disciplined life, 2) laypeople who act as generous, pious patrons, and 3) less wealthy laypeople who distinguish themselves through ritual fasting and inner purification. People of all three categories, if they earnestly desire to be reborn in Amitabha's Pure Land, will have their wish fulfilled upon their death. The monks who make up the first category attain the status of Bodhisattva immediately upon their entry into the Pure Land. However, the laypeople of the two latter categories, after their blessed rebirth, must wait much longer (over 500 years) before gaining Bodhisattva-hood. This is because they have intermittently wavered in their faith and devotion.

The *Foshuo amituo sanye sanfo salou fotan guodu rendao jing* emphasizes the compassion of Amitabha and his power to bring salvation to all who desire it, even laypeople of limited faith and devotion. In the *Xuanyi quanjie falun miaojing*, the three categories of gentlemen all appear to be full-time religious practitioners who earn their immortality through their own virtues and efforts. Overall, the descriptions and teachings of the two texts differ considerably. However, it is interesting that the categories described in both texts seem to be defined to a certain degree by social status and wealth.

22. A longer version is found in the *Taishang zhutian lingshu duming miao-jing* (HY23/TT26), 11b–14a.

23. By this I mean to say that they are not enumerated in the texts that fit my working definition of "Lingbao Scriptures" (see nt. 1).

24. This deity appears prominently in the Shangqing texts as a revealer of scriptures. (See Robinet, *La revelation Shangqing dans l'histoire du taoisme*, 1:127, 187). In Tao Hongjing's *Zhenling weiyi tu*, he is described as the teacher of the Queen Mother of the West and is ranked in the realm of Taiqing.

25. See "Sources of the Ling-pao Scriptures," pp. 470–71.

26. For an in-depth discussion of them, see Eskildsen (1994), pp. 442–48.

27. In Buddhist texts, this term refers to greed, anger, and ignorance. Such could also be what is meant here.

28. This is a name for the internal baby mentioned in the *Wufu xu*, *Laozi zhongjing*, and *Huangting jing*. Here, however, Zidan has his dwelling in the Three Elixir Fields.

29. This refers to a technique of inner visualization carried out in preparation for the recitation of the *Dadong zhenjing*. The adept visualizes the Three Primal

Goddesses of Simplicity in the cranial Jinhua (Golden Flower) Palace. See Robinet, *Taoist Meditation*, pp. 131–34.

30. In a Buddhist context, Anyang refers to the Western paradise of the Buddha Amitabha.

31. This refers to a visualization method described at the end of the *Shang-qing dadong zhenjing* (HY6/TT16–17, 6/16a–18a). It was meant to be carried out after the recitation and practice of the *Dadong zhenjing*. The adept visualizes "one hundred gods," who transform into white *qi*, enter his mouth, pervade the interior of his body, exit from his extremities, encircle and illuminate his body, and finally merge to become the Imperial Worthy Lord of the Dadong. This deity then enters the "Liuhe Palace" in the adept's brain through his mouth. See Robinet, *La revelation du Shangqing dans l'histoire du taoisme*, 2: 36. Also, *Taoist Meditation*, pp. 103–17.

32. This probably refers to the believer whose home is serving as the ritual arena. The participants at the final feast are told to wish for his or her ascension. This perhaps implies that "the host" is recently deceased, and the ritual is conducted for the deliverance of his or her soul at the request of his or her family.

33. See Sunayama Minoru, *Zui-Too Dookyoo shisooshi kenkyuu* (Tokyo: Hirakawa Shuppansha, 1990), pp. 193–94. Also Yoshioka Yoshitoyo, *Dookyoo to Bukkyoo*, 2: 67.

34. See Sunayama Minoru, *Zui-Too Dookyoo shisooshi kenkyuu*, pp. 201–11. The Taixuan faction, according to Sunayama, was a movement that promoted the *Laozi*, the *Xisheng jing*, and the *Miaozhen jing*. Its most prominent figure was Meng Zhizhou of the Liang dynasty, who devised the system of categorizing scriptures into the four *fu*, which complemented the previously devised three Caverns, or *dong*.

35. A detailed discussion of this practice in Chinese Buddhism is Julian Pas, "Six Daily Periods of Worship: Symbolic Meaning in Buddhist Liturgy and Eschatology," *Monumenta Serica* 37 (1986–1987), pp. 49–82.

36. Buddhist texts, in stating the times for worship, are not entirely consistent with each other, but do give times roughly similar to this. See Pas, "Six Daily Periods of Worship: Symbolic Meaning in Buddhist Liturgy and Eschatology," pp. 50, 53–54, 82.

37. Buddhist terms. A passage from *Zhengao* 6, which is mostly borrowed from the *Sishi'erzhang jing*, enumerates the "eight difficulties": "Lord Wang of Xicheng proclaimed, '*It is difficult for a person to avoid the three bad existences* (hell, hungry ghost, animals) *and get to become a human. Once one has gotten to be a human, it is difficult to avoid becoming a woman and to become a man. Once one has become a man, it is difficult to become fully endowed with the six senses and four limbs. [Even] when one has the six senses, it is difficult to get to be born in China*. Once one has been born in China* (italics added), it is difficult to get to live under parents and a ruler who maintains the Tao. Even if one gets to live under a

ruler who maintains the Tao and is born into a family which studies the Tao, it is difficult to get to have a good heart, and it is difficult to get to believe in the inner power of the Tao and long life. Even if you believe in the inner power of the Tao and in long life, it is difficult to get to live during the moment of the Great Peace of Renchen. How can you not be diligent!" (*Zhengao* 6/6b–7a)

"Ten Sufferings" refers to the suffering caused by 1) birth, 2) old age and decrepitude, 3) illness, 4) death, 5) despair, 6) resentment, 7) emotional effects of suffering, 8) worry, 9) fear of death, and 10) transmigration.

38. This interpretation can be deduced from the fact that in some places the text reads "hit your cheek" (*bojia*), rather than "hit yourself" (*zibo*).

39. A Buddhist term referring to three realms that make up *samsara*; the realm of desires (*yujie*), the realm of forms (*sejie*), and the realm of no forms (*wusejie*).

40. See Henri Maspero, *Taoism and Chinese Religion*, pp. 381–86.

41. Here, Henri Maspero (whose translation I have borrowed) has rendered the character *shi* as "hours." However, "times" would probably be the correct translation here, since this sentence refers to the Buddhistic custom of worshiping six times a day.

42. Here I have borrowed Maspero's translation. See *Taoism and Chinese Religion*, pp. 381–82.

43. One of the few faults in Maspero's otherwise masterful work is that he mistakenly understood the Great Peace Sect and Five Pecks of Rice Sect to be two branches of the same organization. He thus uses the name "Yellow Turbans" to refer to both groups, even though only the anti-Han rebels of the Great Peace Sect were known by this name to their contemporaries. His misunderstanding is likely due to the fact that the two groups carried out similar practices and their leaders shared the surname Zhang.

44. See *Taoism and Chinese Religion*, pp. 387–88.

45. The character *shuang* has no common nominal usage. However, as an adjective, it can refer to the brightness of dawn. Following the example of Isabelle Robinet, I have rendered this word as "light," for lack of a better conceivable alternative. See Robinet, *Histoire du taoisme: des origines au XIVe siecle* (Paris: Les Editions du Cerf, 1991), p. 157.

46. See D.C. Lau tr. *Tao Te Ching*, p. 69.

47. *Daode zhenjing zhu* (HY682/TT363) 1/10b. The commentary is ascribed to a Former Han dynasty hermit known as Heshanggong. Opinion among modern scholars about the date of this text is divided. Estimates range from Latter Han to roughly the time of the Lingbao scriptures. Kusuyama Haruki proposes the theory that the commentary was written in two stages. He believes that much of the Heshanggong commentary could date as early as the Latter Han. However, according to him, the portions dealing with physiological theories and macrobiotic methods were clumsily tacked on during the late Six Dynasties (Liang dynasty or later) by Lingbao proponents. See *Rooshi densetsu no kenkyuu* (1979), pp. 5–160.

48. The *Taiji yinzhu baojue* 14a–b clearly endorses the Heshanggong commentary.

49. Livia Kohn observes that the word *shen* (translated earlier as "body") generally is used in Taoist texts to refer to the body that is afflicted with self-involved concerns and needs. *Xing* (translated earlier as "bodily form"), on the other hand, is used to describe the body in its capacity as a microcosm. She thus proposes that *shen* should be translated as "personal body" or "extended self," and *xing* should be translated as "physis" or "physical body." However, she also admits that the usages of the two words do not always conform to this pattern. Here, the two words are used interchangeably. See Livia Kohn, "Eternal Life in Taoist Mysticism," Journal of the American Oriental Society 110.4 (1990), pp. 622–40.

50. See Eskildsen (1994), pp. 485–500.

51. This scripture, which no longer survives as an independent text, appears to have been one of the scriptures cited in Lu Xiujing's catalog. The title resembles catalog entries 13 and 27. The aforementioned story of Aqiu Zeng, found in the *Chishu yujue*, also is found in the *Yunji qiqian* as a quote from this *Dongxuan benxing jing*.

52. This scripture and its concept of *miedu* have been discussed by Stephen Bokenkamp in "Death and Ascent in Lingbao Taoism," *Taoist Resources* 1.2 (1989), pp. 1–20. Bokenkamp has understood *miedu* in a different way than I have. He understands it as a process where rebirth, not resurrection, is achieved. His interpretation does not appear to make sense. If one is to enter a human womb to be reborn, it would be senseless to preserve the corpse in the ground. As we have already seen, the Lingbao movement's understanding of rebirth was that the body would decompose to dust and then light, after which it would reunite with the *hun* soul to be reborn.

7. Criticisms of Heretical Asceticism in the *Yuqing jing*

1. Major examples of such scriptures, aside from the *Yuqing jing*, are the *Taixuan zhenyi benji jing* (HY1103/TT758), *Taishang yisheng haikong zhizang jing* (HY9/TT20–22), *Taishang lingbao yuanyang miao jing* (HY334/TT168–169), *Dasheng miaolin jing* (HY1387/TT1049), *Taishang dongxuan lingbao yebao yinyuan jing* (HY336/TT174–175), and *Taishang dongxuan lingbao shengxuan neijiao jing* (HY1114/TT759).

2. The scripture's full title is *Taishang dadao yuqing jing*. The scripture also is included in the *Daozang jiyao* nos. 26–27. Textual discrepancies between the Taoist Canon and *Daozang jiyao* editions are few and insubstantial.

3. For a discussion of the *Yuqing jing*'s authorship, see Eskildsen (1994), pp. 534–38.

4. The text takes up three full bound volumes in the Taoist Canon. It is divided into ten *juan*, which contain a total of nineteen chapters or *pin* (numbered 1 through 20; the seventh chapter is missing). For an overview of the nineteen chapters and the topics covered in each of them, see Eskildsen (1994), pp. 529–33.

5. See Eskildsen (1994), pp. 588–619.

6. It should be clarified that words such as "heretical" or "heresy" are used in this discussion to refer to beliefs and practices deemed as such by the author(s) of the *Yuqing jing*. "Orthodoxy" refers to what the author(s) considered correct Taoism. In using such words, I am not making any value judgments of my own.

7. Throughout this chapter, this is how I will render the term *waidao*. It was originally a Buddhist term used to refer to non-Buddhist faiths and doctrines. When used in Taoist texts, it refers to non-Taoists. "Infidel" appears to be the most appropriate English word for translating the term. While I fear that certain readers may feel that the word "infidel" is too loaded with connotations of religious dogmatism and conflict (things that people more commonly associate with Western religion), I would contend that such connotations are quite appropriate in light of the harsh polemical tone that pervades this text.

8. In chapter 3, mention was made of the suppression of Taoism in the early sixth century under Emperor Wu of the Liang dynasty. Before and after this incident there occurred cases where emperors heavily persecuted Buddhism. The first of these persecutions occurred during the years 446–452 under the reign of Northern Wei Emperor Taiwu (Taiwudi). The second occurred during the years 574–578 under the reign of Northern Zhou Emperor Wu. The third (most infamous) persecution of Buddhism was the Huichang Persecution of 845 under Tang Emperor Wuzong.

9. The ten ordinances can be paraphrased as follows: 1) Do not be disrespectful or disobedient toward your parents, teachers, and superiors. 2) Do not kill. 3) Do not commit treason. 4) Do not commit adultery, especially incest. 5) Do not blaspheme the Tao. Do not transmit scriptures in an improper way. 6) Do not defile holy altars or act contemptuously in their midst by being naked. 7) Do not deceive or deride those who are poor or who lack families. 8) Do not go about naked beneath the sun, moon, and stars. Do not deceive or deride the aged or the ill. 9) Do not drink liquor excessively. Do not tell lies and do not insult others. 10) Do not do things in a cruel and arbitrary manner. (See 1/8b–9a.)

10. The *Yang*-Nine is a term used in the *Wufu xu* to refer to the Great Kalpa. See Eskildsen (1994), pp. 144, 230–35.

11. The author apparently believed that the universe underwent a preordained sequence of cosmic cycles. Each cycle had its operative element that dictated the type of calamity that would destroy the world. The narrative here takes place in the Fire Kalpa in the inconceivably remote past, which was to be followed by the Water Kalpa. This Water Kalpa is the present cosmic era, which is due to end with a gigantic flood.

12. Here, *kalpa* seems to refer to the cosmic disaster rather than the cosmic cycle.

13. This quite possibly refers to the first Heavenly Master Zhang Daoling, who here takes the form of a deified, cosmic being. The doctrines and methods of the Heavenly Masters Sect are commonly referred to as "Zhengyi meng (= ming)

wei zhi dao santian zhengfa," or "The Way of the Might of the Covenant of the Orthodox Unity, the Orthodox Methods of the Three Heavens."

14. *niji.* I have tentatively understood *ni* 逆 as meaning "beforehand" (there is a verb *nigao* 逆告 , which means to verbally predict something), and *ji* 紀 as corresponding to *ji* 記 , which can mean to remember or have something in mind.

15. A spirit denoted by this character usually is an animistic nature spirit that dwells in a plant, tree, or rock. It also can be the transfigured form of an animal that has reached an unusually old age.

16. These are two of the three realms of *samsara.* The realm of desire is the lowest realm, whose inhabitants possess desires. The realm of form is the realm where desires no longer exist, but where people are still deluded by their perception of forms. Above these two realms is the realm of no forms, a realm where all desires and forms are transcended in a state of deep *samadhi.* By describing the wicked Immortals as citizens of the two lower realms, the text is saying that in spite of their considerable powers, they were still not Perfected beings of the highest caliber. The concept of the three realms was adopted from Buddhism.

17. See nt. 11.

18. This refers to special physical features that are possessed by extraordinary holy beings such as the Buddha and Laozi.

19. Judging from its usage throughout the *Yuqing jing*, the term *Dharma Body* refers to the state where one has achieved the final goal in the religious quest. It is, of course, an originally Buddhist term that refers to the cosmic body of the Buddha that is beyond forms, shapes, and differentiations. It is equivalent to "emptiness" (*sunyata*), the ultimate and absolutely true principle. The *Yuqing jing* appears to be one of the earliest Taoist scriptures to make frequent use of the term.

20. *Jing* may refer to the bodily "essences" or fluids that seep out of the corpse. It also could refer to a soul substance of some kind. It also could be an adjective that modifies the word *shuang.* The meaning of *shuang* is unclear, since it is not normally used as a noun. As may be recalled, the Lingbao scripture, the *Gongde qingzhong jing*, says that the human body decomposes into dust, which then transforms into *shuang*, which I tentatively rendered as "light" (see p. 123).

21. This probably means that the body is both the product and cause of confusion. Confusion causes people to be born into a body of flesh, and the body's needs and impulses keep them confused.

22. This seems to refer to the spiritual and mental capacities that the "infidels" believed to survive the death of the body. However, it is probably actually a mistranscription of 魂識 , which would translate into "*hun* soul consciousness."

23. See Mochizuki Shinko, *Bukkyoo daijiten*, 3,767–68.

24. According to Buddhist mythology, these four gods live on Mt. Sumeru and serve the god Indra in the task of protecting the Buddhist religion. Their names are Dhrtarastra, Virudhaka, Virupaksa, and Vaisravana. See Nakamura Hajime, *Bukkyoogo jiten*, 1: 527–28.

25. For something to be empty means that it is conditioned by causes and has no self-sufficient reality. Buddhism teaches that delusion and suffering come from attachments to things and concepts, and that these attachments result when one does not realize that all is emptiness.

26. See Kenneth K.S. Ch'en, *Buddhism in China: A Historical Survey*, pp. 78–81 and Matsunaga Yukei, *Mikkyoo no Rekishi* (Kyoto: Heirakuji Shoten, 1969), pp. 131–35.

27. On the practice of human sacrifice in Chinese folk cults, see Sawada Mizuho, "Satsujin Saiki" in *Chuugoku no Minkan Shinkoo* (Tokyo: Kosakusha, 1982), pp. 332–73.

28. *Beijing daxue guoxue jikan* 3 (1923), pp. 27–46.

29. The key passage is found in *Weishu, juan* #102 (pp. 2,271–72) and *Beishi, juan* #97 (pp. 3,222–23). According to the *Weishu*, the God of Heaven also was worshipped in the nations of Gaochang (located in the vicinity of present-day Turfan) and Yanzhi (located in the vicinity of present-day Yanzhi County, Xinjiang Province). This seems to indicate that Zoroastrians lived in those nations. Another possibility is that the word *tianshen* is used to describe non-Chinese astral deities in general, rather than just those of Zoroastrianism. Contact with Zoroastrians apparently was also made by the Southern dynasties, since the *Liangshu* (54th *juan*, p. 812) and *Nanshi* (79th *juan*, p. 1,984) describe a Central Asian nation called Guguo, where people worshipped *huoshen* and *tianshen*. This nation sent envoys with tribute to the Liang court in 516 and 521.

30. See Mary Boyce, *Zoroastrians: Their Religious Beliefs and Practices* (London: Routledge, 1979), pp. 23–27, 119.

31. *Buddhism in China: A Historical Survey*, pp. 279–82.

32. Here I have borrowed Chen's translation. See *Buddhism in China: A Historical Survey*, p. 281.

33. Taisho Canon no. 189 (3: 634 middle and bottom).

34. Taisho Canon no. 374 (12: 462 top).

35. HY334/TT168–169. Full title, *Taishang lingbao yuanyang miaojing*. The passage in question here is found in 3/13b line 3 character 13–14a line 5 character 4. Actually, most of the *Yuanyang jing*'s contents were taken from the *Nirvanasutra*. This fact was first brought to the attention of modern scholars by Kamata Shigeo in *Chuugoku Bukkyoo shisooshi kenkyuu* (Tokyo: Shunjusha, 1968), pp. 168–72. Appended to this book is a table displaying the text of the *Yuanyang jing* alongside the matching passages from the *Nirvanasutra*. The *Erjiao lun*, a Buddhist polemical text of 570 C.E., mentions a text called the *Yuanyang jing* and criticizes it for being a plagiarism of the *Lotus Sutra*. This could be the same *Yuanyang jing* in question here, since as Kamata points out, a portion of the *Yuanyang jing* (the "Wenxing pin" chapter in the 4th *juan*) indeed matches the *Lotus Sutra*'s introductory chapter. It is, however, odd that the *Erjiao lun* does not mention any plagiarism from the *Nirvanasutra*. As it has been pointed out by Ofuchi Ninji, two different scriptures

bearing the title *Yuanyang jing* appear to have circulated. Only one (Pelliot 2450) of several Dunhuang manuscripts entitled *"Yuanyang jing"* matches the Taoist Canon version; the others have an entirely different theme and content. See *Tonkoo dookyoo: Mokuroku hen*, pp. 104–5.

36. This refers to a demonifugic talisman endorsed in the Shangqing tradition. See Robinet, *Taoist Meditation*, p. 32.

37. This is a derogatory term that means that someone is worthless and no good, no more useful than a corpse.

38. His full title is "the Golden Perfected Being of the Red Jade Palace, the Latter Age Sagely Heavenly Worthy of the Heaven of Jade Purity."

39. In Hinduism, Brahma is the divine creator. In Buddhism, he is a protector of the Buddhist religion.

40. The origins of this legend date back to the Latter Han or Three Kingdoms periods. Very early versions of it are found in the *Houhan shu* and the *Sanguo zhi*. According to a Buddhist source (the *Chu sanzang jiji*), a Taoist priest named Wang Fu forged a *Huahu jing* (Scripture on the Conversion of Barbarians) during the reign of Western Jin Emperor Hui (291–307 C.E.). The legend is narrated in various sources with considerable variation in how they explain the identity of the Buddha. Some versions say the Buddha was a guise taken by Laozi, some say he was Laozi's disciple Yin Xi, and others say he was a vainglorious king who was converted by Laozi after unsuccessfully trying to burn him to death. See Kusuyama Haruki, *Rooshi densetsu no kenkyuu* (Tokyo: Sobunsha, 1979), pp. 437–72. Kubo Noritada has proposed the novel theory that the first fabricators of the legend, contrary to the common assumption, were Buddhists who had hoped to facilitate the growth of their religion by identifying their Buddha with a saint more familiar to the Chinese public. See *Chuugoku shuukyoo ni okeru juyoo, hen-yoo, gyoo-yoo* (Tokyo: Yamakawa Shuppansha, 1979), pp. 6–24.

41. The Three Vehicles are teachings for: 1) *Sravaka*—Those who train for their own enlightenment after learning the doctrines from someone else. They become arhats after a long period of time. They are practitioners of the Small Vehicle; 2) *Prattyekabuddha*—Those who achieve enlightenment on their own. This refers primarily to those who lived and attained enlightenment prior to the ministry of the historical Buddha; 3) *Bodhisattva*—Those who achieve enlighten-ment through the doctrines of the Great Vehicle and compassionately stay in the world to help others. Practitioners of the Great Vehicle.

42. This speculation finds support in the *Xisheng jing* (The Scripture of the Western Ascension), a famous Taoist text written some time between the mid-fourth century and the end of the fifth century. The *Xisheng jing* opens with the passage, "Laozi ascended to the West to open up the Tao in India. He was called Master Gu (*gu xiansheng*, "the ancient master"); skilled at entering non-action." The *Xisheng jing* also includes a passage that reads, "Laozi said: [Yin] Xi, I tell you once again, Master Gu is myself." See Livia Kohn, *Taoist Mystical Philosophy: The Scripture*

of the Western Ascension (Albany: State University of New York Press, 1991), pp. 235, 255.

43. Special physical traits possessed by superhuman beings.

44. An indestructible body. In Buddhist texts, this refers to the Buddha's Dharma Body.

45. There appears to be a textual corruption here. The character *er* 二 is a mistranscription of *fan* 反 , which would fit more logically into the text. The version of the text in the *Daozang jiyao* (vol. 30, p. 24a) uses the character fan 反 .

46. The ten wishes (paraphrased) were as follows: 1) That the doctrines of the Tao will spread and pervade. 2) That everybody will be able to understand the Tao. 3) That *hun* souls in the netherworld will be released. 4) That the wandering souls of the dead who have no support (descendants to make offerings to them) will gain rebirth. 5) That peace will prevail and crops will be plentiful throughout the world. 6) That subjects will be loyal and sons filial. 7) That all enmities and conflicts in the world will be resolved. 8) That all embryos and seeds in gestation will be safely born and reared to maturity. 9) That all diseases will be healed. 10) That all living beings will be provided with abundant food and clothing (7/12b).

47. The text also describes how flowers and sweet dew came raining down, the earth trembled, the music of immortality filled the air, and unicorns and phoenixes appeared.

48. As a Buddhist term, this refers to 1) killing, 2) stealing, 3) lechery, 4) lying, 5) eloquent deception, 6) slander, 7) double-talk, 8) greed, 9) wrath, and 10) ignorance. The author of the *Yuqing jing* may well have had the same sins in mind.

49. As a Buddhist term, this refers to 1) the killing of one's own mother, 2) the killing of one's own father, 3) the killing of a holy man, 4) harming the body of the Buddha, and 5) causing schism and destruction within the religious organization. Something similar is probably being referred to here in the *Yuqing jing*.

8. Conclusion

1. Certain exceptions should be noted. In southern China (primarily Guangdong Province and Hong Kong) and in overseas Chinese communities, one can find organizations that are at least nominally affiliated with the Complete Perfection Sect but do not practice monasticism. These organizations venerate and worship Lü Chunyang, Wang Chongyang, and other important figures associated with the Complete Perfection Sect. Probably the largest of these organizations is the Ching Chung Taoist Church, which has its headquarters in Hong Kong and several branch temples in North America and Australia.

2. For a study and description of Taoist monastic life prior to communism, see Yoshioka Yoshitoyo, "Taoist Monastic Life" in *Facets of Taoism*, edited by Holmes Welch and Anna Seidel (New Haven: Yale University Press, 1977), pp. 229–52.

3. For a good general survey on internal alchemy, see Joseph Needham, *Science and Civilization in China*, vol. 5, no. 5 (Cambridge: Cambridge University Press).

4. Mt. Mao, the most sacred mountain of the Shangqing Sect, today has two active temples that are inhabited by Orthodox Unity Sect priests. These priests, for their self-cultivation, practice internal alchemy akin to that of the Complete Perfection Sect and apparently do not practice the methods of the original Shangqing texts.

5. See Eskildsen (1989); Yao Tao-chung, "Ch'üan-chen: A New Taoist Sect in North China During the Twelfth and Thirteenth Centuries," Doctoral Dissertation (University of Arizona, 1980); Kubo Noritada, *Chuugoku no shuukyoo kaikaku: Zenshin kyoo no seiritsu* (Kyoto: Hozokan, 1967).

Bibliography

Secondary Sources

Bhagat, M.G. *Ancient Indian Asceticism.* New Delhi: Munshiram Manoharlal, 1976.

Bokenkamp, Stephen. "Sources of the Ling-pao Scriptures." In *Tantric and Taoist Studies*, Vol. 2. Edited by Michel Strickmann. Brussels: Institut Belge des Hautes Etudes Chinoises, 1983, pp. 434–86.

———. "Death and Ascent in Ling-pao Taoism." *Taoist Resources*, 1.2 (1989), pp. 1–20.

Boyce, Mary. *Zoroastrians: Their Religious Beliefs and Practices.* London: Routledge, 1979.

Chakraborti, Haripada. *Asceticism in Ancient India in Brahmanical, Buddhist, Jain and Ajivika Societies from the Earliest Times to the Period of Sankaracharya.* Calcutta: Punthi Pustak, 1973.

Chen Guofu. *Daozang yuanliu kao.* Beijing: Zhonghua Shuju, 1975.

Chen, Kenneth. *Buddhism in China: A Historical Survey.* Princeton: Princeton University Press, 1964.

Chen Yuan. "Huoxian jiao ru Zhongguo kao." In *Beijing Daxue Guoxue Jikan*, No. 3 (1923), pp. 27–46.

DeWoskin, Kenneth J. *Doctors, Diviners and Magicians of Ancient China.* New York: Columbia University Press, 1983.

Eskildsen, Stephen E. "The Beliefs and Practices of Early Ch'üan-chen Taoism." M.A. Thesis. University of British Columbia, 1989.

———. Severe Asceticism in Early Daoist Religion. Ph.D. Dissertation. University of British Columbia, 1994.

Forke, Alfred, Trans. *Lun-heng: Philosophical Essays of Wang Chung.* Leipzig: Otto Harrassowitz, 1907.

Fukui Kojun. *Tooyoo shisoo no kenkyuu.* Tokyo: Risosha, 1955.

———. "A Study of Chou-i Ts'an-t'ung-ch'i," *Acta Asiatica*, No. 27 (1974), pp. 19–32.

————. *Toyo shisooshi kenkyuu.* Tokyo: Shoseki-Bunbutsu Ryutsukai, 1960.

————. *Dookyoo no kisoteki kenkyuu.* Tokyo: Shoseki Bunbutsu Ryuutsuukai, 1964.

Fukui Kojun et al., Ed. *Dookyoo 1: Dookyoo to wa nani ka.* Tokyo: Hirakawa Shuppansha, 1983.

Fukui Kojun et al., *Daojiao*, Vol. 1 (*Dookyoo 1: Dookyoo to wa nani ka*). Translated by Zhu Yueli. Shanghai: Shanghai Guji Chubanshe, 1990.

Gernet, Jacques. *A History of Chinese Civilization.* Translated by J.R. Foster. Cambridge: Cambridge University Press, 1982 (original French edition published in 1972).

Graham, A.C., Trans. *Chuang-tzu: The Seven Inner Chapters and other writings from the book* Chuang-tzu. London: George Allen and Unwin, 1981.

Gulik, R.H. van. *Sexual Life in Ancient China.* Leiden: E.J. Brill, 1961.

Hinson, E. Glenn. *The Early Church.* Nashville: Abingdon Press, 1996.

Huang Zhaohan, Ed. *Daozang danyao yiming suoyin.* Taipei: Taiwan Xuesheng Shuju, 1989.

Ishida Hidemi. "Body and Mind: The Chinese Perspective." In *Taoist Meditation and Longevity Techniques.* Edited by Livia Kohn. Ann Arbor: University of Michigan Press, 1989, pp. 41–71.

Ishii Masako. *Dookyoogaku no kenkyuu.* Tokyo: Kokusho Kankookai, 1980.

Ishii Masako, and Ninji Ofuchi. *Rikuchoo-Too-Soo no kobunken sho-in Dookyo tenseki mokuroku, sakuin.* Tokyo: Kokusho Kankokai, 1988.

James, William. *The Varieties of Religious Experience: A Study in Human Nature.* New York: Modern Library, 1902.

Jiangsu Xinyixueyuan, Ed. *Zhongyao dazidian.* Shanghai: Renmin Chubanshe, 1975.

Jonas, Hans. *The Gnostic Religion.* Boston: Beacon Press, 1958.

Kaelber, Walter O. "Asceticism," in *The Encyclopedia of Religion.* Edited by Mircea Eliade. New York: Macmillan, 1987, 1: 441.

Kaltenmark, Max, Trans. *Le Lie-sien Tchouan.* Beijing: University of Paris, 1953.

————. "The Ideology of the *T'ai-p'ing-ching.*" In *Facets of Taoism.* Edited by Holmes Welch and Anna Seidel. New Haven: Yale University Press, 1979, pp. 19–52.

Kamata, Shigeo. *Chuugoku Bukkyoo shisooshi kenkyuu.* Tokyo: Shunjusha, 1968.

Kaneoka, Terumitsu, Ed. *Tonkoo to Chuugoku Dookyoo.* Tokyo: Daito Shuppansha, 1983.

Kobayashi Masayoshi. "*Reihoo sekisho gohen shinbun* no shisoo to seiritsu." *Toho Shukyo,* No. 60 (October 1982), pp. 23–47.

————. "*Ryuu-Soo ni okeru Reihoo kyoo* no keisei." *Toyo Bunka,* No. 62 (March 1982), pp. 99–138.

————. "*Taijoo reihoo gofu jo* keisei koo: joo." *Toho Shukyo,* No. 71 (April 1988), pp. 20–43.

————. "*Taijoo reihoo gofu jo* keisei koo: ge." *Toho Shukyo,* No. 72 (October 1988), pp. 20–44.

――――. "Jooseikyoo to Reihookyoo no shuumatsuron." *Toho Shukyo*, No.75 (May 1990), pp. 20–41.

Kohn, Livia. "Guarding the One: Concentrative Meditation in Taoism." In *Taoist Meditation and Longevity Techniques*. Edited by Livia Kohn. Ann Arbor: University of Michigan Press, 1989, pp. 123–56.

――――. "Taoist Insight Meditation: The Tang Practice of Neiguan." In *Taoist Meditation and Longevity Techniques*. Edited by Livia Kohn. Ann Arbor: University of Michigan Press, 1989, pp. 191–222.

――――. "Eternal Life in Taoist Mysticism." *Journal of the American Oriental Society*, 110: 4 (1990), pp. 623–48.

――――. *Taoist Mystical Philosophy: The Scripture of the Western Ascension.* New York: State University of New York Press, 1991.

――――. *Early Chinese Mysticism: Philosophy and Soteriology in the Taoist Tradition.* Princeton: Princeton University Press, 1992.

――――. *The Taoist Experience: An Anthology.* Albany: State University of New York Press, 1993.

Kominami Ichiro. "Jin-yaku kara zonshi e." In *Chuugoku ko-Dookyooshi kenkyuu.* Edited by Yoshikawa Tadao. Kyoto: Dohosha, 1992, pp. 3–54.

Kubo Noritada. *Kooshin shinkoo no kenkyuu.* Tokyo: Nihon Gakujutsu Shinkokai, 1961.

――――. "Zenshinkyoo no seiritsu." *Toyo Bunka Kenkyujo Kiyo*, No.42 (1966), pp. 1–60.

――――. *Chuugoku no shuukyoo kaikaku: Zenshinkyoo no seiritsu.* Kyoto: Hozokan, 1967.

――――. *Dookyooshi.* Tokyo: Yamakawa Shuppansha, 1977.

――――. *Chuugoku shuukyoo ni okeru juyoo, hen-yoo, gyoo-yoo.* Tokyo: Yamakawa Shuppansha, 1979.

――――. *Dookyoo no kamigami.* Tokyo: Hirakawa Shuppansha, 1986.

Kusuyama Haruki. *Rooshi densetsu no kenkyuu.* Tokyo: Sobunsha, 1979.

Latourette, Kenneth Scott. *A History of Christianity.* New York: Harper & Brothers, 1953.

Lau, D.C., Trans. *Tao Te Ching.* London: Penguin, 1963.

Levi, Jean. "L'abstinence des cereales chez les Taoistes." *Etudes Chinoises*, No. 1 (1983), pp. 3–47.

Li Shuhuan. *Daojiao dazidian.* Taipei: Juliu Tushu Gongsi, 1980.

Li Yangzheng. *Daojiao jiben zhishi.* Beijing: Zhongguo Daojiao Xiehui, 1985.

Liu Ts'un-yan. "Sources of Zoroastrian and Manichaean Activities in Pre-T'ang China." In *Selected Papers from the Hall of Harmonious Wind.* Leiden: E.J. Brill, 1976, pp. 3–58.

Loewe, Michael. *Ways to Paradise: The Chinese Quest for Immortality.* London: George Allen and Unwin, 1979.

Long Bojian. Kootei naikei *gairon.* Translated from Chinese into Japanese by Maruyama Toshiaki. Ichikawa: Toyo Gakujutsu Shuppansha, 1984.

Maeda Shigeki. "*Rooshi chuukyoo* oboegaki." In *Chuugoku kodai yoosei shisoo no soogooteki kenkyuu*. Ed. Sakade Yoshinobu. Tokyo: Hirakawa Shuppansha, 1988, pp. 474–502.

Maspero, Henri. *Taoism and Chinese Religion*. Translated by Frank Kiermann. Amherst: University of Massachusetts Press, 1981.

Mather, Richard B. "K'ou Ch'ien-chih and the Taoist Theocracy at the Northern Wei Court." In *Facets of Taoism*. Edited by Holmes Welch and Anna Seidel. New Haven: Yale University Press, 1979, pp. 103–22.

Matsunaga Yukei. *Mikkyoo no rekishi*. Kyoto: Heirakuji Shoten, 1969.

Min Zhiting. *Daojiao yifan*. Beijing: Zhongquo Daojiao Xueyuan, 1990.

Miyakawa Hisayuki. *Rikuchooshi kenkyuu: Shuukyoo hen*. Kyoto: Heirakuji Shoten, 1964.

———. *Chuugoku shuukyooshi kenkyuu*. Vol. I. Kyoto: Dohosha, 1983.

Mochizuki Shinko. *Bukkyoo daijiten*. 10 vols. Kyoto: Sekai Seiten Kanko Kyokai, 1956.

Mollier, Christine. *Une apocalypse taoiste du Ve siecle*. Paris: Institut des Hautes Etudes Chinoises, 1990.

Mugitani Kunio. "*Kootei naikei kyoo* shiron." *Toyo Bunka*, No. 62 (1982), pp. 29–60.

Murakami Yoshimi. "Affirmation of Desire in Taoism." *Acta Asiatica*, No. 27 (1974), pp. 57–74.

Nakajima Ryuzo. *Rikuchoo shisooshi no kenkyuu*. Kyoto: Heirakuji Shoten, 1985.

Nakamura Hajime. *Bukkyoo go daijiten*. Tokyo: Tokyo Shoseki Kabushiki Gaisha, 1975.

Nakamura Shohachi, and Yasui Kozan. *Jushu Isho shuusei*. Vol. VI. Tokyo: Meitoku Shuppansha, 1978.

Needham, Joseph. *Science and Civilization in China*. Vol. 2. Cambridge: Cambridge University Press, 1956.

———. *Science and Civilization in China*. Vol. 5, no. 2. Cambridge: Cambridge University Press, 1980.

———. *Science and Civilization in China*. Vol. 5, no. 4. Cambridge: Cambridge University Press, 1981.

———. *Science and Civilization in China*. Vol. 5, no. 5. Cambridge: Cambridge University Press, 1983.

Ngo Van Xuyet. *Divination, magie et politique dans la Chine ancienne*. Paris: Presses Universitaires de France, 1976.

Ofuchi Ninji. "On *Ku Ling-pao ching*." *Acta Asiatica*, No. 27 (1974), pp. 34–56.

———. *Dookyooshi no kenkyuu*. Okayama: Okayama Daigaku Kyoseikai Shosekibu, 1964.

———. *Shoki no dookyo*. Tokyo: Sobunsha, 1991.

———. *Tonkoo dookyoo: Mokurokuhen*. Tokyo: Fukutake Shoten, 1978.

———. *Tonkoo dookyoo: Zurokuhen*. Tokyo, Fukutake Shoten, 1979.

————. "The Formation of the Taoist Canon." In *Facets of Taoism*. Edited by Holmes Welch and Anna Seidel. New Haven: Yale University Press, 1979, pp. 253–67.

Ozaki Masaharu. "Dooshi: Zaike kara shukke e." In *Rekishi ni okeru Minshuu to Bunka*. Edited by the Editorial Committee for the Commemoration of Professor Tadao Sakai's Seventieth Birthday. Tokyo: Kokusho Kankookai, 1982, pp. 205–20.

Pas, Julian. "Six Daily Periods of Worship: Symbolic Meaning in Buddhist Liturgy and Eschatology." *Monumenta Serica* 37 (1986–1987), pp. 49–82.

Qing Xitai, Ed. *Zhongguo daojiao shi*. Chengdu: Sichuan Renmin Chubanshe, 1988.

Ren Jiyu et al. *Zhongguo daojiao shi*. Shanghai: Renmin Chubanshe, 1990.

————, Ed. *Daozang tiyao*. Beijing: Zhongguo Shehuikexue Chubanshe, 1991.

Robinet, Isabelle. *La meditation taoiste*. Paris: Devy Livres, 1979.

————. "Metamorphosis and Deliverance from the Corpse in Taoism," *History of Religions* 19.1 (1979), pp. 37–70

————. *La revelation du Shangqing dans l'histoire du taoisme*. 2 vols. Paris: L'Ecole Francaise d'Extreme-Orient, 1984.

————. "Original Contributions of *Neidan* to Taoism and Chinese Thought." In *Taoist Meditation and Longevity Techniques*. Edited by Livia Kohn. Ann Arbor: University of Michigan Press, 1989, pp. 295–328.

————. "Visualization and Ecstatic Flight in Shangqing Taoism." In *Taoist Meditation and Longevity Techniques*. Edited by Livia Kohn. Ann Arbor: University of Michigan Press, 1989, pp. 157–90.

————. *Histoire du taoisme*. Paris: Les Editions du Cerf, 1991.

————. *Taoist Meditation (La meditation taoiste)*. Translated by Julian Pas and Norman Girardot. Albany: State University of New York Press, 1993.

Rudolph, Kurt. *Gnosis: The Nature and History of Gnosticism*. San Francisco: Harper and Row, 1984.

Saso, Michael. "What is the Ho-t'u." *History of Religions*, No.17 (1978), pp. 399–416.

Sawada Mizuho. "*Ressen den, Shinsen den* kaisetsu." In *Hoobokushi, Ressen den, Shinsen den, Sengai kyoo*. Chuugoku koten bungaku taikei, No. 8. Tokyo: Heibonsha, 1969, pp. 559–70.

————. "Dookyoo seiseihan koo." In *Yoshioka hakase kanreki kinen Dookyoo ronbunshuu*. Tokyo: Kokusho Kankokai, 1977, pp. 381–401.

————. *Chuugoku no minkan shinkoo*. Tokyo: Kosakusha, 1982.

Schafer, Edward H. *The Divine Woman*. Berkeley: University of California Press, 1973.

————. "The Jade Woman of Divine Mystery." *History of Religions*, No. 17 (1978), pp. 387–98.

Schipper, Kristofer. *Concordance du Houang-t'ing king*. Paris: L'Ecole Francaise d'Extreme-Orient, 1975.

————. *Le fen-teng: rituel taoiste.* Paris: L'Ecole Francaise d'Extreme-Orient, 1975.

————. *Concordance du Pao-p'u-tzu nei/wai-p'ien.* Paris: L'Ecole Francaise d'Extreme-Orient, 1975.

————. "The Taoist Body." *History of Religions.* No. 17 (1978), pp. 355–87.

————. "Le Calendrier de Jade: Note sur le *Laozi zhongjing.*" *Nachrichten der deutchen Gesellschaft für Natur- und Volkerkunde Ostasiens.* No. 125 (1979), pp. 75–80.

————. *Index du* Yunji qiqian. 2 vols. Paris: Ecole Francaise d'Extreme Orient, 1981.

————. *Le corp taoiste: Corps physique—corps social.* Paris: Fayard, 1982.

————. *The Taoist Body (Le corp taoiste: Corps physique—corps social).* Translated by Karen Duval. Berkeley: University of California Press, 1993.

Seidel, Anna. "The Image of the Perfect Ruler in Early Taoist Messianism." *History of Religions.* No. 9 (1969), pp. 216–47.

————. *La divinisation de Lao tseu dans le taoisme des Han.* Paris: Ecole Francaise d'Extreme-Orient, 1969.

————. "Imperial Treasures and Taoist Sacraments: Taoist Roots in the Apocrypha." In *Tantric and Taoist Studies.* Vol. II. Edited by Michel Strickmann. Brussels: Institut Belge des Hautes Etudes Chinoises, 1983, pp. 291–371.

————. "*Post-mortem* Immortality—or: the Taoist Resurrection of the Body." In S. Shaked, D. Shuman, and G.G. Stoumsa, Eds. *Gilgul: Essays on Transformation, Revolution and Permanence in the History of Religions,* Leiden: E.J. Brill, 1987, pp. 223–37.

————. "Chronicle of Taoist Studies in the West 1950–1990." *Cahiers d'Extreme-Asie,* No. 5 (1989–1990), pp. 223–347.

Seidel, Anna, and Michel Strickmann, eds. "Taoism" in *Encyclopedia Brittanica* (1994 ed.) Col. 28, p. 388.

Stein, Rolf A. "Religious Taoism and Popular Religion from the Second to Seventh Centuries." In *Facets of Taoism.* Edited by Holmes Welch and Anna Seidel. New Haven: Yale University Press, 1979, pp. 53–81.

Strickmann, Michel. "The Mao-shan Revelations: Taoism and the Aristocracy." *T'oung-pao,* No. 63 (1978), pp. 1–63.

————. "Liang Wu Ti's Suppression of Taoism." *Journal of the American Oriental Society,* No. 98.4 (1978), pp. 467–75.

————. "On the Alchemy of T'ao Hung-ching." In *Facets of Taoism.* Edited by Holmes Welch and Anna Seidel. New Haven: Yale University Press, 1979, pp. 123–92.

————. *Le taoisme du Mao chan; chronique d'une revelation.* Paris: College du France, 1981.

Sunayama Minoru. *Zui-Too Dookyoo shisooshi kenkyuu.* Tokyo: Hirakawa Shuppansha, 1990.

Suzuki Yoshijiro. *Shuu-eki sandoo kei.* Tokyo: Meitoku Shuppansha, 1977.

Vervoorn, Aat. *Men of the Cliffs and Caves: The Development of the Chinese Eremitic Tradition to the End of the Han Dynasty.* Hong Kong: Chinese University Press, 1990.

Voobus, Arthur. *History of Asceticism in the Syrian Orient.* 2 vols. Louvain: Catholic University Press, 1958.

Wang Ming. *Taiping jing hejiao.* Beijing: Zhonghua Shuju, 1960.

Ware, James R. *Alchemy, Medicine and Religion in the China of A.D. 320.* Cambridge: MIT Press, 1966.

Weber, Max. *The Religions of China.* Translated by Hans Gerth. New York: Macmillan, 1951.

Wile, Douglas. *Art of the Bedchamber: The Chinese Sexual Yoga Classics including Women's Solo Meditation Texts.* Albany: State University of New York Press, 1992.

Wimbush, Vincent L., Ed. *Ascetic Behavior in Greco-Roman Antiquity: A Sourcebook.* Minneapolis: Fortress Press, 1990.

Yamada Toshiaki. "*Gofu jo* keisei koo." In *Dookyoo to shuukyoo bunka.* Edited by Akizuki Kan-ei. Tokyo: Hirakawa Shuppansha, pp. 122–35.

———. "Longevity Techniques and the Transmission of the *Lingbao Wufuxu.*" In *Taoist Meditation and Longevity Techniques.* Edited by Livia Kohn. Ann Arbor: University of Michigan Press, 1989, pp. 99–124.

Yao Tao-chung. "Ch'üan-chen: A New Taoist Sect in North China During the Twelfth and Thirteenth Centuries." Ph.D. Diss., University of Arizona, Phoenix 1980.

Yasui Kozan. *Isho.* Tokyo: Meitoku Shuppansha, 1969.

Yoshioka Yoshitoyo. *Dookyoo kyootenshi ron.* Tokyo: Dookyoo Kankookai, 1955.

———. *Dookyoo to Bukkyoo.* Vol. I. Tokyo: Nihon Gakujutsu Shinkookai, 1959.

———. *Dookyoo to Bukkyoo.* Vol. II. Tokyo: Nihon Gakujutsu Shinkookai, 1970.

———. *Dookyoo to Bukkyoo.* Vol. III. Tokyo: Nihon Gakujutsu Shinkookai, 1976.

———. "Taoist Monastic Life." In *Facets of Taoism.* Edited by Holmes Welch and Anna Seidel. New Haven: Yale University Press, 1977, pp. 229–52.

Zürcher, Erik. "Buddhist Influence on Early Taoism." *T'oung-pao,* No. 65 (1980), pp. 84–146.

Primary Sources

Texts from the Taoist Canon

HY6/TT16–17 *Shangqing dadong zhenjing*
HY9/TT20–22 *Taishang yisheng haikong zhizang jing*
HY22/TT26 *Yuanshi wulao chishu zhenwen tianshu jing* (*Chishu zhenwen*)
HY23/TT26 *Taishang zhutian lingshu duming jing*
HY56/TT30 *Taishang yupei jindang taiji jinshu shangjing* (*Yupei jindang jing*)

210 Bibliography

HY87/TT38–39 *Yuanshi wuliang duren shangpin miaojing sizhu*
HY97/TT49 *Taishang lingbao zhutian neiyin ziran yuzi*
HY140/TT60 *Shangqing wozhong jue*
HY173/TT75–76 *Jinlian zhenzong ji*
HY174/TT76 *Jinlian zhenzong xianyuan xiangzhuan*
HY177/TT77 *Taishang dongzhen zhihui shangpin dajie* (*Zhihui shangpin dajie*)
HY244/TT115 *Dadan zhizhi*
HY263/TT131 *Huangting waijing jing zhu* (Liangqiuzi commentary)
HY294/TT138 *Liexian zhuan*
HY296/TT139–148 *Lishi zhenxian tidao tongjian*
HY302/TT152 *Zhoushi mingtong ji*
HY303/TT152 *Ziyang zhenren neizhuan*
HY304/TT153–158 *Maoshan zhi*
HY325/TT167 *Taishang dongxuan lingbao zhihui dingzhi tongwei jing* (*Dingzhi tongwei jing*)
HY330/TT167 *Taishang dongxuan lingbao zhenwen yaojie jing*
HY331/TT167 *Huangting neijing jing*
HY332/TT167 *Huangting waijing jing*
HY334/TT168–169 *Taishang lingbao yuanyang miao jing* (*Yuanyang jing*)
HY336/TT174–175 *Taishang dongxuan lingbao yebao yinyuan jing*
HY344/TT177 *Taishang dongxuan lingbao zhihui benyuan dajie shangpin jing* (*Benyuan dajie jing*)
HY345/TT177 *Taishang dongxuan lingbao jieye benxing shangpin miaojing*
HY346/TT177 *Taishang dongxuan lingbao zhenyi quanjie falun miaojing* (*Zhenyi quanjie falun miaojing*)
HY348/TT177 *Taishang xuanyi zhenren shuo quanjie falun miaojing* (*Xuanyi quanjie falun miaojing*)
HY352/TT178 *Taishang dongxuan lingbao chishu yujue miaojing* (*Chishu yujue*)
HY369/TT181 *Taishang dongxuan lingbao miedu wulian shengshi miaojing*
HY388/TT183 *Taishang lingbao wufu xu* (*Wufu xu*)
HY421/TT193 *Dengzhen yinjue*
HY422/TT193 *Shangqing sanzhen zhiyao yujue*
HY424/TT194 *Shangqing mingtang yuanzhen jingjue* (*Mingtang yuanzhen jingjue*)
HY425/TT194 *Shangqing taiji yinzhu yujing baojue* (*Taiji yinzhu baojue*)
HY442/TT198 *Shangqing housheng daojun lieji*
HY454/TT202 *Taishang dongxuan lingbao shangpin jie jing* (*Shangpin jie jing*)
HY456/TT202 *Taishang dongxuan lingbao sanyuan pin jie gongde qingzhong jing* (*Gongde qingzhong jing*)
HY457/TT202 *Taishang dongxuan lingbao zhihui zuigen shangpin dajie jing* (*Zuigen dajie jing*)
HY508/TT278 *Wushang huanglu dazhai licheng yi*

HY532/TT295 *Taishang zhenren fu lingbao zhaijie weiyi zhujing yaojue* (*Zhaijie weiyi jue*)
HY542/TT296 *Taishang shifang yinghao tianzun chan*
HY596/TT329–330 *Xianyuan bianzhu*
HY666/TT346–347 *Xisheng jing* (comp. by Chen Jingyuan)
HY671/TT352 *Taishang wuji dadao ziran zhenyi wuzheng fu shangjing*
HY682/TT363 *Daode zhenjing zhu* (Heshanggong commentary)
HY725/TT440–448 *Daode zhenjing guangsheng yi*
HY726/TT449–450 *Xisheng jing* (Commentary by Song Emperor Huizong)
HY780/TT558–559 *Xuanpin lu*
HY782/TT560–561 *Yongcheng jixian lu*
HY816/TT568 *Taiqing zhonghuang zhenjing* (*Zhonghuang jing*)
HY835/TT571 *Shenxian shiqi jingui miaolu*
HY861/TT578 *Xiandao jing*
HY872/TT580 *Huangting dunjia yuanshen jing*
HY983/TT618 *Taishang dongxuan lingbao sanyi wuqi zhenjing*
HY1004/TT628 *Zhouyi cantongqi jie*
HY1010/TT637–640 *Zhengao*
HY1026/TT677–702 *Yunji qiqian*
HY1093/TT *Taiping jing*
HY1093/TT746 *Taiping jing chao*
HY1103/TT758 *Taixuan zhenyi benji jing*
HY1106/TT758 *Taishang dongxuan lingbao benxing suyuan jing*
HY1107/TT758 *Taishang dongxuan lingbao benxing yinyuan jing* (*Benxing yinyuan jing*)
HY1114/TT759 *Taishang dongxuan lingbao shengxuan neijiao jing*
HY1117/TT760–761 *Dongxuan lingbao sandong fengdao kejie yingshi*
HY1119/TT761 *Lu xiansheng daomen keliie*
HY1122/TT764 *Daodian lun*
HY1124/TT765 *Shangqing daolei shixiang*
HY1130/TT768–778 *Wushang biyao*
HY1131/TT780–782 *Sandong zhunang*
HY1177/TT868–870 *Baopuzi neipian*
HY1196/TT876 *Santian neijie jing*
HY1238/TT992–995 *Sandong qunxian lu*
HY1301/TT1022–1024 *Taishang dadao yuqing jing* (*Yuqing jing*)
HY1302/TT1025 *Dongzhen gaoshang yudi dadong ciyi yujian wulao baojing* (*Ciyi jing*)
HY1303/TT1026 *Dongzhen taishang suling dongyuan dayou miaojing*
HY1319/TT1030 *Dongzhen taiyi dijun taidan yinshu dongzhen xuanjing*
HY1321/TT1030 *Dongzhen taishang zidu yanguang shenyuan bianjing*

HY1333/TT1032 *Taishang shuo zhihui xiaomo zhenjing* (*Xiaomo jing*)
HY1345/TT1038 *Shangqing gaoshang miemo yudi shenhui yuqing yinshu* (*Yuqing yinshu* 1)
HY1347/TT1038 *Shangqing gaoshang jinyuan yuzhang yuqing yinshu* (*Yuqing yinshu* 2)
HY1349/TT1039 *Shangqing jiutian shangdi shu baishen neiming jing*
HY1353/TT1039 *Shangqing dongzhen zhihui guanshen dajie wen*
HY1365/TT1042 *Shangqing taishang dijun jiuzhen zhongjing* (*Jiuzhen zhongjing*)
HY1387/TT1049 *Dasheng miaolin jing*
HY1393/TT1050 *Shangqing taiji zhenren shenxian jing*
HY1394/TT1050 *Changsheng taiyuan shenyong jing*
HY1396/TT1051 *Dongxuan lingbao ershisi shengtu jing* (*Ershisi shengtu jing*)
HY1400/TT1052 *Dongxuan lingbao changye zhi fu jiuyou yugui mingzhen ke* (*Mingzhen ke*)
HY1419/TT1056 *Daozang quejing mulu*
HY1427/TT1059 *Dongxuan lingbao yuqingshan buxu jing*

Other Primary Sources

Changsun Wuji (d. 659). *Sui shu jingji zhi*. Shanghai: Shangwu Yinshu Guan, 1932.
Chen Shou (233–297). *Sanguo zhi*. Commentary by Pei Songzhi (327–451). Beijing: Zhonghua Shuju, 1960.
Daban niepan jing (*Nirvanasutra*). Translated into Chinese by Dharmakshema in 421. Taisho Buddhist Canon, No. 374, Vol. 12.
Fang Xuanling (578–648). *Jin shu*. Beijing: Zhonghua Shuju, 1974.
Ge Hong (putative author, 283–264). *Shenxian zhuan*. In *Daozang jinghua lu*. Edited by Ding Fubao, 1922. Hangzhou: Zhejiang Guji Chuban She, 1989.
Guoqu xianzai yinyuan jing. Translated ca. 450. Taisho Buddhist Canon, No. 189, Vol. 3.
Li Fang (925–996). *Taiping guangji*. Shanghai: Yeshan Fang, 1926.
———. *Taiping yulan*. Beijing: Zhonghua Shuju, 1960.
Li Yanshou (7th c.). *Bei shi*. Beijing: Zhonghua Shuju, 1974.
———. *Nan shi*. Beijing: Zhonghua Shuju, 1975.
Liu Xu (887–946). *Jiu Tang shu*. Beijing: Zhonghua Shuju, 1975.
Longshi nü jing. Taisho Buddhist Canon, No. 557 Vol. 14 p. 909.
Lu Jia (ca. 216–ca. 172 B.C.E.). *Xinyu*. Sibu Congkan Chubian Suben. Vol. 18. Taipei: T'ai-wan Shang-wu Yin-shu-kuan, 1960.
Ouyang Xiu (1007–1072) and Song Qi (998–1067). *Xin Tang shu*. Beijing: Zhonghua Shuju, 1975.
Sishi-er zhang jing. Taisho Buddhist Canon. No. 784, Vol. 17 p. 722.
Song Wenming (6th c.). *Tongmen*. Dunhuang manuscripts (see Ofuchi Ninji, Ed., *Tonkoo dookyoo: Zurokuhen*). Pelliot 2861 and 2256.

Taiji zuoxiangong qingwen jing shang. Dunhuang Manuscripts. Stein 1351.

Taishang dongxuan lingbao kongdong lingzhang. Dunhuang Manuscripts. Pelliot 2399.

Taishang dongxuan lingbao zhenwen duren benxing miaojing. Dunhuang Manuscripts. Pelliot 3022.

Wang Chong (23–100). *Lun heng.* Shanghai: Renmin Chubanshe, 1974.

Wei Shou (506–572). *Wei shu.* Beijing: Zhonghua Shuju, 1974.

Wu Shu (947–1002). *Shilei fu.* Taipei: Hsin-hsing Shu-chü, 1970.

Xiao Tong (501–531), Ed. *Wenxuan.* Commentary by Li Shan (d. 689). Taipei: T'ai-wan Shang-wu Yin-shu-kuan, 1965.

Xiao Zixian (489–537). *Nanqi shu.* Beijing: Zhonghua Shuju, 1972.

Xu Jian (659–729). *Chuxue ji.* Beijing: Zhonghua Shuju, 1962.

Yao Sulian (557–637). *Chen shu.* Beijing: Zhonghua Shuju, 1972.

———. *Liang shu.* Beijing: Zhonghua Shuju, 1972.

Zhang Hua (putative author, 232–300). *Bowuzhi.* Congshu jicheng chupian, Vol. 1342. Shanghai, Shangwu Yinshu Guan, 1939.

Zheng Qiao (1104–1162). *Tongzhi lü.* Taipei: T'ai-wan Shang-wu Yin-shu-kuan, 1968.

Zhenyi ziran jingjue. Dunhuang Manuscripts. Pelliot 2356.

Index

Note: In the references to endnote material, the numbers in parentheses indicate the page of the main text on which the number of the note is printed.

215

Du Jingchan, 71
Duan jiurou wen, 39
Duke of Thunder, 135
Dunhuang manuscripts, 6, 169 n. 20 (6)
durability, 8
Duyang zapian, 140

earth, worship of, 139
earthbound immortals, 82, 97–98, 102, 104
eating of impurities, 131, 132, 142
eccentricity, 33
Eight Difficulties (*ba-nan*), 118, 194 n. 37 (118)
Eight Gates, 111
Elder of the Primal *Qi*, 54
Elder of the Western Peak, 81
elimination of mentation, 114
elitism, 103, 105
elixir field(s) (*dantian*), 45, 46, 49
Emperor of Heaven, 131
emptiness, 124, 133, 134, 138, 162, 199 n. 25 (138)
empty burial mounds, 131, 138
envy, 106
epidemics, 130, 149, 150
Erjiao lun, 121
Ershisi shengtu jing, 126, 155, 162–163
esoteric biography (*neizhuan*), 84
Ethiopian Moses, 9
evangelism, 104, 106
exorcism, 136
expelling and taking in (*tuna*), 51, 52, 114
expiation, 96, 118–119
extinction and deliverance (*miedu*), 122–123, 126–128, 144, 145

fagara, 60
Famen Temple, 140
family-leaving Taoist monks (*chujia daoshi*), 150
famines, 60, 67
Fan Chai, 32, 33–34
Fang Qianzhi, 39–40
fangshi. See magicians
fasting, 1, 8, 69, 86, 104, 153, 159; after the noon hour, 81, 91, 104, 110, 115, 116,

as condition for scripture transmission, 91–92; drugs and potions for, 11, 21–22, 23, 60–67, 99, 148, 154; for surviving famine, 60, 67; in the *Daoxue zhuan*, 41–42; methods of, 43–68; of Indian ascetics, 141; purpose of, 11, 21–22, 42, 47, 50; special techniques, 11, 22–24, 34, 41, 44–49, 79, 80, 91, 99, 116, 148, 154, 163
Father of the Great One, 56
fatigue, 121; inducing trance, 115; overcoming of, 45
Female-One (*ciyi*), 111
Feng Yanshou, 75
Fengdu, Mt, 90, 188 n. 77 (88)
filial piety, 101
Fire *Kalpa*, 135
fire worship, 135136, 139, 141, 142, 145
fists, clenching of, 45, 49
five agents (*wuxing*), 1, 46, 48, 53, 167 n.1 (1)
five deadly transgressions, 151
five elements. *See* five agents
five flavors, 46
five grains, 154
Five Heavens, 54
Five Monarchs (*wudi*), 89, 101, 162
Five Monarch Demon-Kings, 101
Five Palaces, 127
Five Pecks of Rice School (*wudoumi dao*), 6, 25, 121
five planets, 53
five pungent vegetables, 108
Five *Qi*, 46, 50, 61, 116, 126, 162, 163; method for imbibing the, 53–56
five rocks, 66, 127
Five Sprouts. *See* Five *Qi*
Five Venerables, 89
five viscera (*wuzang*), 44, 45, 46, 47–48, 52, 53, 66
flight into heavens in the *Zhonghuang jing*, 49–50
flood, 127, 132, 162
Flying Celestial Beings, 111, 113
Flying Immortal, 101
"folk ballad in 3000 lyrics" 89